Bourdieu's Politics

Bourdieu's academic work and his political interventions have always proved controversial, with reactions varying from passionate advocacy to savage critique. In the last decade of his career, the French sociologist Pierre Bourdieu became involved in a series of high-profile political interventions, defending the cause of striking students and workers, speaking out in the name of illegal immigrants, the homeless and the unemployed, and challenging the incursion of the market into the field of artistic and intellectual production.

This new study presents the first sustained critical analysis of the political implications of Bourdieu's sociology. Through a close reading of the political speeches and pronouncements of his later years, Jeremy F. Lane provides a detailed exposition both of Bourdieu's critique of neo-liberalism and of his own political position. Bourdieu's theory of politics is also brought into critical dialogue with the work of a range of other commentators of a broadly Marxist or post-Marxist orientation who have also intervened in such debates – theorists such as Stuart Hall, Ernesto Laclau, Chantal Mouffe, Judith Butler, Slavoj Žižek and Jacques Rancière.

The first sustained analysis of Bourdieu's politics will seek to assess the validity of his claims as to the distinctiveness and superiority of his own field theory as a tool of political analysis. It will be of great use to students and researchers in sociology, social theory, cultural studies, French studies and political science.

Jeremy F. Lane is Senior Lecturer in the Department of French at the University of Nottingham. He has published widely on all aspects of the work of Pierre Bourdieu, most notably *Pierre Bourdieu: A Critical Introduction*.

Routledge Advances in Sociology

This series aims to present cutting-edge developments and debates within the field of sociology. It will provide a broad range of case studies and the latest theoretical perspectives, while covering a variety of topics, theories and issues from around the world. It is not confined to any particular school of thought.

1. **Virtual Globalization**
   Virtual spaces/tourist spaces
   Edited by David Holmes

2. **The Criminal Spectre in Law, Literature and Aesthetics**
   Peter Hutchings

3. **Immigrants and National Identity in Europe**
   Anna Triandafyllidou

4. **Constructing Risk and Safety in Technological Practice**
   Edited by Jane Summerton and Boel Berner

5. **Europeanisation, National Identities and Migration**
   Changes in boundary constructions between Western and Eastern Europe
   Willfried Spohn and Anna Triandafyllidou

6. **Language, Identity and Conflict**
   A comparative study of language in ethnic conflict in Europe and Eurasia
   Diarmait Mac Giolla Chríost

7. **Immigrant Life in the U.S.**
   Multi-disciplinary perspectives
   Edited by Donna R. Gabaccia and Colin Wayne Leach

8. **Rave Culture and Religion**
   Edited by Graham St. John

9. **Creation and Returns of Social Capital**
   A new research program
   Edited by Henk Flap and Beate Völker

10. **Self-Care**
    Embodiment, personal autonomy and the shaping of health consciousness
    Christopher Ziguras

11. **Mechanisms of Cooperation**
    Werner Raub and Jeroen Weesie

12. **After the Bell – Educational Success, Public Policy and Family Background**
    Edited by Dalton Conley and Karen Albright

13. **Youth Crime and Youth Culture in the Inner City**
    Bill Sanders

14. **Emotions and Social Movements**
    Edited by Helena Flam and Debra King

15. **Globalization, Uncertainty and Youth in Society**
    Edited by Hans-Peter Blossfeld, Erik Klijzing, Melinda Mills and Karin Kurz

16. **Love, Heterosexuality and Society**
    Paul Johnson

17. **Agricultural Governance**
    Globalization and the new politics of regulation
    Edited by Vaughan Higgins and Geoffrey Lawrence

18. **Challenging Hegemonic Masculinity**
    Richard Howson

19. **Social Isolation in Modern Society**
    Roelof Hortulanus, Anja Machielse and Ludwien Meeuwesen

20. **Weber and the Persistence of Religion**
    Social theory, capitalism and the sublime
    Joseph W. H. Lough

21. **Globalization, Uncertainty and Late Careers in Society**
    Edited by Hans-Peter Blossfeld, Sandra Buchholz and Dirk Hofäcker

22. **Bourdieu's Politics**
    Problems and possibilities
    Jeremy F. Lane

23. **Media Bias in Reporting Social Research?**
    The case of reviewing ethnic inequalities in education
    Martyn Hammersley

Bourdieu's Politics
Problems and possibilities

Jeremy F. Lane

LONDON AND NEW YORK

First published 2006
by Routledge
2 Park Square, Milton Park, Abingdon, Oxon OX14 4RN

Simultaneously published in the USA and Canada
by Routledge
711 Third Avenue, New York, NY 10017

First issued in paperback 2012

Routledge is an imprint of the Taylor & Francis Group, an informa business

© 2006 Jeremy F. Lane

Typeset in Times New Roman by
Newgen Imaging Systems (P) Ltd, Chennai, India

All rights reserved. No part of this book may be reprinted or
reproduced or utilised in any form or by any electronic,
mechanical, or other means, now known or hereafter
invented, including photocopying and recording, or in any
information storage or retrieval system, without permission in
writing from the publishers.

British Library Cataloguing in Publication Data
A catalogue record for this book is available from the British Library

Library of Congress Cataloging in Publication Data
A catalog record for this book has been requested

ISBN13: 978–0–415–64614-7 (pbk)
ISBN13: 978–0–415–36320–4 (hbk)
ISBN13: 978–0–203–01357–1 (ebk)

Politics is that specific activity which only exists because there is no science of politics.

(Jacques Rancière)

Contents

Acknowledgements   xi

Introduction   1

1   Neo-liberalism as 'imposition' and 'invasion'?   11

2   The poetics and politics of practice   36

3   From practical sense to performative politics   54

4   Field theory and political analysis   76

5   Gender politics and the return of symbolic domination   98

6   Aesthetics, politics and the market   120

7   Universalism and the elusive public sphere   141

Conclusion   162

Notes   171
Bibliography   174
Index   187

Acknowledgements

The writing of this book was greatly facilitated by the encouragement and advice I received from a range of colleagues and friends. I should particularly like to thank Susan Brook and Jon Beasley-Murray for the friendship, hospitality and intellectual stimulation they have provided over the past few years. I am grateful to the participants in the Sociology of Culture Reading Group at Nottingham University – Alan Aldridge, Meryl Aldridge, Joseph Burridge, Roger Cox, Christian Karner, David Parker, Nick Stevenson and Claire Tinker – for inviting me to join their stimulating discussions on areas of social theory, which I would not have explored without their encouragement. I should also like to thank both my colleagues in the French Department at Nottingham University and the AHRC for providing the teaching cover and financial support necessary to allow me to bring this project to completion. Final thanks go to the editors of the journals *French Cultural Studies* and *Paragraph* for allowing me to reproduce, in chapters 1 and 2, materials that first appeared, in modified form, as 'Neo-liberalism as "imposition" and "invasion": problems in Bourdieu's politics', *French Cultural Studies*, 14, 42 (October 2003), part 3: 323–35 (© Sage Publications), and 'Bourdieu's Forgotten Aesthetic: the poetics and politics of practice', *Paragraph*, 27, 3 (November 2004): 82–99.

All translations from Bourdieu's work in the pages that follow are my own. For works that have appeared in English translation, citations include page numbers of the original French text followed by the page numbers of the corresponding passages in the English translations.

Introduction

In an interview he gave to the Swiss newspaper *Le Temps* in 1998, Pierre Bourdieu contrasted the 'neutrality' that had marked his early career with the more public and overtly political role he had come to adopt over the course of the 1980s and 1990s. He accounted for the change of heart that had prompted these increasingly frequent political interventions in the following terms:

> I myself fell victim to that moralism of neutrality, of the non-involvement of the scientist. At the time, and wrongly, I forbade myself from drawing some of the obvious consequences of my sociological enquiries. With the self-assurance and the recognition that comes with age, and under the pressure of what I consider to be a genuine political emergency, I was driven to intervene in the terrain of so-called politics. As if one could talk of the social world without being involved in politics!
>
> (quoted in Lahire, ed. 1999: 15)

Bourdieu was surely not arguing here that he had never intervened politically in the decades prior to the 1980s. Indeed, his studies of Algeria during the War of Independence, like his studies of education and cultural policy in postwar France, had all possessed an unmistakably political force. Moreover, from the 1960s onwards, Bourdieu had periodically agreed to contribute directly to public policy decision-making by sitting on various government commissions on state education and cultural provision.[1] The change to which Bourdieu was alluding in this interview related rather to the increasing frequency and intensity of his political interventions in the last decades of his career. This increasing frequency and intensity reflected both a quantitative change, in terms of the number of Bourdieu's political interventions, and a qualitative shift, in terms of the manner in which he understood his own role and public responsibilities as an intellectual.

Examples of Bourdieu's directly political interventions in the last decades of his career are numerous and have been well-documented elsewhere. The documentary film *La Sociologie est un sport de combat*, which gained a general cinema release in France in 2001, focused on Bourdieu's political activities, attempting to bring his message of resistance to neo-liberalism to the widest possible audience. The two brief volumes of speeches and interventions, published in France under the titles *Contre-feux* [*Acts of Resistance*] (1998) and *Contre-feux 2* [*Firing back*] (2001), manifest a similar desire to reach a readership beyond the limited confines of the intellectual field. They bear witness to the range of issues on which Bourdieu felt moved to speak out, from supporting the major French public sector strikes of autumn 1995, to railing against the dismantling of social welfare, bemoaning the incursions of the market into the realms of culture and education, and criticizing the role of supranational organizations such as the World Bank, International Monetary Fund (IMF) and World Trade Organisation (WTO) in 'imposing' their 'neo-liberal *doxa*' on societies throughout the world. The two volumes of *Contre-feux* were published in the 'Liber-Raisons d'agir' series, a series set up and run by Bourdieu with the intention of communicating 'the most advanced state of research on current political and social problems' to the widest possible readership, bringing together 'researchers in the social sciences, sociologists, historians, economists, but also, on occasion, artists and writers, all animated by the committed will [*la volonté militante*] to circulate the knowledge indispensable for political reflection and action in a democracy'.[2] The first volume to appear in the series had been Bourdieu's own polemic against the role played by a media field dominated by market interests in promoting the neo-liberal agenda and hence stifling democratic debate, *On Television and Journalism* (1996c).

While Bourdieu acknowledged that such intense political activity was something of a new departure for him, he nonetheless maintained that each of his political interventions derived its authority from the more detailed, fully worked out sociological studies of the phenomena in question that he or his close collaborators had carried out. Each of the short volumes or pamphlets published in the 'Liber-Raisons d'agir' series was thus intended to represent the distillation of the more detailed sociological, economic or historical researches carried out either by Bourdieu himself or by fellow members of the 'Raisons d'agir' Collective, a group of intellectuals and commentators with similar intellectual and political sympathies. In the case of Bourdieu's own interventions, his protests at the dismantling of social welfare systems drew on the collaborative study of contemporary forms of impoverishment published under his editorship as *The Weight of the World* (1993). His concern for artists' and writers' loss of creative 'autonomy' in the face of market imperatives was informed by his account of the struggles of nineteenth-century French artists to construct an autonomous field of artistic production in *The Rules of Art* (1992a). His polemics against neo-liberalism and the unthinking application of neo-classical economics to public policy decisions were informed by his study *The Social Structures of the Economy* (2000), an analysis of the French housing market and of the French government's application of market principles to social housing policy in the late 1970s. Bourdieu's polemics against the technocratic elite he held responsible for 'imposing' the neo-liberal *doxa* on French and other societies drew on his study *The State Nobility* (1989), an analysis of the role played by the prestigious *grandes écoles* in the production of France's ruling and business elite. Since the mid-1970s Bourdieu had dedicated a series of articles to the analysis of 'the political field', several of which were subsequently anthologized in *Language and Symbolic Power* (1982) and *Propos sur le champ politique* (2000a). These theorizations of the political field informed his analysis of quite how neo-liberalism had come to enjoy its current ascendancy over the political field, both within France and globally. Finally, Bourdieu's interventions on media and journalism drew on the body of work in this domain carried out by several of his close collaborators, work such as Partick Champagne's study of the effects of the mass media on political protest in *Faire l'opinion* (1990) or Dominique Marchetti's analyses of political scandals in France (Champagne and Marchetti 1994; Marchetti 2000), to give but two examples.

Clearly then, there was a symbiotic relationship between Bourdieu's fully worked out sociological studies and what might be termed his more punctual, directly political interventions, the speeches and short articles later anthologized in the two *Contre-feux* and the posthumously published collection *Interventions, 1961–2001: science sociale et action politique* (2002). Indeed, the neo-liberal *doxa* against which Bourdieu railed in such speeches and articles was understood as having been 'imposed' on society through a form of 'symbolic violence' in a manner which Bourdieu considered his own concepts of 'field', 'habitus' and 'symbolic domination' peculiarly well-suited to analyse and explain. As Franck Poupeau and Thierry Discepolo put it in their Introduction to *Interventions*: 'social science and militancy, far from being opposed, can be conceived as the two faces of the same work of analysis, of deciphering and critique of social reality with the aim of transforming that reality' (in Bourdieu 2002: 8).

As Bourdieu himself explained in the interview with *Le Temps*, he had only decided to employ the findings of his sociological studies to such overtly political ends because he had felt 'driven' to do so by what he considered to be 'a genuine political emergency'. The political emergency in question was surely the assault on the social gains of France's postwar compromise, an assault which led Bourdieu to reflect more fully on the effects of the neo-liberal agenda not only in his native France but throughout the world. It might be argued that this assault on the postwar compromise occurred relatively late in France in comparison to other Western nations, such as Britain and the US. What might be termed the delayed arrival of neo-liberalism in France may help explain the timing of Bourdieu's decision to adopt a more actively political role.

By the beginning of the 1980s, of course, the British and American electorates had both elected leaders committed to enacting radical programmes of neo-liberal reform in the economic, social and cultural domains. In 1981, however, French citizens had elected a Socialist president and government ostensibly committed to pursuing a radical programme of Keynesian reflation. Certainly, by 1983–4 and in the face of a flight of capital from the French economy, François Mitterrand and his Socialist administration had abandoned their commitment to Keynesianism in favour of the politics of 'rigour' and 'austerity'. However, Mitterrand would remain, until his death in 1995, the dominant figure in French politics, and Socialist-led administrations would continue to govern France throughout much of the 1980s and 1990s. As W. Rand Smith has argued, the

Socialists' shifting economic policies during their various periods in government from 1981 to 1993 never involved a straightforward embrace of neo-liberalism. Despite their role in 'restructuring' and shutting down large sections of traditional heavy industry, for example, French Socialist governments continued to indulge in significant forms of state intervention, both in industrial planning and in mitigating the effects of closures and job losses (Smith 1998). The role of successive Socialist administrations in France from the 1980s to the mid-1990s thus combined with a strong popular commitment to a centralized state, seen as guarantor of certain fundamental republican rights, to mitigate and delay the effects of the neo-liberal revolution in France.

If Bourdieu's most intensive period of political activism dates from the late 1980s, this is surely because the strength of the phenomena that had delayed and mitigated the effects of neo-liberalism in France was beginning to wane by that time. The legislative elections of 1986 had delivered a right-wing government, which, under the premiership of Jacques Chirac, pursued policies explicitly modelled on those of both Thatcher and Reagan. While the French Socialist Party would return to government periodically over the course of the next decade, their claims to offer any real policy alternatives to the neo-liberal consensus seemed ever less credible. On the international stage, meanwhile, the fall of the Berlin Wall in 1989 and consequent collapse of the Soviet system seemed to some to signal the final triumph of liberal capitalism over any socialist or communist alternatives, however conceived. It certainly appeared to herald an era marked by the unrivalled dominance of US power, in military, cultural and economic terms, finally securing the US's ability to impose the neo-liberal tenets of the 'Washington Consensus' over the economies of every nation-state. This then, in broad terms, was 'the genuine political emergency' to which Bourdieu's political interventions in the last two decades of his career were addressed. Faced with this emergency, with this neo-liberal assault on the institutions of the centralized state and the forms of social protection they guaranteed, Bourdieu increasingly came to adopt what appeared to be a classically French republican mode of discourse. Thus, in his later articles and books Bourdieu could be found stating his allegiance to what he termed 'the French model' or 'French exceptionalism', calling for a 'defence of the Hegelian or Durkheimian vision' of the state as guarantor of certain 'universal' rights and values, claiming 'the state of the French Third Republic' represented 'nearly an exact incarnation' of that model (Bourdieu 1998b: 20).

Bourdieu's adoption of such apparently classically French republican rhetoric seemed to point to a first problem inherent in his political interventions. For, throughout much of his career, most notably in his studies of the relationships between class, education and culture, Bourdieu had carried out a sustained assault on the institutions of French republicanism, rejecting their claims to embody universal ideals and values, arguing that such claims merely served as ideological cover for the function they performed in reproducing and legitimizing class divisions and distinctions. Indeed, Bruce Robbins had accused Bourdieu of 'indolence' in this respect, of only being so 'comfortable' in his denunciations of the role played by state institutions in reproducing social distinctions, because he assumed the state would 'always be there to hate' and could not 'itself require legitimating, at least from left-wing intellectuals like himself'. These were 'lazy assumptions', Robbins had agued, since they ignored the challenges posed to the legitimacy of the state from a range of reactionary forces, from the new racisms and nationalisms, on the one hand, to neo-liberalism and global capital, on the other (Robbins 1993: 109–10). Nicholas Garnham had made a similar point when he had argued that in insisting that the 'objective function' of high culture was to legitimate class privilege, Bourdieu had apparently left no grounds on which to defend high culture against neo-liberal demands that it be 'opened up' to the supposedly more democratic tribunal of market forces (in Calhoun *et al.* 1993: 186–7).

Thus Bourdieu's invocations of the 'French model', of the ideals of French republicanism as a bulwark against neo-liberalism, struck several commentators as perplexing, not to say simply contradictory. Commenting on Bourdieu's support for the protesting students in autumn 1995, François Dubet noted what he considered to be the 'strange about-face' whereby 'the "school of reproduction"' had suddenly become 'the Republican school' in Bourdieu's discourse (in Touraine *et al.* 1996: 121). In similar vein, Bernard Lahire noted the development of what he termed 'a rather strange discourse (from a strict sociological point of view) on what he [Bourdieu] calls "the universal" and which essentially corresponds to artistic and scientific high culture, as well as to the state and the School as public service institutions'. This, according to Lahire, involved Bourdieu 're-baptising as "universal"' phenomena 'he would previously have dubbed "legitimate" cultures or institutions (emphasizing the historical arbitrariness of that legitimacy and its foundation in the misrecognition of a power relation between groups or classes in the social formation)' (Lahire ed. 1999: 12 n.7).

The question of quite how Bourdieu could reconcile his calls for the universal values of the French republican state to be defended with an earlier body of work that had seemed to discredit any such claims to universalism was merely one of a series of criticisms provoked by the political activism of his later career. Such criticisms, expressed both by fellow academics and by journalists, were frequently very hostile, condemning Bourdieu's interventions as over-simplified, arguing they were the expressions of a sociology that was outdated and rigidly deterministic and of a sociologist who was manifesting dangerously totalitarian, even Stalinist tendencies in his dealings with political and intellectual rivals. Bourdieu's study of gender relations, *Masculine Domination* (1998a), was published at the height of the controversy sparked by his more directly political interventions. The fact that the study appeared to present a pessimistic view of relations between the sexes as unchanged and unchanging encouraged certain commentators to move from criticism of his political activism to outright rejection of Bourdieusian sociology as a whole. Perhaps the most notorious example of this kind of hostile response to Bourdieu's sociological theory and political practice was Janine Verdès-Leroux's *Le Savant et la politique: essai sur le terrorisme sociologique de Pierre Bourdieu* (1998). Angry and intemperate, Verdès-Leroux's book combined expressions of surprise at Bourdieu's sudden decision to adopt the role of public or engaged intellectual with accusations that his political interventions, like his sociological theory, betrayed worryingly totalitarian tendencies. As such, Verdès-Leroux's book occupied the most extreme pole on a continuum of similar such criticisms voiced by a range of other intellectuals and media commentators.

Bourdieu's collaborators and sympathizers responded to this onslaught of criticism with a defensiveness which, if understandable, was not always helpful in clarifying the precise nature of his political interventions. For example, one of the more frequent charges made against Bourdieu was that he had begun to overreach himself, illegitimately assuming an authority to speak on all and every social and political issue in a manner that contrasted with his previous commitment to remaining within his own sphere of expertise. Close collaborators typically sought to deflect such charges by arguing that the model of intellectual engagement followed by Bourdieu was not that of a Jean-Paul Sartre, of the 'all-powerful' intellectual abrogating to himself the right to speak on all and every subject in the name of the universal. Rather, they maintained, Bourdieu was following a more modest and limited notion of intellectual engagement, modelled on Michel Foucault's concept of the 'specific intellectual' (Mauger 1995; Pinto 1998: 178). This claim was less than convincing, however. The notion of the 'specific intellectual' was intended by Foucault to signal a break with the claims of French intellectuals to speak in the name of the universal, a break with the tradition of French intellectual engagement from Emile Zola's 'J'Accuse' on (Foucault 1977). However, Bourdieu frequently claimed to speak in defence of or in the name of the universal and repeatedly invoked 'the model invented by Zola' in justification of his own political interventions (1992a: 464–5 [342]; 1994: 38 [29]; 1996c: 91 [82]).

If a model existed for Bourdieu's intellectual engagements, it seemed to lie less with Foucault's notion of the 'specific intellectual' than with the activities of the 'nouvelle Sorbonne' in the late nineteenth century. The 'nouvelle Sorbonne' was composed of a group of intellectuals concerned to replace the old 'impressionistic' methods of literary, historical and philosophical study with the 'rational' methods of the new historical sciences, the history of Charles-Victor Langlois and Charles Seignobos, the literary history of Gustave Lanson and the sociology of Durkheim. These intellectuals justified their political interventions, whether in defence of Alfred Dreyfus or in support of the democratization of education, by reference to their specifically intellectual expertise, their ability to speak in the name of 'universal, scientific' truth rather than the narrow interests of nation, religion or class. Working collaboratively, the intellectuals of the 'nouvelle Sorbonne' sought, for example, to bring the insights of literary criticism, historical and sociological research to bear on the Dreyfus trial, undermining the prosecution's case by reference to the scientific and universal truths to which their specific expertise gave them access (Bompaire-Evesque 1988). It was this kind of collaborative effort, to bring the specific expertise of sociologists, historians and economists to bear on contemporary political debates and hence to speak in the name of universal scientific truth against the partial claims of politicians or neo-classical economists, that was expressed both in the activities of the 'Raisons d'agir' Collective and in the pamphlets their members published in the 'Liber-Raisons d'agir' series.

The claims that Bourdieu adhered to Foucault's model of the specific intellectual thus need to be treated with caution, as do some other responses to the criticisms elicited by his later political activism. For example, the very violence of the reaction to Bourdieu's political interventions has been taken by some as proof of the justice of his claims, of the extent to which his arguments had hit home. For Poupeau and Discepolo, the hostile criticisms of Bourdieu in the mass media were proof of the media's role in silencing any critique of the neo-liberal *doxa*, evidence of the extent to which the media were working 'in the service of the conservative revolution' (in Bourdieu 2002: 383). This argument was expanded upon by Michel Onfray, a sympathizer rather than a close collaborator, in his *Célébration du génie colérique* (2002). Here Onfray argued that the virulence of the criticisms directed against Bourdieu represented an attempt to vilify and silence him, confirming all Bourdieu's claims as to the unchallengeable hegemony of neo-liberal ideas and the complicity of the media in that hegemony (Onfray 2002). There is, however, something too self-serving about the argument that the extent of the criticisms levelled at Bourdieu's interventions merely demonstrated the well-founded nature of his analyses. According to the logic of this argument, any criticism of Bourdieu, whatever its merits, can be taken simply to confirm his point regarding the complete dominance of the neo-liberal *doxa* over the media and intellectual fields. Such an argument rests on a manichean vision of those fields and implies that all criticisms of Bourdieu were voiced by commentators who were either the conscious promoters or the unwitting dupes of the neo-liberal *doxa*. This is to ignore the fact that patient, detailed and persuasive critiques of Bourdieu's politics have been produced by commentators who themselves have authored alternative, but no less critical accounts of neo-liberalism, of its rise to dominance, its mode of operation and of the best ways to combat it. One example of such an approach can be found in the work of Jean-Pierre Le Goff.

In his 2002 study *La Démocratie post-totalitaire*, Le Goff (2002) argues that Bourdieu shares with many contemporary French critics of neo-liberalism an assumption that neo-liberalism operates in a mode analogous to the totalitarian ideologies of 1930s and 1940s Europe. He detects in a range of French critiques of neo-liberalism, Bourdieu's included, a tendency to understand neo-liberalism as being something imposed from above on an unwilling or impotent French citizenry, whether by a domestic technocratic elite or by the operations of supranational bodies such as the IMF and WTO. Le Goff rejects such analyses for a variety of reasons, the most significant of which is his claim that to attribute neo-liberalism purely to the machinations of a distant elite is to overlook the whole range of social, cultural and political changes which the neo-liberal agenda seeks to exploit and through which it seeks to gain some purchase on the hopes, desires and beliefs of French citizenry at large. Here Le Goff draws on his earlier studies of what he terms 'the impossible legacy' of May 1968, by which he means the radical questioning of traditional values, figures of authority and state institutions expressed during the events of May 1968, which fed into the counter-cultural movements of the 1970s, while feeding off and into the more radical forms of postwar French thought, Bourdieu's own work included (Le Goff 2002a). The effects of this radical questioning, he argues, can be seen in current theories of both pedagogy and management, with their shared tendency to demand ever greater 'transparency' and 'accountability', constant 'self-evaluation' and 'self-realization' of employees, students and teachers. The extensive apparatuses of audit and evaluation that such theories seek to put in place represent the concrete manifestation of a new mode of domination that Le Goff names 'la barbarie douce', literally 'gentle barbarism' (Le Goff 1999). Le Goff argues that although this 'barbarie douce' is not directly reducible to neo-liberalism, in its suspicion of the values incarnated in older institutions and traditions, it perfectly complements that economic and political creed. An unintended by-product of the progressive movements of the 1960s and 1970s, 'la barbarie douce' is thus a symptom of the cultural, political and social shifts that allowed neo-liberalism to gain its current hegemony, shifts whose importance Bourdieu's polemics against neo-liberalism fail adequately to acknowledge.

Le Goff's account of 'la barbarie douce' offers a series of similarities with Luc Boltanski and Eve Chiapello's analysis in their study *Le Nouvel Esprit du capitalisme* (1999).[3] Boltanski and Chiapello argue for the need to understand neo-liberalism in relation to the criticisms of and popular disaffection with the centralized form of welfare statism that emerged in France in the postwar period. They argue that in its challenges to the power of the state and its promotion of greater 'flexibility', 'autonomy' and less rigid hierarchy in the workplace, neo-liberalism represents an attempt by the forces of capital to 'recuperate' some of the demands of the French progressive movements of the 1960s and 1970s. As such, they too reject Bourdieu's terms of analysis, but in a perhaps more radical way than Le Goff, since they attribute failings in Bourdieu's analysis of neo-liberalism to certain flawed assumptions underpinning his sociological theory as a whole. Indeed, Boltanski and Chiapello's study forms just one part of the broader collaborative project of the Group for Political and Moral Sociology headed by Boltanski. This project seeks to challenge the assumptions behind 'critical sociology', a form of sociology of which Bourdieu's own is seen as paradigmatic. Boltanski and his collaborators reject the founding assumption of 'critical sociology' that society operates according to a logic of which ordinary agents remain ignorant or unconscious and which only the scientific gaze of the professional sociologist can uncover. They argue rather that all agents are constantly involved in an active process of assessing ways of life, modes of governance and forms of political and social life against their own sets of values, their own 'logics of justification' and 'tests of legitimacy' which evolve over time in response to changing circumstances. The 'new spirit of capitalism' that is the subject of Boltanski and Chiapello's study is thus seen as the result of the institutions that emerged from the French postwar compromise gradually losing their popular legitimacy in the face of grass roots demands that such institutions justify themselves in new ways. It was this loss of legitimacy and these demands for new forms of justification that were recuperated by the forces of capital in pursuit of their neo-liberal agenda, according to Boltanski and Chiapello. A critical sociology, such as Bourdieu's, will always have too 'top-down' a conception of politics and society to grasp the significance of such grass roots shifts and movements, they suggest.

There is of course nothing new in the suggestion that Bourdieu's sociology is insufficiently attentive to the multiple ways in which ordinary agents challenge, resist, modify or act upon the social and cultural structures in which they live. One of the most persistent and patient critics of Bourdieu in this respect has been Jacques Rancière, who, over the course of a series of books and articles, has elaborated an account of the relationship between politics, aesthetics and agency, which he derives, in significant part, from working through some of the flaws he finds in Bourdieu's sociology (Rancière 1983: 239–88; 1998: 74–111; 2003: 353–76). Rancière has had little to say on the specific topic of Bourdieu's directly political interventions. However, his general criticisms of Bourdieu's sociological theory frequently bear on its political implications and potential contradictions. As such, his work is worthy of attention here and will prove helpful in identifying and working through some of the more problematic elements of Bourdieu's theory.

A fundamental premise of the current study is, therefore, that it is perfectly possible to share Bourdieu's concern at the destructive social and political effects of neo-liberalism without subscribing uncritically either to his account of how neo-liberalism came to ascendancy or to his proposals regarding how best to respond to that ascendancy. It follows, then, that not all of the criticisms of Bourdieu's politics can be dismissed as being motivated by a desire to silence him and reassert the neo-liberal agenda as an unchallengeable dogma. On the contrary, some of these criticisms raise valid and urgent questions of both Bourdieu's political interventions and of the sociological theory which underpinned them. Moreover, as the example of the 'specific intellectual' showed, the defensiveness of Bourdieu's supporters has sometimes proved unhelpful in answering such criticisms, since such defensiveness has obscured rather than clarified the true nature of his theory and practice of politics.

There is thus clearly a need for a critical study of Bourdieu's politics, a study which not only clarifies and assesses the nature of the positions he took in the 1980s and 1990s but which also moves beyond such overtly political interventions to analyse the more general theory of politics and society on which they drew. This study, then, does not aim to provide an exhaustive account of *all* of Bourdieu's political interventions throughout the course of his long career, a historical narrative of Bourdieu's politics that imposes some spurious retrospective coherence on those many and varied interventions. Rather, it moves from an analysis of his interventions against neo-liberalism in the 1980s and 1990s and the criticisms they provoked to ask a series of more theoretical questions about the contribution that Bourdieu's sociology might make to political analysis more generally. It thus seeks to assess the contribution that such key Bourdieusian concepts as 'symbolic domination', 'habitus', 'practice' and 'field' might make to what normally falls under the rubric of 'discourse analysis' or the theory of ideology. Bourdieu frequently insisted that his own 'theory of practice' was both distinct from and superior to those theories of ideology and political discourse which drew on the Marxist Gramscian or Althusserian traditions. Assessing the validity of such claims will also bring Bourdieu's work into dialogue with that of a range of Marxist or post-Marxist thinkers who have similarly sought to move beyond conventional theories of ideology, thinkers ranging from Stuart Hall, Ernesto Laclau and Chantal Mouffe, to Judith Butler and Jacques Rancière. Once the theoretical bases of Bourdieu's theory of politics and society have been clarified and assessed, this study will turn to consider his contribution to the analysis of gender politics, his theorization of the relationship between aesthetics and politics, and his understanding of the role of intellectuals and their relationship to a public sphere increasingly dominated by market and mass media interests. This study will also attempt to clarify the precise nature of Bourdieu's universalism, the bases of his frequent claims to speak in the name of or in defence of universal ethical, political, aesthetic and epistemological values. It will seek to elucidate the relationship of this universalism to the tradition of French republican universalism, whose failings Bourdieu had seemed so eager to criticize early in his career.

The attitude to Bourdieu's work adopted in this study will be a *critical* one, in the sense that it will seek to uncover certain problems, inconsistencies and contradictions in his theory and practice of politics. However, this study is not critical in the sense of merely seeking to demonstrate how, where and to what extent Bourdieu's politics went wrong, as it were. Rather, it is animated by the conviction that, whatever its problems, Bourdieu's sociology does have a significant contribution to make to political analysis. Hence, identifying certain problems in Bourdieu's work will serve merely as a precursor to working through such problems, adapting Bourdieu's theoretical concepts in order to highlight the *possibilities* contained in his theory and practice of politics, as much as the problems.

1 Neo-liberalism as 'imposition' and 'invasion'?

In 1998, Bourdieu published a collection of his most explicitly political speeches and interviews under the title, *Contre-feux: propos pour servir à la résistance contre l'invasion néo-libérale*. The title of the English-language version of this collection, *Acts of resistance: against the new myths of our time* (1998), seemed to have lost something in the translation. The loss of the original metaphor, which figured Bourdieu's interventions as a series of 'contre-feux', was surely regrettable. For 'contre-feux' are those small fires lit by fire-fighters to open up a fire break in a forest and hence halt the advance of a larger fire. Bourdieu's original title thus emphasized that his interventions amounted not to a fully developed political programme but rather sought, in the face of the advance of neo-liberalism, to open up a series of spaces for thought and reflection, spaces in which other options might be discussed and an alternative political programme sketched out.[1] The failure to retain the notion of neo-liberalism as an 'invasion', meanwhile, was at once more serious and less surprising. That the English-language publisher and/or translator should have drawn back from offering a literal translation of *Contre-feux*'s subtitle was understandable given that the phrase 'l'invasion néo-libérale', uttered in the French context, left little doubt as to the presumed source of that so-called invasion. The clear implication of this phrase was that neo-liberalism was an inherently non-French phenomenon, emanating from what French commentators tend disparagingly to refer to as 'the Anglo-Saxon world'.

This interpretation seemed confirmed by the sequel to the first *Contre-feux*, entitled *Contre-feux 2: pour un mouvement social européen* (2001), in which Bourdieu argued that the dominance of neo-liberal economics throughout Europe followed 'a logic which recalls that of colonization' (2001: 31). If Continental Europeans were the colonized in this account, then the colonizer was the US; neo-liberalism, according to the title of the essay in which this reference to 'colonization' appeared, represented 'the imposition of the American model' on Europe and the rest of the world (Bourdieu 2001: 25–31). Significantly, this essay, 'L'Imposition du modèle américain', was not included in *Firing back*, the English translation of *Contre-feux 2*, being replaced by a more conciliatory 'Letter to the American reader'. Here Bourdieu was careful to acknowledge the role played by 'American researchers' in highlighting the destructive effects of neo-liberalism, before calling on 'American scholars and activists' to join 'our struggles' and hence 'strip' them 'of the appearance of particularism, even of nationalism' they might otherwise possess (Bourdieu 2003). Clearly then, there was a conscious effort by Bourdieu himself, as well as his publishers and translators, to tone down some of his more overtly anti-American rhetoric for an English-speaking readership. However, this could not conceal his tendency to cast neo-liberalism as a foreign, invading force fundamentally inimical to the political and cultural traditions of France and Continental Europe more generally.

According to Bourdieu, the attempt to apply neo-liberal solutions to economies throughout the world represented an attempt to *impose* as universal an economic model which had its roots in the particular cultural and political traditions of the US. In this context he pointed to what he saw as a typically American emphasis on self-reliance and self-help rooted in Protestantism, which had fostered the ideology of the 'self-made man' flourishing in a 'land of opportunity' and hence encouraged both a weak centralized state and a tendency to take the market to be the primary measure of all worth (Bourdieu 2001: 25–31, 2000: 22–6 [10–13]). Thus Bourdieu concluded, 'what is universally proposed and *imposed* as the norm for every rational economic practice is in reality the universalisation of the particular characteristics of an economy embedded in a particular history and social structure, that of the United States' (2001: 98 [87], my emphasis). In explaining the UK's role in this process of 'imposition', Bourdieu employed a metaphor first used by Charles de Gaulle, when he vetoed British entry to the EEC in the 1960s. Like De Gaulle before him, Bourdieu argued that the UK acted as a 'Trojan horse' for American ideas and interests, enabling neo-liberalism to 'penetrate' Europe more easily (Bourdieu 1999: 54 n.19).

According to Bourdieu's account, the success of this 'imposition of the American model' on European and other states reflected the US's unrivalled economic, political and military dominance since the collapse of the old Soviet bloc (Bourdieu 2001: 25–32). Imposed by means of American power, neo-liberalism was to be understood as a fundamentally intellectual and elite phenomenon. Its tenets had been elaborated in a series of think tanks in the US and UK,[2] think tanks which had then sought to 'impose' their political and economic vision onto Continental Europe and elsewhere:

> The neo-liberal vulgate, an economic and political orthodoxy which has been so universally *imposed* and so unanimously accepted that it seems beyond the reach of discussion and contestation, was not produced spontaneously. It is the result of the prolonged and constant labour of an immense intellectual labour force, concentrated and organised into genuine enterprises of production, dissemination, and intervention.
> (Bourdieu 2001: 7–8 [11–12], my emphasis)

Indeed, throughout Bourdieu's criticisms of neo-liberalism, the terms 'imposed' and 'imposition' recur with remarkable frequency. Thus he argued that the hegemony of neo-liberal discourse was the result of a 'permanent, insidious *imposition*', representing 'a whole set of presuppositions [...] *imposed* as self-evident'. Journalists and think tanks promoting its tenets were involved in a 'work of *imposition*' and it was thus necessary to understand 'the mechanisms through which' this neo-liberal 'doxa' 'is produced and *imposed*' (Bourdieu 1998: 34–36 [29–31], my emphases).

If think tanks played a key role in producing and imposing neo-liberal ideology, so too, according to Bourdieu, did a whole series of supranational organizations, from the World Bank, IMF and WTO, to multinational media corporations.

> [These] new masters of the world [represented] a genuine invisible world government, [a] sort of Big Brother, which is endowed with interconnected databases on all cultural and economic institutions [and] is already there, in action, efficiently going about its business, deciding what we will be able to eat or not eat, see or not see on television or at the cinema.
> (Bourdieu 2001: 88–9 [78–9])

Neo-liberalism was thus an ideology which

> the conservative International of heads and executives of industrial and financial multinationals of all nations intends to impose by relying on the political, diplomatic, and military power of an imperial state gradually reduced to its function of law enforcement in domestic and foreign theatres.
> (Bourdieu 2001: 107–8 [95–6])

Against this 'conservative International', Bourdieu stated his own allegiance to what he termed the 'French model', or 'French exceptionalism'. Such statements of allegiance sometimes took the most classically French republican form, with Bourdieu calling for 'a defence of the Hegelian or Durkheimian vision' of the state as the guarantor of certain 'universal' values. In 'the state of the French Third Republic', Bourdieu found

> nearly an exact incarnation [of this] model, which follows in the tradition of the Enlightenment, attempts to defend a number of choices making up a systematic whole: the choice of 'solidarity' or 'solidarism' over 'individuality' or 'individualism'; the choice of 'social security' against 'individual private insurance'; the choice of the 'collective' over the 'individual'.
> (1998b: 20)

In *Acts of Resistance*, Bourdieu advocated the extension of these French republican values of solidarity and universalism first to the European and ultimately to the global level, imagining a future 'world state', which would guarantee the social rights of all the world's citizens (1998: 119 [104]). Nonetheless, Bourdieu's preferred model remained avowedly French in origin and his analysis of neo-liberalism did appear to rest on a set of nationally overdetermined dichotomies. For example, in *On Television and Journalism* Bourdieu evoked the French experience of the Second World War to illustrate the threat posed by market forces to intellectual autonomy. In an explicit reference to French resistance and collaboration under Nazi occupation, he contrasted certain 'media intellectuals' who 'collaborated' with market forces and the mass media to those truly autonomous intellectuals who 'resisted' such forces and the neo-liberal agenda they promoted (Bourdieu 1996c: 70–3 [60–4]).

Bourdieu's rhetoric and choice of metaphors in his shorter political interventions were thus by no means innocent. In his reference to a 'neo-liberal invasion', as in his allusions to Gaullism and to French resistance and collaboration during the Second World War, he evoked a French nation and republic at threat from foreign forces. As Alex Callinicos has put it, on reading Bourdieu, 'we are left with a sense of neo-liberalism as a programme imposed by elites external to the society they are seeking to transform. Sometimes, these elites appear literally as an alien force'. For Callinicos, Bourdieu's 'powerful commitment to internationalism' and stated opposition to any xenophobia or racism outweighed any concerns that such apparently nationalistic rhetoric might otherwise have provoked (Callinicos 1999: 90). However, such evident internationalism is by no means inconsistent with a French republicanism that has historically identified its own nationalist project with a universalist and internationalist one, claiming democracy, equality and human rights to be inherently French ideals and hence according the French nation the historic mission of spreading those ideals throughout Europe and the wider world. Bourdieu's evocation of the French Third Republic as guarantor of such universal ideals, a model to be extended first to Europe, then to the world, remained deeply marked by this particular brand of French republican universalism. Clearly, the decision not to retain the reference to a 'neo-liberal invasion' in the subtitle of the English translation of the first *Contre-feux*, like the decision to replace the essay 'L'Imposition du modèle américain' with the more conciliatory 'Letter to the American Reader' in the translation of *Contre-feux 2*, represented conscious attempts to play down the more nationalistic connotations of Bourdieu's rhetoric. However, neither the extent of Bourdieu's nationalism, real or imagined, nor the possibility of his rhetoric causing slight to the national self-esteem of his American or British readers are of great importance here. Far more significant is the possibility that this reliance on a dichotomy between 'French exceptionalism', on the on one hand, and a US-led 'neo-liberal invasion', on the other, might ultimately prove profoundly politically disabling.

Bourdieu's claim that neo-liberalism should be understood as the expression of certain fundamental American cultural characteristics surely risked sliding into a kind of essentialism, whereby analysis of the historical and political conditions that facilitated the ascendancy of neo-liberal ideas in the US would be replaced by the straightforward evocation of a hypostatized American national character. For example, if the US's role in promoting neo-liberalism was merely the expression of its inherent cultural characteristics, it would surely be difficult to account for such historically significant experiences as Franklin Roosevelt's New Deal or the social programmes enacted under John Kennedy and Lyndon Johnson, unless as momentary aberrations. An account which understood neo-liberalism to be the expression of certain inherent American cultural and political traditions would necessarily write out of its analysis any examination of the range of political, historical and economic factors which led subsequent US administrations to abandon such interventionism.[3] Similarly, any account which attributed the dominance of neo-liberalism in Continental Europe solely to a combination of unchecked American power and complicit indigenous elites surely risked enacting an equivalent elision of the political and historical factors at work in European societies. In short, evoking the spectre of an all-powerful 'Anglo-Saxon model' to explain the dominance of neo-liberal ideas could too easily serve as a smokescreen, a diversion from more complex considerations and questions. This spectre risked diverting attention from the problems or contradictions inherent in the 'French model' whose universalism it supposedly threatened. It also risked forestalling adequate analysis of the ways in which French society as a whole might have been implicated in the political, economic and cultural changes which accompanied the erosion of the postwar consensus in all Western democracies from, broadly, the late 1970s onwards. Understanding neo-liberalism to be a fundamentally elite and/or foreign phenomenon might, finally, actively serve to conceal those areas where elements of the neo-liberal agenda, far from being simply 'imposed' on French society from above, did prove capable of mobilizing popular support, tapping into aspirations and desires left unsatisfied by the form of welfare statism that emerged from the postwar compromise in France.

Bourdieu's reluctance to acknowledge the full range of cultural, social and political factors that may have contributed to the current dominance of neo-liberal ideas is at the core of the criticisms of his politics offered by Luc Boltanski and Eve Chiapello (1999) and Jean-Pierre Le Goff (2002). Further, his characterization of neo-liberalism as something foreign, imposed from above, contrasts strikingly with some of the most persuasive and influential studies of neo-liberal politics in Britain and the US. Typically, such studies have focused on 'market populism', on the ability of neo-liberalism to mobilize widespread support, exploiting popular discontent at the sometimes restrictive nature of the postwar compromise. In a series of essays written from the mid-1970s onwards, later anthologized in *The Hard Road to Renewal: Thatcherism and the crisis of the left* (1988), Stuart Hall argued persuasively for the need to understand the *popular appeal* of neo-liberalism, in its Thatcherite form. He did not seek to deny the importance of right-wing think tanks in formulating the Thatcherite agenda, nor did he doubt that that agenda served the interests of the ruling class. Yet he insisted that Thatcherism's success could only be understood by reference to its ability to tap into popular frustrations at the failings of the British postwar compromise and to mobilize the aspirations left unfulfilled by the form of welfare statism that compromise had engendered. In their study, *Hegemony and Socialist Strategy*, Ernesto Laclau and Chantal Mouffe offered a similar analysis when they maintained:

> Popular support for the Reagan and Thatcher projects of dismantling the welfare state is explained by the fact that they have succeeded in mobilizing against the latter a whole series of resistances to the bureaucratic character of the new forms of state organization.
>
> (1985: 169–70)

Lawrence Grossberg, in his *We Gotta Get Out of this Place: popular conservatism and postmodern culture* (1992), placed a similar emphasis on the popular and populist bases of Reaganism in the US.

To point to its capacity to garner popular support is by no means to deny that neo-liberalism has frequently taken a coercive form. The 'structural adjustment' programmes of the IMF and the World Bank clearly do represent the imposition of neo-liberal policies by US-based organizations on other countries, notably those of the developing world and the ex-Soviet bloc (Stiglitz 2002; Harvey 2003). The wholesale dismantling of the traditional heavy industries in the developed world, often in the face of the concerted opposition of those workers whose jobs and communities were most at threat, represents another example of neo-liberalism's coercive side. Indeed, it was this very element of coercion that Hall emphasized when he coined the phrase 'authoritarian populism' to describe the Thatcherite agenda (Hall 1988: 150–60). However, to attribute neo-liberal hegemony exclusively to 'the bodies that make up the invisible world government', as Bourdieu (2001: 72 [51]) appeared to, was surely to grasp only one side of a more complex phenomenon and to ignore neo-liberalism's potential for garnering popular support in ways which commentators such as Hall, Laclau and Mouffe, and Grossberg have sought to analyse.

That said, Bourdieu is by no means the only French critic of neo-liberalism and globalization to have figured these phenomena as somehow essentially American in origin and to have evoked the French republican tradition as the best response to them. To give but one notable example, Viviane Forrester's 1996 polemic *L'Horreur économique* employed a similar rhetoric, becoming a bestseller in France and winning a prestigious literary award, the Médicis Prize. The kind of rhetoric employed by Bourdieu and Forrester evidently seemed both attractive and plausible to a large French readership. This very popularity and apparent plausibility should give pause for thought since it may point to something fundamental about the French experience of neo-liberalism, about the particular institutional, cultural and political conditions under which neo-liberal ideas gained ascendancy in France. It might also suggest that Bourdieu's invocations of 'French exceptionalism' and the French Third Republic should not be too hastily dismissed as expressions of a nostalgic, idealized nationalism. Rather, it will be necessary to assess both the significance and possible tactical value of such invocations of the French republican tradition. Drawing primarily on the speeches and short articles anthologized in the two *Contre-feux* and the collection *Interventions: science sociale et action politique* (2002), this chapter will seek to provide a more detailed assessment of the precise nature and significance of Bourdieu's political interventions against neo-liberalism, by setting them in their national context. It will question whether Bourdieu's rhetoric did indeed reflect something specific about the French experience of neo-liberalism. It will also examine whether, such national specificities aside, his characterization of neo-liberalism as an essentially foreign, elite phenomenon did not ultimately forestall adequate analysis of the political questions raised by the ascendancy of neo-liberal ideas.

French neo-liberalism as 'la pensée unique'

In their comparative study of the 'neo-liberal revolution' in France, the UK, Mexico and Chile, Marion Fourcade-Gourinchas and Sarah L. Babb (2002: 570) distinguish between 'the "ideological road" to neo-liberalism, in which neo-liberal commitments were at once early, radical, and highly politicised' and 'a much more "pragmatic" transition' to neo-liberalism. They argue that where the UK followed 'the ideological road', France's transition was more 'pragmatic' and relate this to the fact that 'neo-liberal ideas did not possess strong organizational bases in French society (in contrast with Britain or the United States)'. They go on to point out that mainstream French right-wing parties have not 'been really comparable to the ideological movements which brought Margaret Thatcher and Ronald Reagan to power'. The neo-liberal revolution in France 'took place without much fanfare, behind the scenes, within the technocracy and political elite', as a result of 'the higher administration' coming to see 'in the internationalisation of the French economy (via integration with Europe in particular) the means to pursue its historic mission of modernisation and free the "stalled society" from its rigidities' (Fourcade-Gourinchas and Babb 2002: 567).

Fourcade-Gourinchas and Babb thus identify two significant characteristics of the French experience of neo-liberalism. First, it has been predominantly an elite phenomenon, driven by technocrats rather than by the popular and populist political projects embraced by the Conservative Party in Britain or the Republicans in the US. Alain Caillé makes a similar point when he distinguishes between the 'pure neo-liberalism', which has triumphed in the US and Britain, and the 'liberal-technocratic discourse' prevalent in France (in Caillé and Le Goff 1996: 107). Second, Fourcade-Gourinchas and Babb emphasize the extent to which neo-liberal policies have been adopted in France in response to *external* pressures, to the demands of globalization and the strictures on monetary policy imposed by membership of the EU. Both these characteristics are reflected in the currency of the term 'la pensée unique' in French popular and journalistic discourse as shorthand for neo-liberal globalization. This term, meaning literally 'single thought', has come to be used to describe the hegemonic nature of the neo-liberal agenda, referring to the tendency of politicians of both Left and Right to assert that there are certain immutable economic imperatives in the face of which every government remains powerless.

The phrase 'la pensée unique' was first coined by the journalist and commentator Jean-François Kahn in a series of articles in the early 1990s, before providing the title for a collection of his articles and essays published in 1995, and subsequently being very widely adopted by commentators of many different political shades. The phrase itself is revealing since it evokes another common French phrase, 'le système à parti unique', the one-party system characteristic of totalitarian regimes. Indeed, in a resonant phrase, Kahn described 'la pensée unique' as amounting 'in short, to swapping Stalin for the World Bank' (Kahn 1995: 22). The widespread use of the term 'la pensée unique' in French political and journalistic discourse thus reflects the tendency amongst many French commentators to understand neo-liberalism to be an essentially 'totalitarian' phenomenon, something imposed from above and from abroad on an unwilling French citizenry. As we have already noted, this kind of rhetoric can be found in Forrester's bestseller *L'Horreur économique*; it is also a feature of Ignacio Ramonet's work, both in his editorials for *Le Monde diplomatique* and in his monographs attacking globalization (Ramonet 2000). Although he rarely used the phrase 'la pensée unique' himself, the tone and content of Bourdieu's own polemics against neo-liberalism thus need to be understood as part of this more general trend.

For Bourdieu, if there was one group which epitomized such attempts to impose neo-liberal solutions on French society, it was surely the *Fondation Saint Simon*, a think tank founded in 1982 which grouped intellectuals, journalists, trades unionists and high-ranking civil servants whose political affiliations ranged from the centre left to the centre right (see Bourdieu 1999: 41, 2002: 338, 444, 473). Several of the *Fondation*'s members argued that France's high rate of unemployment was caused by excessive social charges and hence that unemployment could only be reduced and French economy and society 'modernized' through a programme of competitive social deflation. Such a programme could only be enforced through the intervention of an outside body which would oblige French citizens to be more 'realistic' about the need to cut back on the 'overly generous' social security benefits to which they were entitled. Closer European integration and, more specifically, European Monetary Union's strictures on public deficits would provide both this outside body and that necessary dose of 'realism'. The *Fondation* had emerged from a constellation of forces around the French 'second left' of the 1960s, associated with Michel Rocard's *Parti socialiste unifié* (PSU), with the modernizing *Reconstruction* current of the formerly Catholic trade union the *Confédération française démocratique du travail* (CFDT), the journal *Esprit* and the weekly news magazine *Le Nouvel observateur*. As early as the 1960s, Bourdieu had criticized both the sociological and political affiliations of this constellation of intellectuals and politicians, criticisms which culminated in the 1976 article 'La Production de l'idéologie dominante', in which he had first anatomized the form of 'liberal technocratic' discourse peculiar to France (Bourdieu 1967a, 1976). For Bourdieu, conclusive proof of the fundamentally neo-liberal affiliations of the *Fondation Saint Simon* was provided by the decision of several of its members to sign what became known as the 'pétition *Esprit*' in the autumn of 1995, a petition in favour of the reform of French social security contained in the 'plan Juppé'. It was the 'plan Juppé', of course, which sparked the major strikes and demonstrations of late 1995 to which Bourdieu gave his public support.

The programme embraced by the *Fondation Saint Simon*, the currency of the phrase 'la pensée unique' and the technocratic form neo-liberalism has taken in France are all testimony to the difficulties that French right-wing parties have experienced in converting neo-liberal ideas into a winning formula at national elections. For example, the election in 1981 of François Mitterrand and a

Socialist-led government, committed to Keynesian reflationary policies and a significant programme of nationalizations, seemed to signal a decisive rejection of neo-liberalism by the French electorate, occurring, as it did, so shortly after the elections of Reagan in the US and Thatcher in the UK. This exercise in reflation was to prove short-lived, however, and during 1983–4, in the face of a balance of payments crisis and rising unemployment, the Socialists abandoned Keynesianism in favour of the politics of 'austerity'. It might be argued that the conditions under which this policy shift took place had a decisive influence on future interpretations of neo-liberalism in France. First, this dramatic policy shift was the result of decisions made at the governmental level, rather than a response to popular demand, and might therefore be presented as a betrayal by the political elite both of their own ideals and of the electorate who voted them into power. Second, the Socialist government justified its turn to the politics of austerity by reference to *external* economic pressures, to capital flight and the balance of payments crisis sparked by a recently deregulated global monetary system. In this context, the notion that neo-liberalism is an essentially elite phenomenon 'imposed' from abroad on France's citizens would appear to have some validity. Certainly, the policy turn of 1984 in France contrasted strongly with the conditions under which neo-liberal policies were first enacted in the US and Britain, following the election of two politicians whose campaigns had expressly sought to exploit popular disaffection at the perceived failures of previous Keynesian policies, offering overtly neo-liberal solutions to such apparent failures.[4]

In both the UK and the US, mainstream right-wing parties pursuing aggressive neo-liberal agendas were elected to office in the wake of the perceived failure of the preceding Labour and Democratic governments to manage the economic and social problems caused by the economic downturn of the mid-1970s and aggravated by the two oil crises of 1974 and 1979. Hence in Britain and the US neo-liberals were able to blame the economic recessions of the 1970s and 1980s, as well as the social dislocation and perceived national decline they provoked, on previous Labour or Democratic administrations. Restoring national pride and doing away with state interventionism and the discredited policies of the social-democratic postwar compromise could become linked in the discourse of both Thatcher and Reagan. As both Hall (1988) and Grossberg (1992) have shown, the ability of Thatcher and Reagan to articulate popular desires for the restoration of national prestige to the neo-liberal agenda played a significant role in their electoral successes. However, this articulation between neo-liberalism and nationalism could not happen in quite the same way in France. First, the Left had not been in power in France at the onset of the recession. Indeed, the Left was not in power at all in France between 1958 and 1981. Second, state intervention or *dirigisme* tends to be associated, in the French popular imaginary, not with the economic recession of the 1970s and 1980s but with the national prosperity that it is generally credited with having secured during the 'trente glorieuses', the thirty-year period of economic growth that followed the Second World War. Third, the centrality of the memory of De Gaulle, in the 1970s, 1980s and 1990s, to Jacques

Chirac's post-Gaullist *Rassemblement pour la République* (RPR), the dominant grouping on the mainstream Right, meant that that party would always have difficulties simply abandoning the Gaullist heritage of *dirigisme*. Where Thatcher could cheerfully rubbish the legacy of William Heath, her predecessor as Conservative leader, dubbing him a 'wet', complicit in the decline her free-market policies sought to arrest, Chirac could never dare do the same with regard to De Gaulle since the very identity of his party remained linked to the memory of De Gaulle and his belief in the power of a strong interventionist state.

However, if French neo-liberals have failed to articulate their economic creed to an appeal to national identity, the same has not been true of their opponents. Those opposed to free-market economics have often been able to call upon the French republican tradition, figuring their defence of certain fundamental social and political rights as a defence of French national identity. A significant example of this phenomenon is provided by the problems encountered by Chirac, during his term as prime minister from 1986 to 1988. The election of Chirac as prime minister in 1986 did represent a rejection of the failed policies of the Socialist Party, while heralding the accession to power of a right-wing politician openly committed to a free-market agenda. Chirac pushed forward a programme of privatizations explicitly modelled on the analogous policies of successive Thatcher governments in the UK (Becker 1998: 396–401). However, Chirac's efforts to use the premiership as a springboard for the presidential elections of 1988 were foiled by the student protests and public-sector strikes of the winter of 1986–7. The student protests were sparked by anger at proposals to introduce selective entry to French universities. They combined with strikes for better pay and conditions in the public sector fatally to undermine Chirac's authority. Mitterrand, meanwhile, still in post as president, was able to distance himself from his prime minister's policies, meeting delegations of both students and workers, and posing as the guarantor of certain fundamental democratic rights, inscribed in the French Fifth Republic's Constitution. Having outflanked Chirac, Mitterrand was able to win the presidential election of 1988, call new parliamentary elections and replace the right-wing government with a new centre–left coalition. It appeared that neo-liberalism had again been wholeheartedly rejected by the French electorate, in the name, significantly, of core French republican values of social justice and solidarity, exemplified, in this instance, by defence of the fundamental principle of free access to higher education for all who had passed the *baccalauréat*.

Tellingly, when Chirac at last managed to win a presidential election in 1995, he did so on an almost social-democratic programme, accusing left- and right-wing rivals alike of being in thrall to 'la pensée unique' and promising to maintain high levels of public spending in order to heal the 'social fracture' at the heart of French society. As soon as he attempted to enact policies seen to renege on that promise, the reforms to public health insurance and the public sector contained in the infamous 'plan Juppé', Chirac again met with concerted and decisive mass opposition in the form of the public-sector strikes of autumn 1995. These strikes won widespread support even among those members of the general public who were most affected by the disruption to public services they brought. Numerous commentators argued that they were 'strikes by proxy', allowing those private-sector workers, who did not dare to strike themselves for fear of losing their jobs, to express their discontent at Chirac's policies through their solidarity with the strikers (Caillé and Le Goff 1996: 99). Bourdieu, of course, intervened directly in these events, expressing his support for the strikes in classically French republican terms and re-drafting the petition backing the strikers so that a reference to defending 'the general interest' was replaced with a call to defend 'the universal gains of the Republic' (Duval *et al*. 1998: 6). As has been noted, such appeals to the republican tradition, to 'the French model' and to 'French exceptionalism' were to be reiterated in subsequent articles and interventions.

The potency of such appeals rests on the historical link between a kind of social-democratic consensus and a certain notion of French national identity, a link forged and sustained in part thanks to the centrality of republican ideology to the French state education system. That link has been further strengthened by the existence of a very large public sector in France, whose employees enjoy relatively favourable pay and conditions and hence form a large constituency with a vested interest in defending the republican tradition and resisting any neo-liberal assault on the centralized state. Moreover, as Alain Caillé has pointed out, for many private-sector employees the public sector has taken on a talismanic value as a haven of job security and good working conditions in a labour market characterized by 'flexibility', short-term contracts and the constant fear of redundancy. Supporting public-sector employees in their struggles to defend their status thus becomes a way 'to mark one's refusal to let the old model of employment, of which the public services represent the most stable core, gradually disappear' (in Caillé and Le Goff 1996: 99).

There is little doubt that the 1995 strikes played a decisive role in the defeat of the Right at the parliamentary elections of 1997 and the victory of a left-wing coalition government under Lionel Jospin. If that government fell in 2002, after Chirac's re-election as president and the mainstream Right's success at the subsequent parliamentary elections, this had less to do with the popularity of any free-market agenda than with a combination of divisions on the Left and a popular determination to defeat Jean-Marie Le Pen, the *Front national*'s candidate (Budgen 2002). Indeed, recent years have seen Chirac again contrasting neo-liberalism to his own supposed allegiance to a social-democratic French republicanism. In his attempts to persuade the French electorate to vote 'yes' to the EU Constitution in 2005, Chirac claimed that the Constitution was the best way to preserve France's 'republican pact' from the threat of 'an ultraliberal Europe', while ensuring that Europe was constructed 'on values and no longer only on a market'.[5] Although such appeals fell on deaf ears, the fact that a right-wing politician like Chirac should have felt obliged to employ such rhetoric highlights once more the extent of popular opposition to neo-liberalism in France and the potency of French republicanism as a symbol of such opposition.

On the basis of this admittedly simplified and highly condensed account of French politics of the past few decades, it is possible to understand how neo-liberalism has come to be seen, in the eyes of many French commentators, as something inherently foreign, imposed on French society from above. For example, in spite of the fact that privatization has never unleashed the kind of 'market populism' it did under Thatcher in Britain, successive French governments, frequently Socialist governments, have engaged in major programmes of denationalization and industrial restructuring. As Bourdieu noted, this 'withdrawal of the state' under successive Socialist governments has provoked feelings of scandal, stupefaction and despair among many of those working on the front lines of the public services (1998: 10 [2]). Moreover, the strong historical association between the state, the French nation and certain social gains and rights seen as inherent to the republican tradition has meant that those contesting the dogmas of neo-liberalism have frequently done so by means of an appeal to a certain notion of French national identity. This phenomenon may, in turn, help explain Bourdieu's apparent willingness to classify neo-liberalism as something inherently foreign, as an 'invasion', while claiming that 'French exceptionalism', a strong republican state, formed the best bulwark against such an 'invasion'.

The particular history of neo-liberalism in France, as well as the relationship between French national identity, republicanism and certain fundamental social rights, thus provide an important context for understanding the nature of Bourdieu's interventions 'against the neo-liberal invasion'. The fact that a right-wing politician like Chirac has felt obliged to invoke the republican tradition against neo-liberalism on a number of occasions could be taken as evidence of both the extent of popular resistance to neo-liberal ideas in France and of the potency of republicanism as a symbol of such resistance. On the other hand, one could draw very different conclusions from the fact that such discourse has been so widely recuperated, with French politicians from extreme right to extreme left regularly declaiming against 'la pensée unique'. Indeed, it might be argued that the evident rhetorical force of this kind of discourse can serve precisely to deflect attention away from more difficult questions regarding both the inherent failings of French republicanism and the extent of French society's own implication in a neo-liberalism too conveniently characterized as inherently un-French. As Timothy B. Smith has argued, 'social policy nationalism' can be 'a clever ploy' distracting the French population from 'homegrown' problems (Smith 2004: 16). Smith identifies a series of problems inherent to the French welfare state, notably its failure to achieve effective wealth redistribution, its regressive taxation system and the inadequacy of its welfare provision to France's most deprived social groups, the young unemployed, immigrants and the handicapped. He argues that the kind of rhetoric employed by commentators such as Bourdieu serves to conceal these problems by attributing blame for all of France's social problems to the foreign forces of neo-liberal globalization (Smith 2004: 54–87). In short, whatever the specificities of the French experience of neo-liberalism, Bourdieu's adoption of an apparent classically French republican rhetoric remained potentially problematic. It will therefore be necessary to look in more detail at the precise role he anticipated the republican state playing in opposition to neo-liberalism. This, in turn, will enable a clearer assessment of the extent to which he acknowledged or simply skated over the flaws inherent in the French republican state in its current incarnation.

The republican nation-state against neo-liberalism

For Bourdieu, the state needed to be defended inasmuch as it represented 'the trace in reality of past social conquests' (1998: 38 [33]). He sought to distinguish between what he termed 'the left hand' and 'the right hand' of the state, the former comprising the 'street-level bureaucracy' of teachers, social workers and probation officers, increasingly forced to apply the free-market solutions foisted on them by the latter, the 'state nobility' of high-ranking civil servants imbued with the neo-liberal doxa dispensed by one of the more technocratically oriented *grandes écoles* (Bourdieu 1993: 221–3 [183–4]). These 'street-level bureaucrats' constituted,

> the left hand of the state, the set of agents of the so-called spending ministries which are the trace, within the state, of the social struggles of the past. They are opposed to the right hand of the state, the technocrats [*énarques*] of the Ministry of Finance, the public and private banks and the ministerial *cabinets*. A number of social struggles that we are now seeing and will see express the revolt of the minor state nobility against the senior state nobility.
> (Bourdieu 1998: 9–10 [2])

Defending the role of the state thus was a matter of defending the 'social gains' incarnated in the state's 'left hand', while calling for the state as a whole to reassert its autonomy from market forces so that it might once more come to embody the 'universal interest'. The state should intervene in the market to regulate its operations and mitigate the social injustices caused by unrestrained market forces: 'Far from calling for "the withering of the state", we must call on the state to carry out the regulating action capable of counteracting the "fatality" of those social and economic mechanisms which are immanent to the social order' (Bourdieu 2002: 243). As Bourdieu's allusion to the Marxist–Leninist thesis regarding 'the withering of the state' indicated, his target was not merely neo-liberalism here. His reassertion of the 'public service ethos' at the heart of the state and of the state's role as guarantor of the 'universal interest' against the partial interests of the market was directed against both neo-liberalism and Marxism. On several occasions in his later writings, Bourdieu pointed to what he saw as an affinity between neo-liberalism and Marxism: both were forms of economism and it was necessary 'to reaffirm the role of the state against the two forms of submission to the necessity of economic laws which flow from these two forms of economism' (2002: 242–3). Neo-liberals who contested the role of the state did so in the name of a 'Marxist vision that paradoxically they take as their own' (Bourdieu 1998b: 20). It was this affinity between

Marxism and neo-liberalism that explained why 'so many people' of Bourdieu's generation 'have so effortlessly passed from a Marxist fatalism to a neo-liberal fatalism: in both cases economism forbids responsibility and mobilisation by cancelling out politics' (1998: 56 [50]). Bourdieu thus situated his own position on the state as being 'in opposition to this Marxist vision' (1998b: 20), as much as it was in opposition to a neo-liberalism characterized by

> the withering of the hegelo-durkheimian vision of the state as a collective instance charged with acting as consciousness and collective will, responsible for making choices in conformity with the general interest and for contributing to efforts to reinforce social solidarity.
>
> (2000: 23 [11])

As the phrase 'the hegelo-durkheimian vision of the state' indicated, Bourdieu's conception of the state drew on elements of both Hegel's *Philosophy of Right* (1821) and Durkheim's *Professional Ethics and Civic Morals* (1957). From Hegel he took the notion of the state as 'higher authority' and guarantor of the universal interest above the partial or particular interests of its citizens. This notion is broadly consistent with Durkheim's emphasis on the state's responsibility 'to work out certain ideas which apply to the collectivity', ideas which possessed a 'more conscious and deliberate character' than those contained in the '*conscience collective*' (in Giddens ed. 1972: 192). Moreover, as Steven Lukes points out, for Durkheim the state had a 'special responsibility' in safeguarding social solidarity by imposing

> rules of justice on economic exchanges, to ensure that 'each is treated as he deserves, that he is freed of all unjust and humiliating dependence, that he is joined to his fellows and to the group without abandoning his personality to them'.
>
> (1973: 272)

Bourdieu's critique of neo-liberalism echoed Durkheim's emphasis on the role of the state not only in regulating the market and mitigating its injustices but also, to quote Durkheim, in acting as 'the very organ of social thought', as the 'collective agency which [. . .] is more fully aware of what it is attempting to do', generating 'representations' that are 'more self-conscious, aware of their causes and aims' than the 'collective representations that are diffused in every society' (in Giddens ed. 1972: 192). One of Bourdieu's most frequent charges against neo-liberalism was that in reducing everything to the workings of the market, it neglected to take account of the social costs of its public policy prescriptions, justifying such neglect by invoking the 'scientific proofs' derived from the abstract econometric models of neo-classical economics (Bourdieu 1998: 60 [54]). If the state were to perform the function Durkheim had attributed to it, arriving at rational decisions made in the general interest, then a calculation of the social costs should be included in the decision-making process, a calculation based on the properly 'scientific' findings of sociology rather than the pseudo-science of neo-classical economics. As Bourdieu put it, 'we must at all costs ensure the gains of science enter the realm of public debate, from which they are tragically absent' (2001: 9 [13]).

Bourdieu's emphasis on the progressive role of the state was, finally, intended as a corrective to what he saw as a common misuse of the term 'globalization'. He fully acknowledged the significance of certain new global forces, of multinational corporations, massive international capital flows and supranational organizations such as the World Bank, IMF and WTO (1998: 43–4 [38]). However, he distinguished this 'descriptive meaning of the concept' from its 'normative, or better, performative meaning', whereby 'globalization' was invoked as an irreversible process in the face of which further market liberalization represented the only possible option (2001: 95 [85]).[6] Against this 'normative' or 'performative' use of the term, Bourdieu emphasized that globalization was a historical process and that individual states and their politicians thus possessed the power to control or counter its damaging effects.

Reasserting the role of the nation-state was not seen as an end in itself. Rather the nation-state, particularly for 'so-called developing countries such as South Korea or Malaysia', represented 'the only force that, in the absence of a world state and of a world bank financed by a tax on the international circulation of speculative capital' could be opposed 'to the stranglehold of the multinationals' (Bourdieu 2001: 38 [23]). Reserving 'a special place for the state, the national state' was thus merely a preliminary to the organization of a 'supranational, in other words European', state, itself seen as a 'stage on the way to a world state' (Bourdieu 1998: 119 [104]). At the European level, construction of this new supranational state would involve a complete reform of the existing EU, rendering its institutions genuinely democratic and transforming its economic policy (Bourdieu 2001: 11 [15]). Economically, Bourdieu's proposals seemed to represent classical Keynesianism applied at the European level, calling for the financing of 'a major public programme of social and economic development based on the willed establishment of a coherent body of European "framework laws", notably in the fields of education, health, and social protection' (2001: 15 [55]). Arguing that 70% of the trade of European nations took place with other European nations, Bourdieu proposed that a pan-European trade union movement should fight for a shared minimum wage, minimum employment rights and protection. Such measures aimed to mitigate intra-European competition and hence end 'social dumping', i.e. the movement of investment and manufacturing plant to those countries with the lowest wages and weakest social protection (1998: 41, 70 [36, 64]). At the international level, while anticipating the extension of such measures worldwide, Bourdieu called for 'the establishment of an international system of taxation of capital (levied particularly on very short-term speculative flows)', effectively a form of Tobin tax, and 'the reconstruction of a monetary system capable of guaranteeing stable relations between economies' (2001: 15 [55]).[7] He regretted that globalization had led to unification of the global market taking place 'without a state – counter to the wish of John Maynard

Keynes to see the creation of a world central bank issuing a neutral reserve currency and capable of guaranteeing trade on an equal footing between all countries' (2001: 107 [95]).

It would be a mistake to expect a fully worked out political programme to be contained within Bourdieu's various political speeches and articles. Indeed, he explicitly refused to provide any such programme, stating that this was the role of 'parties' and 'apparatuses', to whose deliberations and debates intellectuals should merely contribute their specific expertise (1998: 62 [56]). Nonetheless, on the basis of his published statements, it is clear that Bourdieu was committed to deepening and extending the social gains of the welfare state and the postwar compromise. This approach explicitly defined itself against Marxism, was profoundly influenced by Keynes and, in its invocation of the 'hegelo-durkheimian vision of the state' as guarantor of 'social solidarity', remained strongly tinged with a particular form of left-wing French republicanism. As we have already noted, there was nothing parochial about these proposals. However, Bourdieu's goal of applying an avowedly French republican model first at the European, and subsequently at the global, level did raise a number of both practical and theoretical problems. First, as Callinicos (1999: 93) has pointed out, this 'projection of the French myth of the republican state as the embodiment of the general interest onto a European scale bears little relation to the reality of a European Union riven by national conflicts and social tensions'. Second, the greatly weakened state of trade unions throughout the EU makes Bourdieu's vision of a social-democratic Europe constructed on the basis of a pan-European union movement seem rather unrealistic. Finally, on the practical level, the extent of popular resistance, notably in France, to EU expansion even as far as Turkey provides but a foretaste of the immense difficulties to be encountered by any attempt to extend a 'European social model' to encompass all the nations of the world. There was surely a danger that Bourdieu's plan would stall at the European level, and the measures taken to prevent 'social dumping' would hence merely form a series of protectionist barriers.

At the theoretical level, there did appear to be something paradoxical in Bourdieu's championing of the French republican state as guarantor of the universal interest and bulwark against neo-liberalism in this way. For, his analyses of higher education in the 1960s and 1970s had constituted a sustained critique of that same republican state's failure to live up to its universal ideals, a wholesale rejection of what Bourdieu himself had acerbically termed 'the Jacobin ideology' (2002: 55–61). It was unclear, therefore, how Bourdieu's belated championing of the French republican model could be reconciled with that earlier assault on 'the Jacobin ideology'. Moreover, to champion the state in this way was surely to risk overlooking the force neo-liberalism derived from exploiting popular discontent at that state's failings. In an interview with Günter Grass given late in his life, Bourdieu acknowledged this risk:

> We are paradoxically led to defend what is not entirely defensible. But is it enough to demand a return to 'more state'? In order to avoid falling into the

trap laid by the conservative revolution, I think we have to invent another kind of state.

(Bourdieu 2002a: 71)

Bourdieu's distinction between the left and right hands of the state might be taken as evidence of an attempt to specify the form this other kind of state should take. However, this hardly amounted to a wholesale re-thinking of the role and operation of state power. On the contrary, his appeals to the 'hegelo-durkheimian vision of the state' suggested a continued adherence to the most classical conception of the state's proper role and function.

Bourdieu's appeals to 'the French model' of the state as guarantor of the universal interest thus appeared to involve him overlooking his own, earlier, trenchant critiques of that state's failure to live up to its universal ideals. This apparent contradiction suggested that, at the very least, Bourdieu's championing of the universalism of the French republican state necessitated his adopting a rather idealized vision of its actual mode of functioning, turning a blind eye to the inherent failings he had earlier been eager to highlight. His intervention in support of the 1995 strikes represents one area where the political problems posed by such an idealization seemed to manifest themselves in particularly striking form.

Republican univeralism and its limits

As we have already seen, Bourdieu expressed his support for the strikes of 1995 in classically French republican terms, re-drafting an early version of the petition he signed so that it referred to the strike movement not merely as defending 'the general interest' but as struggling for 'the defence of the most universal gains of the Republic'. The problem with this kind of rhetoric was that the form of health insurance and the public-sector pay and conditions that the strikers were attempting to defend were not in fact universal in any genuine sense. Immigrants in France are prevented from enjoying the relatively favourable pay and conditions enjoyed by French public-sector workers, since acquiring the status of 'fonctionnaire' or civil servant is dependent upon French citizenship. Further, in 1995 France's health insurance system was anything but universal in its coverage. At the time of Alain Juppé's proposed reforms to the social security system, approximately 1% of the population had no access to state health care coverage, instead depending on the charitable sector. More significantly, French social security typically covers only the first 75–80% of standard health care costs, the remaining percentage being covered by supplementary mutual insurance schemes that are work-related. It is the poorest paid, the self-employed, farmers and farm labourers who usually lack such supplementary insurance, while the wealthiest and best-paid groups in France tend to be fully covered (Smith 2004: 144). Like health insurance, unemployment benefits in France have traditionally been linked to employment, claimants receiving a percentage of their former salary over a limited time period.

This necessarily disadvantages the young and long-term unemployed. Indeed, since the 1980s, between 40% and 50% of France's unemployed have not qualified for unemployment insurance in any given year (Smith 2004: 12). Designed for an era of full employment, the French benefits system was ill-adapted to conditions of long-term structural unemployment. Far from being universal, the system disadvantaged some of France's most vulnerable groups – immigrants, the low-paid, the young unemployed. Juppé's package of social security reforms included proposals to extend healthcare insurance to the 1% of the population at the time without coverage and to bring health spending under closer parliamentary control, in order, he claimed, to redistribute such expenditure more equitably. It was on this basis that the signatories of a rival petition to Bourdieu's had lent their qualified support to Juppé. The signatories of the '*Esprit* petition', so-called because it was launched by contributors to the journal of that name, thus maintained that Juppé's reform 'went in the direction of social justice' (in Ross ed. 1996: 4).

To point out that the strikers in 1995 were acting to defend gains that were not universal is not to question the legitimacy of their struggle to hold onto the particular pay and conditions they had managed to acquire over previous decades. It is also not to support the actions of the signatories of the *Esprit* petition, particularly as Juppé's health reforms formed part of a larger package aimed at reducing overall social spending and eroding workers' rights more generally. Rather it is to argue that the strikes of 1995 posed a series of urgent political questions concerning the inherent weaknesses of the French social security system and the kinds of reform necessary to render that system more equitable. In proclaiming the current, flawed system to represent 'the most universal gains of the Republic', Bourdieu surely risked eliding such urgent political questions, failing to offer solutions to that system's evident failings in favour of a defence of the status quo. Granted, in the heat of the moment and for tactical reasons, evocations of the universal interest may have been appropriate, leaving detailed discussion of the system's flaws to another day. However, in the months which followed the strikes, Bourdieu never acknowledged the flaws in the existing social security arrangements, much less did he sketch an alternative reform to that proposed by Juppé. It would surely have been possible, for example, to acknowledge that the signatories of the *Esprit* petition had identified certain failings in the health insurance system, before criticizing their support for Juppé's plan and suggesting an alternative set of reforms in its place. However, Bourdieu appeared to deny that the signatories of the *Esprit* petition had raised any valid political questions at all, reducing the position they had taken to an expression of the networks of political and intellectual power in which they were enmeshed. Hence he argued that the force of their position rested not on 'a sequence of demonstrations' but rather on 'a chain of authorities, which runs from the mathematician to the banker, from the banker to the philosopher-journalist, from the essayist to the journalist' (Bourdieu 1998: 61 [55]).

According to Bourdieu, then, the authority of the signatories of the *Esprit* petition related not to the inherent validity of their arguments but merely reflected the power and prestige or capital they derived from their position within the political and intellectual fields. This claim was taken up by five of his close collaborators in an analysis of the strikes of 1995 they published in the 'Liber-Raisons d'agir' series, entitled *Le Décembre des intellectuels français* (1998). The authors of this study employed the full resources of Bourdieu's 'field theory' to argue that the dispute between those intellectuals who had signed the *Esprit* petition and the signatories of the 'Bourdieu petition' was the expression of a fundamental division structuring the French intellectual field. This division, which Bourdieu had first identified in *Homo Academicus* (1984a), reflected the opposition between the 'spiritual' and 'temporal' poles of the intellectual field, between 'autonomous' intellectuals, whose authority derived from their properly 'intellectual capital' accumulated by conforming to 'universal' criteria of 'scientific' enquiry, on the one hand, and 'heteronomous' intellectuals, who 'compensated' their lack of intellectual capital by their involvement in journalism and the mass media and their proximity to political power, on the other. The signatories of the *Esprit* petition were positioned closer to the 'temporal' pole of the intellectual field; their proximity to sources of media and political power predisposed them to bring 'heteronomous' forces to bear on the intellectual field, playing a key role in importing and imposing neo-liberal ideas, participating in 'the broader movement of conservative restoration, whose "avant-garde" is American' (Duval *et al.* 1998: 115). The struggle between the 'universal gains of the Republic' defended by the strikers and Juppé's market-led reforms was thus played out in microcosm in the intellectual field in the conflict between the 'universal' intellectual values incarnated by the signatories of the Bourdieu petition and the particular 'heteronomous' interests expressed by the signatories of the *Esprit* petition. The authors of *Le Décembre* pointed out that taking social security spending under direct parliamentary control and hence removing trade union representation from the committees making spending decisions might well pave the way for the future privatization of health services (Duval *et al.* 1998: 68). This was something of a moot point. Arguably, given the very low levels of union membership in France, securing direct parliamentary control of social security budgets might be seen as a fundamentally more democratic measure, better serving the universal interest. More significantly, however, at no point in over 100 pages of analysis did the authors of *Le Décembre* acknowledge the flaws inherent in the supposedly universal system of social protection they had defended, nor did they offer any alternatives to the reform of that system to which the signatories of the *Esprit* petition had lent their qualified support. In short, they never engaged with the substantive political issues raised by the strikes of 1995. Rather, the different positions taken regarding the future of the social welfare system were reduced to the straightforward expression of positions occupied in the intellectual field, of the varying forms and amounts of power and capital possessed by the intellectuals concerned.

The position Bourdieu took during the 1995 strikes and the analyses both he and his collaborators subsequently offered of those strikes thus exemplified his analysis of neo-liberalism more generally. Neo-liberal ideas were identified as fundamentally American in origin and their arrival in the French political arena attributed primarily to the actions of a complicit intellectual elite, pursuing their own partial or particular interests to the detriment of the universal values promoted by autonomous intellectuals, such as Bourdieu himself, and safeguarded by the French republican tradition. As has been demonstrated, the problem with such an analysis was its elision of the properly political issues raised by neo-liberalism. The potential for neo-liberals to identify genuine flaws in the French welfare state, exploiting them to their own ideological ends, offering false solutions to real problems, in just the way Juppé had attempted to do, was overlooked here. Eric Fassin, while distancing himself from the position taken by the signatories of the *Esprit* petition, has criticized the signatories of the Bourdieu petition precisely for their failure to acknowledge the limitations of the strike movement or to formulate positive proposals that would overcome such limitations. Regretting the strikers' focus on public-sector jobs reserved for French citizens, he notes 'the blinding absence of the figure of the immigrant' from the movement, concluding that 'the public sector is indeed "truly French"' (in Ross ed. 1996: 9). Etienne Balibar, himself a signatory of the Bourdieu petition, makes a similar point when he notes that 'what was characteristic of the strikes of December 1995' was 'once again their confinement or blockage at the level of the national. To my French compatriots I say, "More effort required"' (Balibar 2002: 126). This remark appears in an essay in which Balibar attempts to re-think the relationship between national or ethnic identity and citizenship and the social rights it confers, so that the latter might no longer be dependent on the former. As Fassin argues, the French left needed to recognize the 'political nature of what was at stake' in the strikes and to formulate an alternative project for reform. Otherwise, it risked reducing the alternatives on offer to a false dichotomy between the maintenance of the existing flawed system or its reform along neo-liberal lines (in Ross ed. 1996: 11). As we have sought to demonstrate, Bourdieu's rhetoric and terms of analysis, his reliance on a dichotomy between French republican universalism and neo-liberalism as a foreign 'imposition', actively worked to forestall the kind of political analysis which Balibar and Fassin attempt.

The urgent political issues raised by the strike movement of 1995 thus demonstrate that neo-liberalism in France cannot be understood to be an essentially foreign phenomenon, 'imposed' on French society from above. Rather, neo-liberalism needs to be understood, in properly political terms, as an attempt to offer solutions to genuine problems or contradictions that are inherent to French society. That such solutions are ideological, in the sense of representing false solutions to real contradictions, is not in doubt here. However, the fact that this is a matter of false solutions to *real* contradictions points to the need to conduct a political analysis and to suggest alternative solutions in a manner in which the terms of Bourdieu's analysis, with its dichotomies between the universal and the particular, French republicanism and a US-inspired neo-liberalism, did not seem to allow.

Of course, Bourdieu's rhetoric had not always been so overtly republican nor had he always appeared so reluctant to question the claims of republican institutions to embody universal values. On the contrary, his earlier work in the sociology of culture and education had involved a sustained critique of state institutions and a debunking of their claims to universality. As we have already seen, Bourdieu accused Marxists who in the 1960s and 1970s had called for 'the withering of the state' of complicity with the neo-liberal project, preparing the ground for the neo-liberal assault on the state by undermining the faith paced in its institutions. He seemed reluctant, however, to concede that his own critique of 'Jacobin ideology' might itself have contributed to a more general climate of distrust towards state institutions. This is not to accuse Bourdieu of straightforward *complicity* with neo-liberalism nor is it to deny any validity to his earlier critiques of state educational institutions. Rather, it is to suggest that Bourdieu was, like all of us in the developed world, himself *implicated* in the cultural, social and political shifts that the neo-liberal *doxa* has sought to exploit and mobilize.

Consider, for example, the interview Bourdieu gave to *Libération* in December 1986, at the time of the mass student protests against the Chirac government's proposals to introduce selective entry to French universities. Bourdieu argued that these proposals formed an integral part of Chirac's broader neo-liberal agenda and the force of the students' reaction against it reflected their rejection of the government's attempts to submit all education to the immediate demands of the labour market. One manifestation of this neo-liberal assault on education, according to Bourdieu, was what he termed the 'disqualification of any form of *gratuitous* research, whether artistic or scientific'. He went on to imagine the dismay of a mother on hearing her son wanted to study an arts subject at university in this climate of the 'disqualification' of the 'gratuitous':

> When a bourgeois or even petty bourgeois mother talks about her son who wants to study history, not to mention philosophy or classics, you'd think she was announcing a catastrophe. Humanities students are seen as a waste of time and money. And not only to those in 'government circles', whether of right or left, but also to their own families, and often to themselves.
>
> (Bourdieu 2002: 214)

Bourdieu's defence of 'gratuitous' research in the humanities was somewhat perplexing here. For, in studies such as *The Inheritors* and *Reproduction*, he had argued that it was precisely its gratuitousness that secured 'legitimate culture's' role in social reproduction, insisting that that role was 'most clearly manifested in the teaching of the humanities' (Bourdieu 1964b: 19 [8]). To appreciate the gratuitous pleasures of 'legitimate culture' and hence master the values dispensed and rewarded by the education system, Bourdieu had maintained, presupposed the possession of certain attributes characteristic of the bourgeois habitus, of the capacity to stand at a leisurely distance from the realm of immediate material need, an ability to 'suspend' all considerations of the practical utility of forms of knowledge and education. By treating these typically bourgeois attributes of wealth and leisure or *skholè* as though they were at once universal characteristics and objective measures of intellectual ability, the education system could perform its function in reproducing and naturalizing class distinctions. As Bourdieu put it in *Sociology in Question*:

> The school, the site of *skholè*, leisure [...] is the site par excellence of what are called gratuitous exercises, where one acquires a distant, neutralizing disposition towards the social world, the very same one which is implied in the bourgeois relation to art, language, and the body.
>
> (1980b: 177 [120])

At times, then, Bourdieu appeared to argue that the 'gratuitous' pleasures of 'legitimate culture' merely expressed the tastes and aversions, values and ethos of the bourgeoisie, in short their habitus. For example, in *Reproduction* he stated that 'legitimate culture' was 'nothing other than the dominant cultural arbitrary', itself defined as the cultural arbitrary 'which most fully, though always indirectly, expresses the objective interests (material and symbolic) of the dominant groups or classes' (Bourdieu 1970a: 38, 23 [23, 9]). If legitimate culture was indeed merely an arbitrary construct expressing the objective interests of the dominant classes, then there would appear to be no justification for the state, in its role as guarantor of the universal public interest, to subsidize the development, expression and transmission of such narrow, class-based values. Furthermore, it would surely be possible to present the market, in opposition to the class-based realm of 'legitimate culture', as offering a more objective measure of inherent ability, representing a realm in which vested interests or inherited abilities would no longer prevail. In this sense, it might be argued that Bourdieu's own critique of 'legitimate culture' had itself played a significant role in undermining popular perceptions of the value of pursuing apparently gratuitous research in the humanities. Indeed, it would be perfectly possible to draw on Bourdieu's findings on education to construct an argument in favour of its 'marketization'.

As Ahearne argues,

> with the repeated insistence throughout *Reproduction* that legitimate culture simply 'is' arbitrary, it is easy to forget the note (afterthought?) in the preface that the notion of pure arbitrariness is a logical construction without empirical referent that is necessary for the construction of the argument.
>
> (2004: 50)

What this points to is a more general ambiguity throughout Bourdieu's work on culture and education as to whether it was *the content of legitimate culture itself* which was entirely arbitrary, class-based and hence to be rejected, or whether it was merely *the manner in which that culture was dispensed and taught* that was problematic and hence in need of reform. At times, in his works on education and culture of the 1960s, such as *The Inheritors* and *The Love of Art*, Bourdieu seemed to be pursuing a classically French republican project, calling for a 'rational pedagogy' to be adopted so that the implicit, class-based assumptions of a cultural education abandoned to the silent workings of the habitus would be replaced by a rational, genuinely universal and democratic system, bringing the benefits of high culture to all. In the opening sections of *Reproduction*, however, he had rejected any such 'rational pedagogy' as 'utopian', arguing, first, that no educational system would be allowed to operate in a manner 'contrary to the interests of the dominant classes who delegate its pedagogic authority to it'. Second, he claimed that inasmuch as a measure of rationalization might improve the educational chances of individual members of the dominated classes, this would only serve to reinforce education's role in social reproduction, since individual cases of successful working-class students, however statistically rare, served to support the ideological myth of School as the guarantor of equality for all (Bourdieu 1970a: 69–70 [53–4]). Nonetheless, he continued to advocate an 'explicit pedagogy' as a means of mitigating the class bias inherent to education in the main body of the text and this advocacy was to be evident in the more concrete proposals on educational reform he made throughout his career (Bourdieu 2002: 199–226).

Bourdieu's position on education was thus marked by considerable ambiguity; he oscillated between a radical critique of French republicanism as pure ideology and an embrace of reforms which appeared to be inspired by the very egalitarian republican ideals whose utopianism he elsewhere rejected. Such ambiguities might be read as exemplifications of what Le Goff has termed the 'impossible legacy' of the political and theoretical radicalism of the 1960s and 1970s. As we have seen, Le Goff argues that progressive critiques of the educational system, such as Bourdieu's own, worked in concert with contemporary critiques of their rigidities and hierarchical structures to undermine faith in a range of private- and public-sector institutions, from businesses to political parties. This kind of progressive discourse fed directly into what Le Goff terms 'la barbarie douce', the new form of social domination and control exercised via the extensive apparatus of audit and evaluation imposed on public- and private-sector organizations alike in the name of ensuring greater transparency and accountability. He maintains that while this 'barbarie douce' is not directly reducible to neo-liberalism, it is 'rather, symptomatic of the breakdown in the guiding values which used previously to structure common life and collective action, something which today makes opposing neo-liberalism more difficult' (Le Goff 1999: 10). According to Le Goff, the fact that Bourdieu's progressive critiques of French education could have fed into an atmosphere conducive to the neo-liberal assault on the state should be taken as an evidence of the contradictions inherent to those critiques. The radicalism of the assault on existing institutions and structures, he argues, was not matched by a coherent vision of what to put in their place and this opened the way to neo-liberal solutions.

Boltanski and Chiapello (1999) might offer only a slightly different interpretation of this. For them, Bourdieu's critiques of education might be seen as forming part of a more general disaffection with the rigid, centralized and hierarchical structures of French society, a disaffection expressed in critical discourses emanating from across society, from grass roots social movements, just as much as from philosophers, sociologists and artists. These critical discourses then coalesced to provoke a generalized demand that French institutions find new and more convincing forms of justification and legitimation, adapting themselves to become less hierarchical and repressive. Such demands were then 'recuperated' by the forces of capital into a 'new spirit of capitalism', an emphasis on labour mobility and flexibility, 'flatter' management structures, constant creativity and change in the workplace that was wholly consonant with the neo-liberal agenda. It is not necessary to accept their analyses uncritically to acknowledge that Le Goff and Boltanski and Chiapello argue convincingly for the need to take full account of the range of cultural, political and social shifts internal to French society that have facilitated the rise of neo-liberal ideas. In this respect, such analyses invite comparison with the accounts of neo-liberalism in the UK and US offered by Hall (1988) and Laclau and Mouffe (1985). For, despite the different theoretical traditions on which they draw, what all these commentators share is an emphasis on the need to understand the ways in which neo-liberalism exploits popular disaffection with the institutions and ways of life that emerged from the postwar compromise. In both Hall and Laclau and Mouffe's modified Gramscian vocabulary, this involved an effort to construct a new 'commonsense', a shared set of assumptions about the perceived inefficiencies of state institutions that formed one key element in neo-liberalism's overall 'hegemonic project'.

Boltanski and Chiapello pose the most explicit challenge to Bourdieu in this respect. They argue that weaknesses in Bourdieu's critique of neo-liberalism are not limited to his shorter, directly political interventions but reflect deeper problems in his full-blown sociological theory. They claim that it is only by abandoning certain founding assumptions of Bourdieu's 'critical sociology' that an adequate account of neo-liberalism's ability to exploit popular desires and disaffections could be given. Commentators like Hall or Laclau and Mouffe, who work within a broadly Gramscian tradition, pose a similar challenge to Bourdieu, albeit implicitly. For Bourdieu always maintained that his own 'field theory' or 'theory of practice' contained a set of analytical tools that were at once distinct from and superior to any theories of ideology derived from the Marxist tradition. Such claims raise a set of more detailed theoretical considerations than this chapter has yet examined. They broach the question as to whether the failings we have identified in Bourdieu's shorter political interventions can be attributed solely to the demands of rhetoric or the necessity for a certain amount of simplification or whether, on the contrary, such failings reflect deeper flaws in his theoretical apparatus. Only by extending our enquiries outwards, as it were, from Bourdieu's short, directly political interventions to embrace his more detailed contributions to social theory, will it be possible to engage more fully with this range of more theoretical questions. This, in turn, will enable us to begin to assess the contribution that Bourdieu's social theory might have to make to political analysis more generally.

2 The poetics and politics of practice

In Chapter 1, we noted the striking contrast between Bourdieu's account of neo-liberalism and the analyses offered by a range of other commentators, from Boltanski and Chiapello, to Hall, and Laclau and Mouffe. What seemed to be lacking from Bourdieu's analysis was any acknowledgement of the popular appeal of certain neo-liberal policies, of their ability to tap into and exploit popular aspirations or frustrated desires. In this sense, Bourdieu's account seemed to exemplify the kind of critique of neo-liberalism that remained, in Boltanski and Chiapello's words, 'blind to what it is that makes the new form of capitalism seductive for so many people' (1999: 29). Despite their different theoretical positions, Hall, Laclau and Mouffe, and Boltanski and Chiapello have all attempted to explain this seductive force by recourse to a notion of *ideology*. Boltanski and Chiapello's conception of ideology is an original one that derives from the collective efforts of the Group for Political and Moral Sociology to develop a theoretical apparatus which will account for the various 'logics of justification' and 'tests of legitimacy' according to which agents judge the political, social and cultural structures they encounter on a daily basis. Both Hall and Laclau and Mouffe, on the other hand, work within broadly Gramscian and Althusserian traditions, which they adapt and modify in different ways. Bourdieu's own 'theory of practice' has frequently been compared to these Gramscian and Althusserian traditions (Hall 1977; Garnham 1980; Eagleton 1991; Butler 1997a: 210 n.13). Yet this is an affiliation that Bourdieu himself was always keen to reject.

Indeed, Bourdieu typically claimed that his own theory of practice offered a set of analytical tools at once distinct from and superior to those contained in Marxist or *marxisant* theories of ideology. For Bourdieu, conventional theories of ideology, with their implicit focus on ideas and representations, necessarily overlooked the key role played by embodied affect, custom and habit in securing agents' adherence to the status quo, a role which concepts such as 'habitus' and 'practice' were able to elucidate and explain. The values contained within what the Marxist tradition might term a 'dominant ideology' operated, according to Bourdieu, 'on the hither side of words or concepts'. Such values were realized in unreflective custom and habit as much as, if not more than they were articulated in any normative discourse. Their appeal was staged less at the level of rational persuasion than at that of affective investment; their efficacy reflected less their capacity for ideological mystification than the fact that they were embodied or incorporated in agents' unspoken and hence unquestioned practices, customs and habits. Social practices which reflected the dominant values thus had 'something ineffable' about them, being 'the product of an "art", "pure practice without theory" ', as Bourdieu put it, quoting Durkheim (Bourdieu 1977a: 2).

In seeking to communicate the 'ineffable' nature of social practice, this 'art' or 'pure practice without theory', Bourdieu had recourse throughout his work to a series of metaphors drawn from the realms of music and poetry. Indeed, Jonathan Loesberg has argued that the concepts of 'habitus' and 'practice' are themselves 'modelled on the aesthetic', being structured by the very 'purposefulness without purpose' that Kant had taken to be the defining characteristic of the aesthetic object (Loesberg 1993). This chapter will examine and expand upon Loesberg's claim that the concepts of practice and habitus are structured analogously to an aesthetic object. Arguing that Bourdieu's frequent allusions to the realms of music and poetry need to be taken entirely seriously, it will examine what advantages such an aestheticized reading of social practice might hold over more conventional theories of ideology. This will involve a shift of focus away from Bourdieu's directly political interventions to concentrate on aspects of his fully fledged social theory. This shift of focus will facilitate a first assessment of the contribution that Bourdieu's theory of practice might have to make to political analysis more generally. For reasons of space, this chapter will examine the concepts of habitus and practice largely in isolation from the closely allied concept of 'field'. It should be noted that there is something artificial in this separating out of the concepts of habitus and practice, on the one hand, and the tenets of field theory, on the other. For, if Bourdieu's contribution to political theory is to be properly understood, habitus can only ever be thought in its inter-relation with the particular fields in which it is invested, while the logic of practices can only ever be grasped inasmuch as they are seen as interventions in one or other of those same fields. Once this chapter has elucidated the theoretical assumptions behind Bourdieu's concepts of habitus and practice, it will be possible to explore their relationship with the equally central concept of field in the chapters which follow.

The aesthetics of practice

To claim that the aesthetic is at the heart of Bourdieu's theory of practice might initially seem absurd given that in his writings on culture and class Bourdieu appeared to suggest that any claim to the specificity of the aesthetic was merely so much bourgeois bad faith. Moreover, in his works of Kabyle anthropology, he appeared to define practice itself in direct opposition to the aesthetic. Thus, in studies such as *The Love of Art* (1969) and *Distinction* (1979), Bourdieu argued that the aesthetic, in its classic Kantian formulation as the realm of 'disinterested' pleasure, amounted to nothing more than the expression of a typically bourgeois, leisurely, contemplative attitude to the world, contingent upon the bourgeoisie's distance from the realm of material necessity. Elevated to the level of a supposedly universally communicable experience and hence taken as an objective measure of inherent moral and intellectual worth, the capacity for disinterested aesthetic contemplation could thus serve to naturalize, legitimize and reproduce existing class divisions and social distinctions. Furthermore, the leisurely, contemplative distance on the world demanded by 'legitimate aesthetics' was, for Bourdieu, merely an expression of a more general, typically bourgeois, attitude to the world he termed 'the scholastic point of view'. This attitude was equally evident in the 'theoretical distortions' Bourdieu found in so much social anthropology and, most notably, in Claude Lévi-Strauss's structural anthropology. If anthropology and aesthetics were to be seen as analogous activities, it was, Bourdieu argued, because each tended to treat the objects of its study in the same way. The bourgeois aesthete, distanced from the realm of immediate material necessity and hence able to view the world through a leisurely, contemplative gaze, tended to view art works as things of beauty in and of themselves, with no regard to their practical utility, in a 'disinterested manner', as objects possessed of a 'purposefulness without purpose', to use Kant's terminology. Anthropologists, meanwhile, thanks to their professional status, enjoyed a certain material well-being that placed them at an equivalent social distance from the societies they studied, predisposing them to adopt a similarly contemplative attitude to the social activities they analysed, treating those activities as 'an autonomous self-sufficient object, that is a purposefulness without purpose – without any other purpose, at any rate, than that of being interpreted, like a work of art'. Playing on the etymology of the terms scholastic, from the Greek *skholè* or leisure, Bourdieu thus argued that both Kantian aesthetics and anthropology exemplified the distortions inherent in the 'scholastic point of view'; both were products of 'the scholastic situation, in the strong sense of *skholè*, of *otium*, of inactivity' (Bourdieu 1980a: 53 [31]).

This analogy between anthropology and aesthetics was made clear in the opening paragraphs of *Outline of a Theory of Practice*. Indeed, these opening paragraphs might suggest, on first reading, that Bourdieu's theory of practice, with its attendant concepts of habitus, field and strategy, defined itself precisely in opposition to the aesthetic. Bourdieu opened this anthropological study of Kabyle society by identifying the 'theoretical distortions' inherent in the objectifying distance that separated anthropologists from the societies they studied:

> The practical privilege in which all scientific activity arises never more subtly governs that activity (insofar as science presupposes not only an epistemological break but also a *social* separation) than when, unrecognised as privilege, it leads to an implicit theory of practice which is the corollary of neglect of the social conditions in which science is possible. The anthropologist's particular relation to the object of his study contains the makings of a theoretical distortion inasmuch as his situation as an observer, excluded from the real play of social activities by the fact that he has no place (except by choice or by way of a game) in the system observed and has no need to make a place for himself there, inclines him to a hermeneutic representation of practices, leading him to reduce all social relations to communicative relations and, more precisely, to decoding operations. [. . .] And exaltation of

the virtues of distance secured by externality simply transmutes into an epistemological choice the anthropologist's objective situation, that of the 'impartial spectator', as Husserl puts it, condemned to see all practice as spectacle.

(Bourdieu 1977a: 1)

Seeking to clarify quite what he meant both by the 'theoretical distortion' characteristic of so much anthropological discourse and by the 'social separation' that occasioned that distortion, Bourdieu turned to the domain of art:

It is instructive to glance at the case of art history, which, never having broken with the tradition of the *amateur*, gives free reign to celebratory contemplation and finds in the sacred character of its object every pretext for a hagiographic hermeneutics superbly indifferent to the question of the social conditions in which works of art are produced and circulate.

(Bourdieu 1977a: 1)

However, it would be wrong to assume that the critique of the contemplative aesthetic attitude with which Bourdieu opened *Outline*, along with his consequent emphasis on the *practical* aspects of social action, amounted to a wholesale rejection of the aesthetic *per se* or a straightforward opposition between aesthetics and practice. For in seeking to explain precisely what it was that aesthetics overlooked by reducing art works to the status of autonomous objects of beauty, Bourdieu turned, in apparently paradoxical fashion, to a certain notion of art and the aesthetic:

To treat a work of plastic art as a discourse intended to be interpreted, decoded, by reference to a transcendent code analogous to the Saussurian '*langue*' is to forget that artistic production is always *also* [. . .] the product of an 'art', 'pure practice without theory', as Durkheim says, or to put it another way, a *mimesis*, a sort of symbolic gymnastics, like the rite or the dance; and it is also to forget that the work of art always contains something *ineffable*, not by excess, as hagiography would have it, but by default, something which communicates, so to speak, from body to body, i.e. on the hither side of words or concepts, and which pleases (or displeases) without concepts.

(Bourdieu 1977a: 1–2)

Social practice, then, rather than being reduced to the status of a code to be deciphered, as structuralism would have it, was to be understood by analogy to a work of art, a work of art, moreover, described in the most apparently classically Kantian of terms. The capacity to 'please (or displease) without concepts', like the quality of ineffability attributed to practice here, recalled nothing so much as the classic Kantian definition of the aesthetic object. The absolute centrality to Bourdieu's sociology of this notion of practice as aesthetic, as an 'art', 'something ineffable', was highlighted by the fact that the aforementioned passage was reproduced verbatim not only in Bourdieu's final work of Kabyle anthropology, *The Logic of Practice*, but also in *Distinction* (Bourdieu 1979: 86 [80]; 1980a: 58 [34]). The importance of this analogy between practice and art therefore appeared indisputable and Loesberg's contention that the concepts of both habitus and practice are structured analogously to the Kantian aesthetic object would seem entirely legitimate (Loesberg 1993).

As Loesberg points out, in the Preface to *The Logic of Practice*, Bourdieu described Kabyle practices in unmistakably aesthetic terms. Such practices manifested 'the coherence without apparent intention and the unity without an immediately visible unifying principle of all cultural realities that are informed by a quasi-natural logic'. As such, Bourdieu suggested, they possessed 'the "eternal charm" of "Greek art" to which Marx refers' (1980a: 28 [13]). Moreover, in the main body of the text, Bourdieu's descriptions of Kabyle practice were replete with allusions to aesthetic forms, most notably to poetry and music. His analysis of the 'mythopoetry' of the Kabyle house, of the social and symbolic connotations of hearth and threshold, stable and sleeping quarters, was greatly indebted to Gaston Bachelard's earlier study of the poetics of domestic space, the *Poetics of Space*.[1] The final chapter of *The Logic of Practice* extended the insights of the analysis of the Kabyle house to an account of the mythico-ritual structure of Kabyle society as a whole. It took its title, 'Le Démon de l'analogie' in the original French, from a prose poem of the same name by the symbolist poet Stéphane Mallarmé. Where Mallarmé's poem explores the relationship between masculine and feminine principles, while suggesting analogies between the ineffability of poetic and musical languages, Bourdieu's analysis described a social and affective universe overdetermined by gendered hierarchies which themselves had an ineffable quality, being incorporated into Kabyle agents below the level of representation, 'on the hither side of words and discourse'. The metaphors Bourdieu used here were not merely poetic but also musical, his analysis replete with allusions to 'orchestra conductors', 'improvisation', 'virtuosity', and 'non-written musical scores' (Bourdieu 1980a: 333–439 [200–70]).[2]

Given that Kabylia was defined by Bourdieu as a pre-capitalist society, it might be tempting to assume that the 'eternal charm' he found in Kabyle practices reflected a certain nostalgia. For Marx, of course, the 'eternal charm' of Greek art reflected its ability to offer a glimpse of a society and of a mode of material and artistic production now lost; Greek art's eternal charm was thus 'inseparably linked with the fact that the immature social conditions which gave rise, and which alone could give rise, to this art cannot recur' (Marx 1857:217). The nostalgia implicit in Marx's formulation might suggest that Bourdieu too was drawing a straightforward distinction between the aesthetic or poetic richness of 'traditional' Kabyle society and the degraded rationality of advanced Western capitalism. However, any such straightforward opposition would appear to be belied by a passage in *The Social Structures of the Economy*, Bourdieu's study of the housing market in contemporary France, in which he analysed the 'poetic effects' mobilized by advertisements for new homes in France. These effects, he argued, obeyed an analogous logic to the mythopoetry at the heart of the practices and rituals of the Kabyle social world (Bourdieu 2000: 38 [23]). Further, in *Pascalian Meditations*, Bourdieu maintained that the play of 'connotations and harmonics' characteristic of the 'practical logic' at the core of the Kabyle mythico-ritual system was reproduced in analogous form in the discourse of neo-liberalism, 'when, for example, we put into play vague sets of imprecise metaphors and approximate concepts – liberalism, liberation, liberalization, flexibility, free enterprise, deregulation, etc.' (1997c: 71 [57]). The efficacy of neo-liberal discourse, therefore, was not reducible to its purely rational force of persuasion. Rather the play of assonance and alliteration between terms such as 'liberalism' and 'liberation' combined with the connotation of 'liberty' contained in both terms to lend neo-liberal discourse an efficacy that related as much to the domain of emotion and poetic imagination as to that of rational argument. In an earlier essay in *Language and Symbolic Power*, Bourdieu had identified an analogous play of assonance, alliteration and connotation at work in Heidegger's philosophy and politics, in the relations the latter sought to establish between such apparently linked notions as *Sorge* (care), *Sorgfalt* (carefulness), *Fürsorge* (solicitude) and *Sozialfürsorge* (social welfare). The associations Heidegger posited between such terms were located 'in the sensory form of the language itself', Bourdieu argued; hence that language staged an appeal at the aesthetic or poetic, rather than strictly rational, level (1982: 173 [140]). Ideological discourses, whether neo-liberalism or Heideggerian philosophy, thus mobilized the material, aesthetic nature of language to make their tenets not simply believed or assented to, at the level of rational consciousness, but also, and more importantly, *felt*. As Bourdieu put it:

> [the] association by alliteration or by assonance, which establishes quasi-material relations of resemblance of form and of sound, can also produce formally necessary associations likely to bring to light a hidden relation between the signifieds or, more probably, to bring it into existence solely by virtue of the play on forms.
>
> (1982: 173 [141])

Bourdieu's recourse to poetic and aesthetic categories in his theory of practice represented his attempt to capture the essence of what he termed 'symbolic' forms of domination and violence, that is to say forms of domination resting on the imposition of arbitrary social hierarchies and conventions, an imposition achieved neither through outright coercion nor freely given consent. If such conventions were adhered to, he argued, it was because they operated at the level of 'practice', engaging a series of embodied, affective and somatic investments and it is, of course, precisely this somatic level of experience to which the term 'aesthetics', in its etymological sense, refers. In *The Logic of Practice*, Bourdieu identified traditional Kabyle society, a society lacking any of the juridical or coercive apparatuses of the modern State, as 'the site *par excellence* of symbolic violence'. Yet, as the examples of both *The Social Structures of the Economy* and *Pascalian Meditations* demonstrate, he believed symbolic violence or domination to be playing an equally important role in advanced capitalist societies. Bourdieu's reliance on a certain notion of the aesthetic to elucidate the logic of practice and the workings of symbolic domination might be read as simply contradictory, as striking evidence of his need to rely on a concept of the aesthetic he elsewhere dismissed as so much bourgeois bad faith. However, without ruling out any such conclusion, it might be argued that a more fruitful line of enquiry would be to examine what both the theoretical bases and possible political implications of such an aestheticized reading of social practice might be. This is particularly the case given the frequency with which Bourdieu claimed his own theory of practice and symbolic domination to be both distinct from and superior to existing Marxist or *marxisant* theories of ideology.

A first indication as to the theoretical basis for the analogies that Bourdieu drew between the aesthetic and social practice is provided by Bourdieu's reference to Husserl's notion of the 'impartial spectator'. This reference revealed the extent to which Bourdieu's critique of structural anthropology, as of objectivism more generally, and his consequent emphasis on the practical, the 'immediate', embodied, or 'doxic' roots of social action were indebted to the phenomenological tradition. As Bourdieu acknowledged in *Pascalian Meditations*, his attempt to avoid the pitfalls of the scholastic point of view represented an effort to historicize the insights of phenomenology, re-reading them in sociological terms:

> Phenomenological description, though indispensable in order to break with the scholastic vision of the ordinary vision of the world, and while it comes close to the real, is liable to stand in the way of a full understanding of practical understanding and of practice itself, because it is totally ahistorical and antigenetic. One therefore has to return to the analysis of presence in the world but historicizing it [. . .] and secondly one has to examine the question of the social conditions that have to be fulfilled to make possible the experience of the social world as self-evident which phenomenology describes without providing itself with the means of accounting for it.
>
> (1997c: 175 [146–7])

Terry Eagleton has pointed out that if aesthetics is understood in its etymological sense to refer to the realm of the somatic and the perceptual, Husserlian phenomenology involves an inherently aesthetic project, inasmuch as it seeks 'to rescue the life-world from its troubling opacity to reason, thereby renewing an Occidental rationality which has cut alarmingly adrift from its somatic, perceptual roots' (Eagleton 1990: 17). Even allowing for Bourdieu's criticisms of phenomenology's 'ahistoricism', it was clear that in his critique of 'the scholastic vision', as in his elaboration of a theory of practice, he was pursuing a similar aesthetic project.

However, Husserl's phenomenology was not merely aesthetic in the sense of staging a return to the somatic roots of human experience; it also showed close similarities to Kant's more specialized definition of the aesthetic in his *Critique of Judgement*. As Merleau-Ponty pointed out in *Phenomenology of Perception* (1945), if phenomenology rejected the transcendental idealism of Kant's *Critique of Pure Reason* for its 'intellectualism', the phenomenological account of 'intentionality' did nonetheless have much in common with the *Critique of Judgement*. For in Kant's Third Critique Merleau-Ponty found a model of perception and practice that relied neither on the disembodied categories of the understanding nor on a deliberative model of rational judgement or cognition:

> Here the subject is no longer the universal thinker of a system of objects rigorously interrelated, the positing power who subjects the manifold to the law of the understanding, in so far as he is able to put together a world – he discovers and enjoys his own nature as spontaneously in harmony with the law of the understanding. But if the subject has a nature, then the hidden art of the imagination must condition the categorial activity. It is no longer merely the aesthetic judgement, but knowledge too which rests upon this art, an art which forms the basis of the unity of consciousness and consciousnesses. Husserl takes up again the *Critique of Judgement* when he talks about a teleology of consciousness. It is not a matter of doubling human consciousness with some absolute consciousness which would assign to the former its aims, from the outside. It is a question of recognizing consciousness itself as a project of the world, meant for a world which it neither embraces nor possesses, but towards which it is perpetually directed – and the world as this pre-objective individual whose imperious unity decrees what knowledge shall take as its goal. This is why Husserl distinguishes between intentionality of act, which is that of our judgements and of those occasions on which we voluntarily take up a position – the only intentionality discussed in the *Critique of Pure Reason* – and operative intentionality (*fungierende Intentionalität*), or that which produces the natural and antepredicative unity of the world and of our life, being apparent in our desires, our evaluations, and in the landscape we see, more clearly than in objective knowledge.
> (Merleau-Ponty 1945: xix–xx, trans. modified)

If Husserl's account of intentionality was to be compared to Kantian aesthetics in this way, it was because like the Kantian aesthetic object, perception was, for Husserl, inhabited by a certain purposefulness without consciously deliberated purpose, a certain intentionality without conscious intention. What determined this intentionality without conscious intention was the subject's pre-predicative or doxic immersion in the world, a presence in the present or being-in-the-world prior to all predication or deliberative judgement. As Husserl explained in *Experience and Judgement* (1948), the ego's perception of any object consisted of a series of past apperceptions or 'retentions', which provoked a series of 'anticipations' or 'protentions', an 'aiming' or 'tending towards', an 'interest' in accumulating knowledge about those aspects of the object as yet unknown, a 'progressive *plus ultra*'. Hence Merleau-Ponty's reference to Husserl's 'teleology of consciousness', perception and consciousness were always aiming towards a goal or *telos*, yet that goal was never consciously posited as such; consciousness was thus characterized by the very 'purposefulness without purpose' that Kant had attributed to the aesthetic. As Husserl put it, the 'interest' in accumulating more knowledge had 'nothing to do with a specific act of will' but rather was inherent in the ego's being-in-the-world, inherent in 'every act of the turning-toward of the ego, whether transitory or continuous, every act of the ego's being-with (*inter-esse*)' (Husserl 1948: 80–6).

In his own phenomenological studies, Merleau-Ponty placed greater emphasis on the *embodied* nature of this kind of intentionality. For Merleau-Ponty, to understand consciousness or perception purely in terms of deliberative judgement or rational cognition was to ignore that these intellectual operations had as their necessary foundation the ante-predicative, pre-logical, 'practical knowledge' derived from the body's being-in-the-world. The body was not merely a blank screen, passively registering external stimuli as empiricism would have it, rather it exerted a grip on the world; it was actively engaged in the world, tending towards that world and seeking to make sense of it, accumulating practical knowledge about the world. This embodied, 'practical knowledge' constituted a series of incorporated 'sedimentations', of habitual ways of acting, viewing and evaluating the world which related more to the realms of affect, desire and taste than to the domain of deliberative judgement. This 'practical knowledge' was the product of that 'operative intentionality', identified by Husserl, which, to quote Merleau-Ponty, 'produces the natural and antepredicative unity of the world and of our life, being apparent in our desires, our evaluations, and in the landscape we see, more clearly than in objective knowledge'. As with Husserl, then, so with Merleau-Ponty intentionality had a teleological structure; in its tending towards the world the body aimed towards a certain *telos*, yet since that *telos* was never consciously posited, embodied practice was endowed with a kind of purposefulness without purpose. In this, intentionality was analogously structured to Kant's aesthetic object and hence Merleau-Ponty's argument, in *Phenomenology of Perception*, that the body, as the repository of an incorporated practical knowledge, should be compared less to a physical object than to a work of art, a painting, a musical composition, a poem or a novel (1945: 174–5).

If Bourdieu's analyses of Kabyle practice were full of allusions to poetry, to Bachelard's *Poetics of Space* and Mallarmé's 'Le Démon de l'analogie', to music, to 'improvization', 'virtuosity' and 'orchestral scores', or to art and the aesthetic generally, this was because his theory of practice remained hugely indebted to these phenomenological accounts of intentionality and its aesthetic characteristics. As we have already seen, Bourdieu sought to re-read the insights offered by phenomenology in more historicist, materialist or sociological terms and the phenomenological concepts of 'doxa' and 'practical knowledge', of 'interest', and 'intentionality' played a central role in his account of the 'strategies' which were generated by the meeting of 'habitus' and 'field'. Thus in *The Logic of Practice* he attributed to the Kabyles an inherent 'interest' in conserving and accumulating 'symbolic capital' through judicious 'strategies' in the realms of gift exchange and marriage. This 'interest' did not reflect a conscious striving for personal gain but rather a pre-reflexive or doxic adherence to 'the *illusio* in the sense of *investment* in the game and its stakes, of *interest* for the game, of adherence to the presuppositions – *doxa* – of the game'. Kabyle participants in the social 'game' or field deployed their 'practical sense' or knowledge of which moves would prove most profitable, 'an almost bodily tending towards the world [...], a proleptic adjustment to the demands of a field, what, in the language of sport, is called the "feel for the game" as a "sense of placement", art of "anticipation", etc.' (Bourdieu 1980a: 111 [66]). According to this model of social action, then, the habitus, that repository of incorporated practical knowledge, would, when deployed in any particular social field, generate a series of practices which each possessed its characteristic 'sense', its meaning and direction or intentionality. As such, each practice would possess a certain purposefulness without conscious purpose, an intentionality without deliberate intention, obeying

> the logic of all the actions that are reasonable without being the product of a reasoned design, still less of rational calculation; informed by a kind of objective finality without being consciously organised in relation to an explicitly constituted end; intelligible and coherent without springing from an intention of coherence and a deliberate decision; adjusted to the future without being the product of a project or plan.
> (Bourdieu 1980a: 85–6 [50–1])

As Loesberg (1993: 1039) points out, at such moments the habitus 'is read as that most familiar of literary objects, the organic whole that operates purposively without purpose'.

For Kant, of course, the aesthetic, elaborated in the Third Critique, was intended to mediate between the realms of pure reason and personal morality, explored in the First and Second Critiques, respectively. The aesthetic, as Eagleton (1990: 17) puts it, represented 'an elusive third way between the vagaries of subjective feeling and the bloodless rigour of the understanding'. The habitus, in Bourdieu's work, played an equivalent role, mediating between the realms of subjective freedom and structural law or objective necessity, overcoming the opposition between subjectivism and objectivism in social theory. According to Eagleton, it is because of its claim to mediate between subject and object, feeling and reason in this way, that the aesthetic becomes a central category for understanding the workings of bourgeois ideology. As he puts it:

> The ultimate binding force of the bourgeois social order, in contrast to the coercive apparatus of absolutism, will be habits, pieties, sentiments, and affections. And this is equivalent to saying that power in such an order has become *aestheticized*. It is at one with the body's spontaneous impulses, entwined with sensibility and the affections, lived out in unreflective custom. Power is now inscribed in the minutiae of subjective experience, and the fissure between abstract duty and pleasurable inclination is accordingly healed. To dissolve the law to custom, to sheer unthinking habit, is to identify it with the human subject's own pleasurable well-being, so that to transgress the law

would signify a deep self-violation. The new subject, which bestows on itself self-referentially a law at one with its immediate experience, finding its freedom in its necessity, is modelled on the aesthetic artefact.

(Eagleton 1990: 20)

It was precisely this non-coercive form of social integration, what Bourdieu termed 'symbolic domination', which operated through sentiment, habit and custom, that the concepts of habitus and practice sought to describe. The habitus was that structure in which objective social or economic chances were internalized into agents' subjective dispositions, in such a way that they adjusted their expectations or 'practical anticipations' to reflect the objective chances of those expectations being met. This allowed those agents to find their freedom in (social) necessity, by that process Bourdieu described as 'amor fati', the love of one's (socially determined) fate.[3] As we have seen, in accordance with its aesthetic characteristics, the habitus was related to the realms of affect, taste and aversion. The affective charge of the habitus also reflected its temporal structure. As an internalized structure of practical anticipations, the habitus generated an affective charge through its production of a communal sense of what kinds of behaviour were acceptable or not, what sorts of ambition reasonable or unreasonable.

Thus, for example, in his studies of French higher education, Bourdieu argued that the low objective chances of working-class students entering university had been internalized into a 'working-class ethos', a practical sense of what kind of educational path one might reasonably hope to pursue. Any aspiration to escape that social destiny would then risk collective condemnation as unacceptable pretension, a transgression of communally maintained values, so that, to quote Eagleton, 'to transgress the law would signify a deep self-violation'. Working-class identity, in such an account, was thus not simply the expression of that class's position in the relations of production, a position which would give birth to a revolutionary consciousness were it not for the workings of bourgeois ideology and the false consciousness it engendered. Working-class identity was, rather, a matter of shared tastes and aversions, desires and expectations, reflecting an 'ethos' based on shared 'habits, pieties, sentiments and affections', through which that class bestowed on itself 'self-referentially a law at one with its immediate experience', to quote Eagleton's description of the aesthetic. As such, again to quote Eagleton, the working-class habitus was 'modelled on the aesthetic artefact'. The concept of the habitus was thus an attempt to capture and explain that interweaving of 'the ethical and the affective' that Bourdieu placed at the core of the workings of 'symbolic domination' (1977a: 190).

The politics of practice

The effects of the aesthetic, affective structures of the habitus could not merely be read in a set of cultural or social identities. For such affective structures also influenced agents' political affiliations and electoral 'choices' in a manner which, Bourdieu suggested, conventional theories of ideology failed to acknowledge.

Thus in his 1977 article 'Questions de politique', Bourdieu argued that much of the electoral appeal of Jacques Duclos, the French Communist Party's candidate at the 1969 Presidential elections, rested on the 'affinity' between his habitus and 'hexis', his bearing, dress, manners and patterns of speech, and the habitus and hexis of the predominantly working-class voters whose votes he attracted. In 1969 the ruling Gaullists offered their electoral rivals unprecedented access to state-run television channels previously notorious for their censorship of any criticism of the government. This unprecedented exposure through an audio-visual medium, Bourdieu suggested, meant that Duclos' electoral appeal owed as much, if not more, to the pre-discursive affinities of embodied affect and custom, as to the persuasive power of a rational, explicit political programme (Bourdieu 1977b: 74). This insight might, of course, be extended from questions of class identity and party politics to other forms of social identity or political affiliation.

For Bourdieu, any theory of ideology would necessarily miss the mark if it attempted to explain the status quo in terms either of the mystifications of 'false consciousness' or of reasoned consent freely given. A whole series of identities, whether those defined in terms of class, ethnicity, gender or sexuality, clearly derive much of their force from affective investments. In order for such forms of identity and affiliation to exist and endure, the principles behind them need not be made explicit, much less consented to, whether that 'consent' springs from deliberative judgement or ideological delusion. To take the example of national identity, it is clear that agents' attachment to their country of origin is never reducible either to the set of positive attributes possessed by that country or to a set of rational arguments which have convinced those agents to love their homeland, as though a sense of national belonging were the product of a rational choice or a series of deliberative judgements. There is, then, 'something ineffable' in national identity, to quote Bourdieu, an affective bond irreducible to any discourses of nationalism that might be produced by government agencies, political parties or national literatures. National identity is, rather, a matter of certain shared tastes and aversions, customs and embodied practices, which obey an analogous logic, while not always possessing identical characteristics, to the tastes and aversions at the core of the working-class habitus, as Bourdieu defined it. For Bourdieu, the importance of affect to such social identities was evident in the immediate physical responses of 'shame, humiliation, timidity, anxiety, guilt', with their 'visible manifestations, like blushing, stuttering, clumsiness, shaking', that might be provoked in certain social situations in which those identities were in play or at stake (Bourdieu 1998a: 44–5 [38]).

Bourdieu's turn to the work of Pascal, notably in his 1997 study *Pascalian Meditations*, should be understood as part of his attempt to find a model for this kind of submission to the status quo based on habit, custom and affect rather than rational argument. Pascal's *Pensées* is a Christian apologetics which refuses to ground religious belief in a rational choice or deliberative judgement. According to Pascal, belief preceded any rational choice, being rooted in the intuitive understanding and emotional investment proper to that realm of the human psyche he termed alternately 'heart' or 'imagination'. Such belief was strengthened by the experience of regular worship, by 'custom', 'habit' and embodied ritual. Although not grounded in a rational choice, religious belief nonetheless possessed its own rationality; it might be brought to consciousness of its own historical and spiritual justification through an apologetics like the *Pensées*. Thus Pascal was convinced that Christian belief was reasonable and certain but that such a conviction could never be reached by rational argument alone. In seeking proof for his claim that religious belief could not be explained in purely rationalistic terms, Pascal turned to a series of secular laws and customs whose operation, he claimed, were equally revealing of the importance of affect, 'heart' or 'imagination', and embodied habit, 'the automaton'. As he put it, in a fragment quoted by Bourdieu (1997c: 23–4 [12]) in *Pascalian Meditations*:

> For we must make no mistake about ourselves: we are as much automaton as mind. As a result, demonstration is not the only instrument for convincing us. How few things can be demonstrated! Proofs only convince the mind; habit provides the strongest proofs and those that are most believed. It inclines the automaton, which leads the mind unthinkingly along with it. [. . .] It is, then, habit that convinces us and makes so many Christians. It is habit that makes us Turks, heathen, trades, soldiers, etc. [. . .]; it is too much trouble to have truths always present before us. We must acquire an easier belief which is that of habit. With no violence, art or argument it makes us believe things and so inclines all our faculties to this belief that our soul falls naturally into it.
>
> (Pascal 1966: 274, trans. modified)

Bourdieu could thus invoke Pascal in support of his contention that obedience to any social convention or law could never be entirely justified by rational argument.[4] Belief in or rather adherence to one's native social universe came from enacting a series of customs and rituals, which trained the body more than they educated the mind. Submission to existing conventions was ensured by a kind of 'bodily dressage' whose effects were visible in the characteristic 'hexis', the bearing and deportment, of the different genders, classes or social groups, as well as in their habitus, their shared assumptions, expectations, tastes and aversions. Discourses or rational arguments seeking to justify such customs and rituals came later, as it were, constituting a set of secondary rationalizations, '*post festum* rationalisations destined to justify an unjustifiable investment, to oneself as much as to others' (Bourdieu 1997c: 123 [102]). Such 'secondary rationalizations' merely sought to conceal the 'violence without any justification', the 'historical arbitrary' that lay at the foundation of any given social order. As Pascal put it, again in a passage quoted by Bourdieu:

> Custom creates the whole of equity, for the simple reason that it is accepted. It is the mystical foundation of its authority: whoever carries it back to first principles destroys it. Nothing is so faulty as those laws which correct

faults. He who obeys them because they are just, obeys a justice which is imaginary and not the essence of the law; it is quite self-contained, it is law and nothing more.

(in Bourdieu 1997c: 114 [94])

To return again to the example of national identity, it is clear that the borders of a nation-state can never be justified in purely rational terms. Indeed, any attempt to justify such borders in rational terms will be a mere 'secondary rationalization', which paradoxically risks revealing the extent to which those borders are historically arbitrary, the result of a founding act of 'violence without any justification'.

Bourdieu's distinction between an affective investment in a particular social identity and the '*post festum* rationalizations', which attempt to justify such an investment, opens up productive ways of thinking about those instances where consciousness and practice appear to be in contradiction with one another. For within such an analytical framework, it becomes possible to think about cases of disjuncture between what is known and what is felt, the explicit principles agents claim to adhere to and the practices and customs they actually engage in. For example, it would be possible to imagine agents who are explicitly committed to ending all forms of racial prejudice, sexism and homophobia, agents capable of producing rational arguments to demonstrate why such prejudices are both unjust and without rational foundation. Yet this would not necessarily prevent those same agents from finding themselves, in particular social situations, giving in to the very feelings of prejudice they have rationally disavowed. Drawing on the terms of Bourdieu's analysis, it would be possible to argue that such phenomena reflect precisely the fact that these forms of prejudice are rooted less in rational argument than in affect, in the feelings of disgust, fear or disavowed envy that an encounter with the 'other' may provoke. It is the lack of affinity between such agents' habitus and the habitus of other nationalities, genders and sexualities that is at the root of these feelings of fear and disgust. Discourses which attempt to rationalize such affective responses by appeal to the pseudo-sciences of racial classification, to various forms of biologism, or to religious doctrine come later, as it were, serving as 'secondary rationalizations' of an initial 'unjustifiable investment'. Critical discourses which aim to prove the lack of rational foundation for such prejudices, on the other hand, will always miss the mark in some sense, since the prejudices in question are not ultimately grounded in reason but in affect.

It was for these reasons that Bourdieu claimed, in *Pascalian Meditations*, that 'little by little' he had 'come to banish the use of the word "ideology"' from his work (1997c: 216 [181]). The concept of ideology, according to Bourdieu, was too tied up with the realm of ideas and reason to grasp the importance of the pre-predicative, affective, embodied forms of practice. Moreover, it led inevitably into theories of social change based 'on that intellectual conversion that is called the "awakening of consciousness" [*prise de conscience*]' and, as such, inevitably led back to a model of political agency based on deliberative judgement and rational action (Bourdieu 1997c: 211–12 [177]). For Bourdieu, it was but one further

> effect of the scholastic illusion to describe resistance to domination in the language of consciousness – as does the whole Marxist tradition and also the feminist theorists who, giving way to habits of thought, expect political emancipation to be the automatic effect of an 'awakening of consciousness' [*prise de conscience*] – ignoring, for lack of a dispositional theory of practices, the extraordinary inertia which results from the inscription of social structures in bodies.
>
> (1997c: 205 [172])

It might be argued that Bourdieu was guilty here of oversimplifying conventional theories of ideology, the better to emphasize the originality of his own concepts of habitus and practice. For example, in his famous essay on 'Ideology and ideological state apparatuses', Althusser insists that ideology should not be understood as a set of disembodied ideas. On the contrary, ideology must be seen as something immanent in material social practices and rituals, so that belief in or adherence to a given social order must be understood as following from, rather than preceding, such practices and rituals. To illustrate his argument, Althusser paraphrases a fragment of Pascal's *Pensées* on religious belief: 'Kneel, move your lips in prayer and you will believe' (Althusser 1984: 42). That Bourdieu conspicuously failed to refer to this fragment of the *Pensées* in his *Pascalian Meditations* was surely significant, signalling an eagerness to distance himself from Althusser, regardless of the theoretical affinities this shared recourse to Pascal might have revealed. Certainly, Bourdieu developed the implications of this Pascalian inversion of belief and action in much more detail than Althusser ever did. Further, Bourdieu's critique of Althusser's notion of 'ideological state apparatuses' did reveal clear differences between the two thinkers.

According to Bourdieu, the Althusserian account of ideology incorrectly imputed 'submission to the law and the maintenance of the symbolic order to a deliberately organised action of propaganda or to the (no doubt significant) efficacy of "ideological state apparatuses" working for the dominant class' (1997c: 201 [168]). Bourdieu did not seek to deny the important role played by those institutions, Church, school, Judiciary, and so on, which Althusser had named 'ideological state apparatuses'. On the contrary, such institutions would form important participants within any given field, elaborating and transmitting their own particular ideologies. Bourdieu's point, rather, was that agents' participation in the social field involved an affective investment that operated below the level of such explicit ideological appeals. In other words, it is clear that institutions such as the Church, the armed forces, the monarchy and the School are important participants in any nationally defined social field, dispensing doctrines and ideologies that may serve to bolster the status quo. However, according to Bourdieu, such ideologies were to be understood as merely so many secondary rationalizations, which could serve to obscure the more fundamental 'pre-reflexive investment' in the 'illusio' of the social field, in the stakes of the struggles for recognition and status that took place within that field. In other words, in order to exist socially at all, agents must have some minimal investment in the social field. Even if they attempt to reject entirely the values of the field as it currently exists, agents will nonetheless find themselves defined by the very values they rebel against. Agents cannot have a social existence anywhere outside of a pre-existing field of social identities. They may take up a variety of different positions in that field; they may even manage to create a new position for themselves. Yet agents can only situate themselves in relation to the pre-existing field in which they invest and intervene. The same would be true of any of the relatively autonomous fields in which agents participate; in order to participate in such fields, agents must invest in their stakes, even if that investment ultimately leads to a re-drawing of the coordinates of the field or an attempt to reject its founding values. In this sense, ideological state apparatuses could be seen by Bourdieu to exert an important influence within any given field, acting as poles of attraction around which agents or groups clustered, dispensing ideological justifications for the positions they occupied. Yet, these were secondary phenomena contingent upon that initial act of pre-reflexive investment in the social game, without which no agent could have any social existence as such.

One reason Bourdieu rejected Althusser's notion of 'ideological state apparatuses' was, thus, that an emphasis on the explicit or normative ideas and values dispensed by such apparatuses risked obscuring the role of embodied practices and pre-reflexive investments in social reproduction. A second reason was Bourdieu's contention that the 'the notion of "apparatus" reintroduces pessimistic functionalism'. Althusser's notion of an 'apparatus' implied the existence of 'an "infernal engine", programmed to bring about certain ends'. Such a notion would only be applicable in those rare cases where the values of an apparatus had gained absolute ascendancy, and the struggles over such values which normally took place in any given field had thus come to an end. As Bourdieu put it: 'A field becomes an apparatus when the dominant agents have the means to nullify the resistance and reactions of the dominated' (Bourdieu 1980b: 136 [88]). The concept of field was thus intended to offer a more dynamic and open-ended account of social and political interactions than that which Bourdieu found in Althusser's theory of ideology and ideological state apparatuses.

According to Bourdieu's notion of 'symbolic domination', then, power was more diffuse and dispersed than the concept of an 'ideological state apparatus' allowed: 'power is differentiated and dispersed (this is probably what Foucault meant to suggest, no doubt in opposition to the Marxist vision of the centralized, monolithic apparatus, with his rather vague metaphor of "capillarity")' (1997c: 123 [102]). Power was immanent to the entire social field and its various sub-fields. Agents, in making an affective investment in the stakes of each of those fields, invested a kind of social libido in those stakes, in the struggles to conserve or accumulate the forms of capital on offer there. As Bourdieu put it in an interview of 1990: 'the role of sociology is to analyse the work that social spaces make the libido, analysed by psychoanalysis, undergo [. . .] and I study how the social world channels, orients, manipulates, constitutes, and institutes these drives, working and transforming them' (Bourdieu 2002c: 53). This notion of the relationship between 'social spaces' and the 'social libido' suggested that Bourdieu was sketching a highly dynamic account of the social world. According to this account, agents and groups were constantly investing in and having their social libido transformed by any number of a variety of different relatively autonomous fields. We have already seen that while feelings of national identity may operate according to an analogous logic to that at work in working-class identity, the characteristics of each form of social identity may not be identical. Since every agent simultaneously invests in any number of different fields, being at once British and working class or middle class and a woman, or Black and gay, the potential for moments of friction or contradiction between these different investments is inherent to any differentiated society. As Bourdieu put it in *Language and Symbolic Power*, no agent could ever find 'within himself, the source of an infallible knowledge of the truth of his condition and his position in the social space'. Rather, 'the same agents' could 'recognize themselves in different discourses and classifications (according to class, ethnicity, religion, sex, etc.)'. It was in this 'margin of uncertainty' between the objective position occupied by agents in social space and the multiple ways in which that position could be symbolized and understood that political struggle proper took place (Bourdieu 1982: 156–7 [132–3]).

However, the apparent dynamism of Bourdieu's account of the social and political fields as sites of shifting and ambiguous affective investments appeared to be contradicted by his simultaneous insistence on what he termed 'the extraordinary inertia which results from the inscription of social structures in bodies'. As we have already seen, this insistence on the *inertia* of embodied practice seemed to reflect the common-sense assumption regarding the possibility of there being a kind of time lag between affect and reason. For example, different forms of prejudice, manifest in an unreflective response of disgust or aversion in the face of an unfamiliar 'other', might prove hard to shift by the force of rational persuasion alone. Indeed, such apparently automatic responses might even co-exist with an explicit commitment to ending any such forms of prejudice. However, while anecdotal evidence might lend some support to these assumptions, it would not follow that the realm of embodied affects and practices need always be characterized by such inertia. For, if the aestheticized, pre-predicative, non-deliberative modes of social experience identified by Bourdieu did indeed play such a central role in securing submission to the status quo, there appeared to be no a priori reason to assume that such decisive modes of experience might not play an equally important role in provoking social or political change. This then raises the question of how Bourdieu theorized social or political change more generally and of what role he attributed to affect and embodied practice in provoking such change. It is to a discussion of these questions that Chapter 3 will turn.

This chapter picked up on Bourdieu's use of a series of musical, poetic and artistic metaphors to illustrate the workings of habitus and practice, seeking to examine what the implications of such an aestheticized reading of social practice might be. It concluded that by understanding habitus and practice to be structured analogously to the Kantian aesthetic object, Bourdieu was able to highlight the central importance of the realms of affect, of taste and aversion, of custom and embodied habit to the functioning of any social order. Moreover, this emphasis on the aestheticized nature of social practices meant that Bourdieu's 'theory of practice' could offer important insights into social and political practice, insights which are not offered by more conventional theories of ideology. Indeed, on the basis of this account of the politics and poetics of practice, it might be argued that Bourdieu's theory of practice provides a set of powerful tools for understanding a political phenomenon such as neo-liberalism. For, as Lawrence Grossberg has argued, the appeal of a politician like Ronald Reagan reflected his ability to mobilize the American electorate's deep affective investment in a particular notion of national identity, as much as his capacity to offer a rationally persuasive solution to the nation's political and economic problems. As Grossberg puts it, the 'victory, however limited, of the new conservatism has been built on an affective politics, on sentimentality and passion, in which meaning and political positions have become secondary' (Grossberg 1992: 269). Grasping the logic of this 'affective politics', he argues, demands moving beyond the conceptual vocabulary of 'hegemony' and 'ideology' inherited from the Gramscian and Althusserian traditions. One aspect of the Reaganite project clearly did involve mobilizing voters' affective investment in quite traditional notions of American national identity. However, that project also comprised elements of radical change, notably an assault on the welfare state and an embrace of the dynamism of market forces in a way which promised to erode well-established conventions and hierarchies. This again raises the question of the relationship between affective investments in existing social arrangements and political change.

As this chapter has shown, Bourdieu's apparent insistence on 'the extraordinary inertia' of embodied practice would seem to raise doubts as to the usefulness of his theory of practice when it comes to understanding the role played by affect in provoking significant social or political change. On the one hand, Bourdieu's account of the politics and poetics of practice seemed to offer an extremely dynamic vision of the social world as the site of multiple and potentially contradictory libidinal investments. On the other, Bourdieu's insistence on 'the extraordinary inertia which results from the inscription of social structures in bodies' seemed to suggest a much more static understanding of the social world. Chapter 3 will examine this apparent contradiction in more detail by focusing on Bourdieu's theorization of the passage from practical sense to political change in his various writings on the political field.

3 From practical sense to performative politics

In Chapter 2, we saw that, for Bourdieu, the concepts of habitus and practice were able to capture something fundamental about social experience that more conventional theories of ideology tended to overlook. Bourdieu's theory of practice was an attempt to explain adherence to the status quo at a level below that of consciousness, by reference to the realm of 'doxa', to that 'practical sense' of the inherent correctness of existing social convention which operated 'on the hither side of words or concepts'. This involved him rejecting the concept of ideology as an explanation of the manner in which social conformity was secured and reproduced. It also involved a rejection of any account of social or political change based on what he termed 'the metaphysics of the *prise de conscience*' (Bourdieu 1984: 6 n.6: [1991: 289–90 n.6]). Logically, having insisted on the importance of non-deliberative modes of judgement to the reproduction of the status quo, Bourdieu would have to theorize political change in a manner which also eschewed recourse to notions of deliberative judgement or rational calculation. As he put it in 'Social space and genesis of "classes"' (1984), his task became that of understanding 'the shift from the practical sense' groups possessed of their position in social space to that practical sense's 'properly political manifestations', without 'succumbing to the mythology of the "awakening of consciousness" [*prise de conscience*]' (1984: 9 [1991: 243–4]).

This chapter will focus on Bourdieu's attempts to theorize such a non-deliberative account of political change in his various essays on the political field, notably those anthologized in *Language and Symbolic Power* and *Propos sur le champ politique*. It will argue that in elaborating such a non-deliberative model of political change, Bourdieu sketched out an account of the performativity of political discourse which suggested a series of parallels with Laclau and Mouffe's 'post-Marxist' theory of hegemony. Accordingly, Laclau and Mouffe will be used as a kind of foil to Bourdieu throughout this chapter, a point of comparison and contrast, serving to uncover certain problems and contradictions at the core of the latter's theory of the political. The work of Jacques Rancière, who has also elaborated a theory of the performative force of political discourse, will serve a similar purpose here in highlighting and examining certain problems in Bourdieu's theorization of the political. Recourse to such theorists should be seen as essentially tactical, however; as will become clear, it does not represent an uncritical endorsement of their various standpoints.

Performative politics

Bourdieu's most concise definition of the political was that it represented a 'struggle to impose the legitimate principle of vision and division' of the social world (1987: 159 [134]). This 'vision and division of the social world', which opposing political forces were attempting to *impose*, was, according to Bourdieu, at the core of the 'practical taxonomies' incorporated, at the pre-predicative level, into the dispositional structures of the habitus. It was these 'practical taxonomies' which formed the structure of shared tastes and aversions, assumptions and expectations, the categories of thought and action of any given social group. Thus, for example, Bourdieu described the spatial and affective universe of Kabylia as being overdetermined by a structure of binary oppositions between light and dark, day and night, east and west, dry and wet, the world of work outside in the fields and the domestic interior. Each of these binaries expressed a hierarchical relationship between its first term, coded as masculine, and the second term, coded as feminine. Incorporated into the Kabyles' habitus as a set of 'practical taxonomies', of categories of thought and action, they served to naturalize and reproduce the fundamental social division in Kabyle society, that between men and women (Bourdieu 1980a). Bourdieu found an analogous set of binary oppositions, a vision and division of the social world obeying an analogous 'practical logic', at work in his massive study of taste and class in France, *Distinction*. Oppositions between the modest and the vulgar, the understated and the ostentatious, the refined and the tasteless functioned as a set of practical taxonomies naturalizing and reproducing class distinctions in advanced capitalist societies (Bourdieu 1979). In 'La Nouvelle vulgate planétaire' (2000a), an article co-written with Loïc Wacquant, he argued that neo-liberalism contained an analogous 'vision and division of the social world', 'imposing' a set of binary oppositions between the market and the state, freedom and constraint, flexibility and rigidity, dynamism and immobility (Bourdieu 2002: 448).

For Bourdieu, then, political change was possible only through changing agents' vision or representation of the social world, through altering the nature of the practical taxonomies which determined their judgements and actions. As Bourdieu put it in *Language and Symbolic Power*:

> Specifically political action is possible because agents, who are part of the social world, have a (more or less adequate) knowledge of this world. This action aims to produce and impose representations (mental, verbal, visual or theatrical) of the social world which might be capable of acting on this world by acting on agents' representation of it. Or, more precisely, it aims to make or unmake groups – and, by the same token, the collective actions they can undertake to transform the social world in accordance with their interests – by producing, reproducing or destroying the representations that make groups visible for themselves and for others.
>
> (1982: 149 [127])

For Bourdieu, then, political action was possible through changing existing representations of the social world in such a way as to mobilize agents or classes into political groups. Such a mobilization would involve enabling a shared set of practical dispositions, which had thus far 'remained in a state of individual or serial existence', to become the basis for collective political action (1984: 6 [1991: 236]).[1]

At the core of Bourdieu's conception of politics was the contention that social groups did not mobilize into political forces through a collective 'awakening of consciousness' regarding their objective class position. Rather their group identity would have to be constructed, made public and explicit by means of the 'imposition' of a new vision and division of the social world. To 'impose' new representations of the social world, to impose a new vision and division of that world, involved what Bourdieu termed an 'act of *nomination*'. The term 'nomination', here, needs to be understood by reference to its etymological root in the Greek word 'nomos', meaning both law and boundary. This act of nomination represented the arbitrary imposition of a social law or boundary, a 'magic, and properly social, act of *diacrisis*' (Bourdieu 1982: 137), which divided the social world between masculine and feminine principles, in the case of Kabylia, or the values of the dominant and dominated classes, in the case of advanced capitalist societies, or state and market, in the case of neo-liberal discourse. Bourdieu cited the examples of Marxism and of movements for regional or ethnic identity as political ideologies which worked by such acts of nomination. Marxism *named* the primary social division as being that between bourgeoisie and proletariat, understanding all further social conflicts and political grievances in terms of that primary division. A movement for regional identity, on the other hand, *named* the primary social division as being that between the region and the encompassing nation-state, understanding all social conflicts and grievances in terms of that primary division. Neither of these acts of nomination was purely descriptive, according to Bourdieu, since each worked to produce performatively the reality it named: 'the *performative* utterance, the political pre-vision, is in itself a pre-diction which aims to bring about what it utters' (1982: 150 [128]). In naming or imposing the division between region and nation-state or proletariat and bourgeoisie as the fundamental organizing principle of the social field, regionalists or Marxists did not simply name two pre-existing positive entities, a region or a class. Rather, that 'act of nomination' worked performatively to produce the very reality it apparently merely described, potentially transforming every agent who fell within the boundaries of a defined region or class into a mobilizable or mobilized political group. This capacity of theories of the social world such as Marxism or regionalism to change collective representations of the social world, and through such change to change the social world itself, Bourdieu termed 'the theory effect' (1982: 157–8 [132]).

It was because of this emphasis on their inherently performative nature that Bourdieu had insisted, in the earlier article 'Questions de politique' (1977), that political ideas or theories should be known as 'idées-force', 'force-ideas' or 'power-ideas', whose force related not merely to their inherent persuasiveness but also to the social forces they were able to mobilize:

> Political opinion is not a pure judgement, a purely informative utterance capable of imposing itself by the intrinsic force of its truth, but an *idée-force*,

containing a claim to realise itself, by being acted upon, all the greater the more powerful and numerous is the group which it mobilises through its properly symbolic efficacy.

(Bourdieu 1977b: 64)

Political ideologies and slogans thus had a kind of 'magic' efficacy (Bourdieu 1982: 109 [111]). In his study of magic, Marcel Mauss (1950) had explained the effectiveness of magic in so-called primitive societies not by reference to the nature of the rituals themselves or to the truth content of magic beliefs but rather by reference to the social institutions and structures which fostered and sustained belief in magic ritual. Similarly, Bourdieu located the efficacy of political discourse and its 'social magic', less in its inherent characteristics than in the broader social field from which it emerged. Thus the force or power of *idées-force* related to the 'symbolic authority' enjoyed by the individual expressing those ideas, an authority mandated to that individual by either or both the political organization and the mobilized group in whose name he or she spoke. The ability to mobilize a given group related, in turn, to what Bourdieu termed 'a determined principle of pertinence', namely 'the degree to which the discourse, which announces to the group its own identity, is founded in the objectivity of the group to which it is addressed' (1982: 141). The symbolic authority and performative force of any political discourse was thus contingent on its ability to offer 'a unitary expression' of the experiences, of the shared ethos and affective investments, the shared 'doxa' and 'practical sense' of the group to which it appealed and which it constituted (Bourdieu 1982: 152 [1991: 129]). It was in this way, then, that the shared ethos and affective investments at the core of a class habitus could become an active force for political change; rendered explicit through an act of nomination, a class's 'practical sense' of their position in social space could form the basis of a group mobilization, with its attendant 'properly political manifestations'.

Bourdieu's political conception would seem, then, to represent an extremely dynamic vision of the social field as the site of constant struggles over the meaning of the social world, of permanently shifting representations around which different groups coalesce and mobilize. As Bourdieu put it in 'Social space and genesis of "classes" ', any social theory 'must take account of agents' representation of the social world and, more precisely, of the contribution they make to the construction of the vision of this world, and, thereby, to the very construction of this world' (1984: 4 [1991: 234]). Bourdieu's thinking here seems to offer a series of striking similarities with the post-Marxist theory of hegemony elaborated by Laclau and Mouffe. For Laclau and Mouffe, 'hegemony' names the process whereby political ideologies attempt to 'hegemonize' the social field by establishing one of a range of 'floating signifiers', such as 'class', 'race', 'gender' or 'nation', as a 'nodal point' or 'point of suture', the point from which society makes sense and around which a political movement can coalesce. Hegemony then operates by drawing a series of 'equivalences' between that hegemonized signifier and a set of adjacent political issues. To take the example of Thatcherism, the signifier 'Great Britain' might form the nodal point for a politics promising to restore British national pride through the improvement of national economic performance, itself seen as equivalent to and inseparable from cutting public expenditure, privatizing nationalized industries, curbing the powers of trades unions and 'rolling back' the state. In a more progressive vein, demands for the emancipation of the working class, for example, might be seen as equivalent to and inseparable from demands for the emancipation of women, or, in the face of Nazi aggression, defence of democracy might be seen as inseparable from defence of national sovereignty, and so on (Laclau and Mouffe 1985).

Laclau and Mouffe see their theory of hegemony as breaking with the economism and essentialism inherent in classical Marxism, which, they claim, ignores the extent to which political identities are not predetermined by position in relation to the material conditions of production but must always be 'discursively constructed' (1985: 1–5). As such they reject the classically Marxist contention that all social and political activities are 'determined in the last instance' by the economy. This, they claim, leads to a kind of essentialism according to which particular social classes, notably the proletariat, are taken to have a set of inherent or essential 'objective interests', which exist prior to their discursive construction. Politics, in such an account, then becomes a matter of the ruling class seeking to conceal those objective interests from the proletariat through the 'false consciousness' engendered by ideology. The Party, on the other hand, in its role as revolutionary vanguard, works to represent and publicize the 'objective interests' of the proletariat, seeking to achieve the transformation of that class's identity from a 'class in itself' to a 'class for itself'. Laclau and Mouffe reject the essentialism of this account, replacing the notion of the 'representation' of existing 'objective interests' with that of the 'discursive construction' of such interests and their subsequent 'articulation' into a new hegemonic project. Replacing 'the principle of representation with that of articulation', they argue, means that unity between agents and groups 'is then not the expression of a common underlying essence but the result of political construction and struggle' (Laclau and Mouffe 1985: 65).

In the opening paragraph of 'Social space and genesis of "classes" ', Bourdieu outlined what appeared to be an analogous project, claiming his emphasis on the performative construction of social groups and classes was the fruit of 'a series of breaks with Marxist theory'. He pointed first to his wish to break with a 'substantialist' mode of analysis, which took classes to be substantive entities defined by a set of positive attributes, rather than 'relational' entities, whose existence was defined in opposition to other groups and fractions within a 'multidimensional' social space. Second, he sought 'a break with economism, which leads to the reduction of the social field, a multidimensional space, to the relations of economic production'. Both 'substantialism' and economism led to the errors of 'objectivism', which ignored the importance of the 'symbolic struggles which are played out in different fields and where what is at stake is the very representation of the social world' (Bourdieu 1984: 3 [1991: 229]). In short, Bourdieu seemed to be arguing, like Laclau and Mouffe, that class identity, and hence potentially political identity also, was not the expression of a pre-given essence, defined by position in the relations of production, but was rather the product of discursive construction and symbolic struggle in any number of different fields, from the economic to the cultural, the political, the educational and so on.

There are, however, a number of fundamental differences between Bourdieu's account of performative politics and Laclau and Mouffe's post-Marxist theory of hegemony. Laclau and Mouffe assume the discursive construction of the social and political world to be a process in which all agents are implicated. Bourdieu, however, maintained that there was a set of strict socio-economic conditions limiting the extent to which different social groups could contribute actively to the performative utterance and hence imposition of new visions and divisions of the social world. As Bourdieu put it, in order to 'put an end to the metaphysics of the "awakening of consciousness" [*prise de conscience*] and class consciousness, a sort of revolutionary *cogito* of the collective consciousness of a personified entity', it was vital for any theory of politics 'to examine the social and economic conditions which make possible that form of distance from the present of practice which the conception and formulation of a more or less elaborated representation of a collective future presupposes' (1984: 6 n.6 [1991: 289–90 n.6]). Throughout his work, Bourdieu insisted that to formulate a rational project for an alternative future agents or groups had to stage a 'break' or 'rupture' with the embodied structures of the habitus, suspending their immediate investment in the realm of pressing material needs, in order to achieve a critical distance on the social world. The capacity to stage such a 'break', he argued, was unequally distributed among the social classes. Only those with the time and money to stand back from the realm of material necessity could stand back from and achieve critical distance on their own social universe.

Bourdieu thus distinguished between a rational consciousness of the social world, an ability to formulate coherent political projects for the future, dependent on a certain level of material wealth, and the 'doxic' level of consciousness available to the dominated classes in society. This 'doxic' level of consciousness implied a 'practical sense' of the social world, an implicit sense of what one could or could not hope to achieve in the future, a sense of one's place and one's limits which worked to naturalize and reproduce the status quo (Bourdieu 1984: 5 [1991: 235]). However, while Bourdieu acknowledged that this 'practical sense' did imply an 'act of construction', a 'practical representation' of the social world, he insisted that this was 'closer to a "class unconscious" than to a "class consciousness" in the Marxist sense' since 'the essential part of experience of the social world and of the labour of construction it implies takes place in practice, without reaching the level of explicit representation and verbal expression' (1984: 5 [1991: 235]). Bourdieu emphasized that this 'practical sense' of the social world involved a 'sense of realities' which 'in no way' implied 'a *class consciousness* in the social-psychological sense [...], i.e. an *explicit* representation of the position occupied in the social structure'. Bourdieu's reference to a 'sense of realities' here reflected the role he took the temporal structure of the habitus to play in the reproduction of the status quo. Bourdieu argued that as long as the 'practical expectations' internalized in the habitus were in accord with the 'objective chances' of those expectations being met, the social world would appear immediately self-evident, natural and beyond question. As long as there was a 'correspondence between [...] objective structures and mental structures', this would secure the 'kind of original adherence to the established order' Bourdieu termed 'the originary doxa' (1982: 150 [127]). Sketching an account of the general conditions of possibility of political change, Bourdieu stated that in order for this situation to end and the established order to be challenged or denounced, two conditions had to be fulfilled. First, there had to be an 'objective crisis' which would bring an end to the correspondence between practical expectations and objective chances and hence cause agents to undergo a 'practical *épochè*', to 'suspend' their investment in the self-evidence of the doxa. Second, there had to be a 'conjuncture' between this objective crisis and 'critical discourse', the discourse elaborated by intellectuals which would exploit the collective energies released by the practical *épochè*, channelling and directing those energies towards rational goals (Bourdieu 1982: 150 [128]).

Bourdieu's own sociological studies provided two clear examples of instances where the first of these two breaks had occurred, where agents had undergone a collective practical *épochè* or suspension of their investment in the originary doxa. In each case, Bourdieu had attributed the failings of the political movements which emerged from such objective crises or moments of practical *épochè* to the absence of an adequate critical discourse, elaborated by intellectuals. Thus, in his very early work on the political consciousness of the Algerian peasantry and sub-proletariat during the War of Independence, Bourdieu had sought to challenge Frantz Fanon's claims that these two classes represented a revolutionary political force. Bourdieu argued, on the contrary, that the peasantry and sub-proletariat existed in conditions of such poverty that they were unable to move beyond a purely 'practical' apprehension of their immediate material needs so as to construct a rational political project for the future. The War and its dislocations had shattered the earlier 'peasant experience of time', disrupting its repetitive cyclical rhythms. Hence an objective crisis had provoked the first of those two breaks with 'doxic immediacy' which Bourdieu saw as the necessary precursors to any political change. However, the result of this objective crisis in the earlier peasant experience of time had been to throw the peasantry and sub-proletariat into a state of economic insecurity. Constrained by a host of immediate, pressing needs, these two social classes lacked the material well-being necessary to achieve 'critical distance' on their world and hence to conceptualize a 'rational project' for an alternative future (Bourdieu 1962a,b, 1963, 1963a). Given the inability of the peasantry or sub-proletariat to form any such rational project for the future, Bourdieu argued that only 'the workers' elite' expressed 'rational and *universal* demands and claims' and that the working class was the only revolutionary class in Algeria (1963a: 381). It thus fell to this 'revolutionary elite' to engage in 'a complete and total action of education' directed towards the peasantry and sub-proletariat (Bourdieu 1964: 176–7).

Bourdieu's analyses had drawn on a variety of theoretical traditions, from Weber's conception of rational calculation to Husserl's phenomenological studies of temporality. The political conclusions of these analyses and their emphasis on the pedagogical role to be played by the workers' elite, however, owed a clear debt to Lenin. In *What is to be done?* (1902), Lenin had rejected the 'populist' assumption that the Russian working class possessed a spontaneous and inherently revolutionary consciousness. On the contrary, Lenin argued, the workers were imbued with a 'trade union consciousness', which limited their political activity to the making of purely corporatist demands aiming at the satisfaction of their desires for immediate material improvement. In such circumstances, it fell to the intelligentsia and the Party, as revolutionary vanguard, to educate the workers and imbue them with a genuinely revolutionary consciousness. As Robert Service puts it, the 'central statement' of *What is to be done?* was that 'workers could never in themselves gravitate towards socialism', needing 'indoctrination and guidance from middle-class intellectuals who, [...] through their education and greater leisure, were in a position to develop socialist theory' (in Lenin 1902: 22).

Bourdieu's account of the events of May 1968 in *Homo Academicus* employed analogous terms of analysis. He emphasized the role played by the rapid postwar expansion of French universities in shattering or 'suspending' the previously unchallenged temporal rhythms governing study, graduation and employment, for students, and promotion and career development, for lecturers. An objective crisis had thus provoked a practical *épochè* in students' and lecturers' previously unquestioned adherence to the doxic order; the forms and content of what was learnt, the mode of teaching, the hierarchical structures of the institution could all now be questioned. Bourdieu (1984a) attributed the failings of the May movement, meanwhile, to the inadequacies of the critical discourse on the universities elaborated by student and lecturers' unions alike, who failed to grasp the real nature of higher education's social role and of the crisis it was undergoing. It is significant in this light that, throughout the events of May themselves, Bourdieu's own research group, the *Centre de sociologie européenne*, was one of the only such groups to keep working, producing a series of analyses of the situation in French universities, of critical discourses that were clearly intended to play an analogous pedagogic role to that he had anticipated the workers' elite playing in Algeria (Bourdieu 2002: 63–8).

Intellectuals: from Lenin to Socrates

Thus, at the heart of Bourdieu's understanding of the role to be played by intellectuals in political change was his conviction that a certain material well-being was the precondition for gaining that measure of critical distance on the world which enabled one to formulate and express an alternative vision and division of the social world. The dominated classes in society, who lacked that material well-being, thus also lacked the capacity to formulate and express alternative visions of society. Intellectuals, on the other hand, enjoyed both the measure of economic wealth and the professional capacities which enabled them to elaborate a coherent social critique. Moreover, as 'the dominated fraction of the dominant class', occupying a dominated position within the 'field of power' homologous to the dominated position occupied within the broader social field by the dominated classes, certain intellectuals were disposed to contribute to 'the production and diffusion, notably in the direction of the dominated classes, of a vision of the social world which breaks with the dominant vision' (Bourdieu 1984: 9 [1991: 244]). As Bourdieu put it:

> Those who occupy the dominated position in social space are also situated in dominated positions in the field of symbolic production and one cannot see where they could acquire the instruments of symbolic production necessary to express their own point of view on the social world, if the very logic of the field of cultural production, and the specific interests engendered there, did not have the effect of inclining a fraction of the professionals engaged in that field to offer to the dominated, on the basis of a homology of position, instruments of rupture with the representations generated in the immediate complicity between social structures and mental structures, which tend to ensure the continued reproduction of the [unequal] distribution of symbolic capital.
>
> (1984: 9 [1991: 244])

The intercession of intellectuals was thus apparently necessary before the dominated classes could express or elaborate a coherent alternative political vision. Only intellectuals had the ability to articulate 'the truth of those who have neither the interest, nor the leisure, nor the necessary instruments to re-appropriate the objective and subjective truth of what they are and what they do' (Bourdieu 1997c: 228 [191]). Only intellectuals had access to 'the instruments of rupture' necessary to secure an objective distance on social reality and gain a rational or scientific knowledge of its laws of functioning.

As the phrase 'instruments of rupture' indicated, Bourdieu was drawing here on Gaston Bachelard's notion of the 'epistemological break' constitutive of science. For example, Bachelard argued that the insights of post-Einsteinian science had only been gained by staging a 'break' with the theoretical assumptions about space and time contained in Newtonian physics and Euclidean geometry. At the level of technology, the use of certain experimental apparatuses or instruments of rupture staged a similar break, this time with the forms of perception available through use of the five senses. There was a qualitative difference, an 'epistemological break', between the forms of knowledge available to a scientist using an electron microscope and the knowledge available to someone using even a conventional microscope, which merely magnified an existing faculty of sight (Bachelard 1934). Bourdieu sought to apply this concept of the epistemological break to his analysis of the social world, positing a qualitative difference between ordinary agents' 'practical sense' or 'practical knowledge' of that world and the scientific or rational knowledge available to intellectuals through their critical distance on that world. It was because of this insistence on the qualitative difference between 'practical' and 'scientific' knowledge that Bourdieu rejected as a 'myth' Gramsci's notion of the 'organic intellectual'. For Bourdieu, Gramsci's notion that the working class might possess its own organic intellectuals ignored the fact that to be working class was, by definition, to lack the economic means to become an intellectual. Hence, in a lecture of 1989, 'Pour une Internationale des intellectuels', Bourdieu argued that intellectuals would only succeed in safeguarding their critical autonomy by 'sacrificing once and for all the myth of the "organic intellectual" ' and engaging in 'a rational action of defence of the economic and social conditions of the autonomy of those privileged social universes where the material and intellectual instruments of what we call Reason are produced and reproduced' (Bourdieu 2002: 266). A certain socio-economic privilege thus appeared to be the precondition for genuinely intellectual activity and, as such, needed to be preserved if intellectual autonomy was to be safeguarded.

As has been demonstrated, Bourdieu's understanding of the political role of intellectuals clearly owed a debt to Lenin, at least at its initial inception. In his later work, Bourdieu 'softened' this Leninist approach,[2] figuring the role of intellectuals in a more Socratic mode as representing an effort to render explicit dispositions, resentments, fears, emotions that already existed within the dominated classes at the implicit, embodied, doxic level, in the form of a set of shared practices or an 'ethos'. As Bourdieu put it in an interview of 1990:

> In order to explain what I have to say in sociology, I could use the parable of Socrates and the little slave: I think that the sociologist is someone who, at the cost of a labour of enquiry and interrogation, using modern means and techniques, helps others give birth to something they know without knowing it.
> (Bourdieu 2002c: 14–15)

It was this more Socratic notion of intellectual activity that was evident in *Language and Symbolic Power*. Here Bourdieu described the 'political labour of representation' as consisting in the effort to 'bring to the objectivity of a public discourse or an exemplary practice a way of seeing and living the social world until then relegated to the state of practical disposition or often confused experience (malaise, revolt, etc.)' (1982: 152–3 [130]). Progressive intellectuals, he argued, would seek to challenge the established order, the doxa, by elaborating a 'critical' or 'heretical' discourse which rendered explicit the previously unspoken experiences of exploitation and suffering endured by the dominated classes, making of them the basis of a movement for political change. The dominant class, on the other hand, would attempt to perpetuate the 'doxic relation to the social world', hoping to 'restore the silence of doxa', through the imposition of 'orthodoxy or straightened opinion' (Bourdieu 1982: 154–5 [130–1]).

In the earlier article 'Questions de politique', Bourdieu had argued that this process of Socratic 'anamnesis' represented his alternative to accounts of political agency which rested on the notion of a *prise de conscience* or 'awakening of consciousness':

> The awakening of consciousness is not the bursting forth of an originary act but the progressive discovery of what is contained, in practical state, within the class habitus. It is the appropriation by oneself of oneself; it is the taking

into one's own hands, by means of its coherent explanation in an adequate language, of everything which, unconscious and uncontrolled, is exposed to mystification and being deliberately misconstrued.

(1977b: 80)

It was the task of intellectuals to provide this 'coherent explanation' and hence transform 'the systematicity "in itself" of practices and judgements generated from the unconscious principles of the ethos' into 'the conscious and almost forced systematicity of the political programme or party' (Bourdieu 1977b: 71–2). Hence a political consciousness 'in itself', could only become 'for itself', explicitly formulated, 'by proxy', by the intercession of an intellectual or spokesperson, a delegate authorized by the group to speak in their name (Bourdieu 1977b: 72 n.37).

As Bourdieu argued in the essay 'Delegation and political fetishism', delegation was a necessary evil, a form of 'political fetishism' in which agents attributed a power to their delegates that in fact derived from themselves (1987: 186 [1991: 204]). While Bourdieu imagined a 'utopia' in which all in society would have an equal 'capacity to produce discourse on the social world and thus a capacity for *conscious* action on that world' (1977b: 55), he maintained that in current circumstances recourse to a delegate or spokesperson remained necessary for the dominated classes (1987: 186 [1991: 204]). Bourdieu concluded 'Delegation and political fetishism' by asserting that in the face of the currently inevitable 'usurpation which is always potentially present in delegation', the 'final political revolution, the revolution again the political clericature', was 'yet to be carried out' (1987: 202 [1991: 219]). The precise nature of this 'final political revolution' remained unspecified in 'Delegation and political fetishism'. However, by the time of the publication of *Pascalian Meditations*, such ambiguity seemed to be cleared up by Bourdieu's much more straightforward evocation of a classically French republican vision. Noting the unequal distribution of political opinions among agents of different classes, Bourdieu returned to the example of the Third Republic and its faith in the power of universal secular, free and obligatory education, regretting that the principles behind this model for ensuring the political equality of all citizens had been 'gradually forgotten' (1997c: 83 [68]).

According to Bourdieu, then, the intercession of intellectuals or mandated delegates in political movements was a necessary evil, whose effects could be mitigated, if not entirely overcome by recourse to the French republican ideal of secular, free and obligatory education for all. Yet Bourdieu's insistence on the vital role played by intellectuals in elaborating a critical discourse and hence directing political movements towards rational goals surely risked returning him to an account of social or political action based on a model of deliberative judgement or rational consciousness. As has been demonstrated, Bourdieu argued that his account of the role played by intellectuals in transforming practical sense into explicit discourse was an attempt to escape what he termed 'the mythology' or 'the metaphysics of the *prise de conscience*'. Indeed, in an interview given in 1984, he claimed to adhere to a model of political change that was 'nearer to

Fourier and to his art of using the passions than to Marx' (Bourdieu 2002: 197). Developing models of social and political change based on a kind of *Fouriériste* 'politics of the passions' would, of course, have been entirely consistent with the justified emphasis Bourdieu had placed on the role of non-deliberative, affective, pre-predicative modes of social experience in his theory of practice. However, this allusion to Fourier was to remain an isolated one in his work, its potentially productive implications never being developed in a systematic way. Rather, the fully developed models of political change Bourdieu did offer seemed to rely on the very 'mythology of the *prise de conscience*' he was seeking to reject. Far from abandoning the problematic of the *prise de conscience*, of consciousness as necessary precursor to any political agency, Bourdieu appeared merely to have set limits on which groups in society were considered capable of achieving the requisite level of rational consciousness. The *prise de conscience* was still seen as necessary, its achievement simply being delegated to intellectuals in the form of the 'epistemological break' which separated their scientific theorizing from the purely 'practical knowledge' available to ordinary agents. It is here that the full implications of Bourdieu's contention as to the 'extraordinary inertia' of the habitus become clear. For, according to this account, the affects, embodied customs, tastes and aversions incorporated into any agent's habitus would remain marked by an 'extraordinary inertia' until such time as they were raised to the level of explicit rationality in intellectual discourse. This suggested not only that political agency was still being understood according to a model of deliberative judgement or rational consciousness, but also that Bourdieu's account of such agency was structured by the very oppositions between the rational mind of the intellectual and the embodied practice of the dominated class, between subject and object, mind and body, he claimed his theory of practice to have overcome.

Certainly, these kinds of opposition were implicit in the Socratic model of intellectual activity to which Bourdieu claimed allegiance. Bourdieu's turn from an earlier Leninist to a later Socratic model may appear to suggest that he was adopting a more modest, less doctrinaire vision of the political role of the intellectual. However, that later Socratic model still rested on an assumption of intellectual superiority. In Plato's the *Meno*, which contains 'the parable of Socrates and the little slave' to which Bourdieu referred, Socrates always knows in advance the laws of geometry whose latent presence in the young slave's practical knowledge he seeks to uncover and demonstrate. Intellectuals or philosophers know and can thus render explicit the truths that their interlocutors simply practise mutely. In short, there is a structural inequality written in to the Socratic dialogue from the very start. Moreover, what Socrates discovers in his dialogue with the young slave in the *Meno* is, of course, a practical knowledge of the laws of geometry, the latent existence of an essential, unchanging truth.

Anamnesis and essentialism

In understanding progressive intellectual activity as 'anamnesis', as rendering explicit or public the shared practical sense or ethos of a dominated social group,

66   From practical sense to performative politics

Bourdieu risked implying that that ethos constituted a fixed identity, an essence, a positive entity which pre-existed both those progressive discourses that raised its hidden principles to the status of an explicit political programme and those reactionary discourses seeking to re-establish 'the silence of doxa'. Bourdieu emphasized that there was always the possibility of a discontinuity between the practical sense of ordinary agents and the various attempts of intellectuals to give expression to that practical sense, a 'margin of uncertainty resulting from the discontinuity between the silent and self-evident truths of the ethos and the public expressions of the logos'. It was within this 'margin of uncertainty' that political struggle proper took place since it was this which prevented each agent from finding 'within himself, the source of an infallible knowledge of the truth of his condition and his position in the social space'. This in turn meant that 'the same agents' could 'recognize themselves in different discourses and classifications (according to class, ethnicity, religion, sex, etc.)' (Bourdieu 1982: 156–7 [132–3]). However, it was noticeable that, according to this account, the margin of uncertainty related merely to a contingent epistemological problem rather than being seen as a transcendental condition of possibility of politics itself. In other words, Bourdieu continued to assume that there was an essential 'truth' reflecting agents' objective position within social space, an 'in itself' of any given class identity. That 'in itself' of class identity could only become a politically mobilizing force, an identity 'for itself', on condition that it were transformed by intellectuals or mandated delegates into a rational, explicit political programme. If there was always a margin of uncertainty in this process of rationalization and explication, this was because of the difficulty of knowing that truth absolutely and not because, as Laclau and Mouffe would argue, that truth exists nowhere as an essential identity or set of objective, predetermined interests outside the range of competing ideologies that seek to construct it discursively.

As we have seen, Bourdieu argued that the efficacy of a political discourse depended on a 'determined principle of pertinence', namely 'the degree to which the discourse which announces to the group its own identity is founded in the objectivity to which it is addressed'. Indeed, in *In Other Words*, he identified this 'principle of pertinence' as being just one of two vital preconditions for the 'symbolic effectiveness' of any performative political utterance. The first such precondition was that an individual or group making a political claim or demand needed to possess sufficient symbolic capital or authority if that claim was to be successful: 'like every form of performative discourse, symbolic power has to be based on the possession of symbolic capital'. Prior possession of sufficient symbolic capital was thus seen as a necessary condition for the success of any political utterance since the 'power of imposing on other minds a vision, old or new, of social divisions depends on the social authority acquired in previous struggles' (Bourdieu 1987: 163–4 [137–8]). Second, the 'effectiveness' of any such utterance depended on 'the degree to which the vision proposed is based on reality'. Bourdieu continued:

> Evidently, the construction of things cannot be a construction *ex nihilo*. It has all the more chance of succeeding the more it is founded in reality: that is [...] in the objective affinities between people who have to be brought

together. The theory effect is all the more powerful the more adequate theory is. Symbolic power is a power of creating things with words. It is only if it is true, that is, adequate to things, that a description can create things. In this sense, symbolic power is a power of consecration or revelation, a power to conceal or reveal things which are already there.

(1987: 164 [138])

The danger inherent in such an account was its apparent assumption that there resided in the *doxa*, in the affinities and practical dispositions of the habitus, a unitary core of shared experience and emotion, a fixed social identity and a truth at once primary and pre-reflexive, waiting merely to be uncovered. Hence, politics risked being understood not as the collective construction of meanings and interpretations of social reality but rather as a struggle between those dominant groups seeking to conceal and those intellectuals seeking to express the fundamental truths of a shared experience or ethos. In *Sociology in Question*, Bourdieu offered two concrete examples of the manner in which 'the scientific gaze' could be 'disseminated' in order to enable a dominated group to 'assume and even lay claim to its own identity, to claim the right to be what it is'. The examples in question, 'slogans like the American blacks' "Black is beautiful" and the feminists' assertion of the right to the "natural look" ', nicely illustrated the dangers of essentialism here (Bourdieu 1980b: 42 [23]). For while such an assumption and assertion of a dominated habitus and identity may prove an important first step in political mobilization, the categories mobilized here, 'Blackness' and 'natural woman', are not themselves unproblematic; they will subsequently need to be questioned, subjected to resignification or be discursively reconstructed and deconstructed in different ways.

As these two examples demonstrated, the assumption behind Bourdieu's theory of political change was that the values contained within the habitus or ethos of a dominated group would be inherently progressive and hence that it was sufficient merely to publicize and validate such values. Yet a dominated group's shared 'practical dispositions' and 'confused experience', their 'malaise' and sense of 'revolt', could surely not always be relied upon to translate into a progressive political agenda, merely by dint of being brought 'to the objectivity of a public discourse'. Intellectuals or political movements, such as the *Front national* (FN) in France, might be more than happy to bring the discontents of dominated groups 'to the objectivity of public discourse', but only in order to articulate that discontent to the most reactionary of political programmes. Indeed, the rise of the FN can serve as a useful example here, illustrating further limitations in Bourdieu's theory of politics. First, the 'symbolic effectiveness' of FN discourse can in no way be attributed to its leader's prior possession of significant amounts of 'symbolic capital' or 'social authority'. In the years between its foundation in 1972 and its first electoral breakthrough in the municipal elections at Dreux in 1983, Jean-Marie Le Pen and his colleagues were marginal figures in the French political field, almost completely ignored, possessing little or no symbolic capital. Indeed, as late as 1981 Le Pen was unable to secure sufficient endorsements from other elected politicians in France to be permitted even to stand as a candidate in the presidential elections of that year. The symbolic capital Le Pen and his colleagues acquired in the course of the 1980s and 1990s was derived from their electoral successes, from the 'symbolic effectiveness' of their discourse, not vice versa, as Bourdieu would have it. Second, the rise of the FN reveals the limitations of Bourdieu's assumption that the effectiveness of any political utterance depends, in any straightforward way, on its truth content, where the relationship between truth and discourse or representation is understood according to a model of adequation.

In *Propos sur le champ politique* Bourdieu argued that the FN had succeeded in the French political field to the extent that it had managed 'to impose' a new 'vision and division' of the social world. This new vision and division was based on a primary opposition between French nationals and foreigners, an opposition which had displaced the older opposition between rich and poor or bourgeois and proletariat as a fundamental explanation for France's social problems (Bourdieu 2000a: 61–3). Clearly, however, the power of the FN's discourse does not reflect, in any straightforward sense, its power 'to reveal things which are already there'. It is not true, as the FN's case strikingly demonstrates, that a 'description can create things' only 'if it is true, that is adequate to reality', as Bourdieu assumed. The FN's descriptions of various 'threats' to French society – immigrants, AIDS sufferers, EU bureaucrats – possess a power which cannot be related directly to their truth content, just as their appeals to national identity cannot be understood to express the reality or truth of some predetermined interest, an interest which had previously remained implicit or unspoken as the 'doxic' core of an experience shared by all French citizens. Rather, the FN attempts to give those often un-stated, ineffable feelings of national identity a very particular discursive construction, hence altering their very nature, rather than simply expressing them or rendering them public. Bourdieu, on the other hand, when he figured neo-liberalism as an 'invasion', was, whether consciously or not, attempting to stage a different appeal to French national identity, giving a different discursive construction to the national interest, reflecting republican notions of equality, universal human rights and social solidarity. In neither case could French national identity be seen to represent a predetermined objective interest or fundamental truth which was subsequently being expressed or represented in political discourses of lesser or greater epistemological precision. There is no fundamental truth to be revealed or concealed here since French national identity exists nowhere outside of the competing discourses that seek to construct it in different ways. Hence the 'symbolic effectiveness' of these competing constructions of French national identity cannot simply be explained by reference to their varying 'power to conceal or reveal things which are already there'. As Laclau and Mouffe put it, 'the field of politics can no longer be considered a "representation of interests", given that the so-called "representation" modifies the nature of what is represented' (1985: 58).

In Laclau and Mouffe's terms, then, FN discourse would be understood as corresponding to a particular 'discursive construction' of national identity. The 'hegemonic project' of the FN would be understood to involve the attempt to hegemonize the political field around the 'nodal point' of French national identity

From practical sense to performative politics 69

and *grandeur* so that defence of that *grandeur* would involve seeing off a number of supposedly equivalent threats, in the form of immigrants, AIDS sufferers, global capital, a corrupt political elite and meddling EU bureaucrats. The limitations of this model are contained in the adjective 'discursive' in the collocation 'discursive construction' since this risks returning us to a model of politics based on discourse, on the force of rational persuasion and the power of deliberative judgement. In this sense, Laclau and Mouffe's concept of hegemony risks overlooking the realms of affect, desire, aversion and affinity, of the almost intuitive practical sense of how things should be, realms to which a xenophobic, nationalistic party such as the FN so clearly appeals.

Indeed, one of the most striking characteristics of Le Pen's speeches is the extent to which they include statements of affiliation or evocations of past experience which, if judged according to the criterion of logical or rational argument, appear to be self-evidently contradictory. Thus, for example, in the late 1990s Le Pen welcomed De Gaulle's grandson onto his platform, while adopting the Gaullist formula of 'a Europe of nations' in support of his anti-EU stance. At the same time, however, the FN leadership included several ex-members of the clandestine terrorist organization, the OAS, which had attempted to assassinate De Gaulle for his role in conceding Algerian independence. Le Pen has himself frequently evoked his own past as a paratrooper fighting for Algeria to remain French and his role in formulating Tixier-Vignancour's programme for his 1965 presidential bid, a programme which included an explicit commitment to returning the newly independent Algeria to French control. Similarly, Le Pen has consistently sought to play down the crimes committed during both the Holocaust and the German Occupation of France, in a manner that flirts with Holocaust denial. At the same time, he evokes memories of the role he claims to have played as a teenager in the Resistance against Nazi Occupation. It would surely be naïve to imagine that such contradictions betray mistakes, errors or unconscious slips on Le Pen's part. Rather what they suggest is that he has understood the extent to which the appeal of the FN rests not on rational argumentation but on affect. To use Bourdieu's own terminology, FN discourse could be seen as so many 'secondary rationalisations' and '*post festum* justifications' of an 'initial, unjustifiable investment' in nationalism, xenophobia and racial prejudice. The performative force of Le Pen's evocations of contradictory traditions in French nationalism depends neither on their truth content nor on their force of rational persuasion but on their ability to appeal to, mobilize and give a particular construction to the affects, tastes and aversions incorporated in the habitus of a significant section of the French electorate. It is here that Bourdieu's theory of practice does seem to have significant advantages over more conventional theories of ideology. However, this advantage can only be secured at the price of a significant modification of his theorization of the relationship between habitus and field, between the practical taxonomies incorporated in the habitus and the objective reality to which they seek to give form and meaning.

In *In Other Words*, Bourdieu defined the habitus as 'at once a system of models for the production of practices and a system of models for the perception and appreciation of practices. And in both cases, its operations express the social position in which it was constructed' (1987: 156 [131]). It is the notion of *expression* that needs to be jettisoned here and replaced with that of *construction*. The 'models', 'practical schemata' or 'taxonomies' of the habitus need to be understood not as the straightforward *expression* of an external reality, of objective position within the social field, models whose potential symbolic force depends on their adequation to essential truths. Rather, such models or schemata need to be understood as *constructions* of that reality, whose relation to it is necessarily *contingent*, never essential. This does not mean that all political discourses possess the same symbolic force regardless of their characteristics and in all historical circumstances. Certain statistical correlations might be observed between a particular discourse and the tendency or probability of a given social group to embrace that discourse at a given historical moment. However, this will be a matter of statistical *correlation* and *probability*, not of causal determination. The criterion of *plausibility* might similarly be employed as one measure of the efficacy of any such discourse, where plausibility implies that any assessment of a discourse's relation to what can be known of social reality must always be made in a relative way rather than in terms of an absolute measure of adequation to the truth. Plausibility would have to be understood in an extended sense, here, as referring to any political programme's ability not only to persuade voters, at the rational level, but also to engage their affective investments, hopes, tastes and aversions. The failure to grasp the contingent and constructed nature of the values contained in the habitus risked leading Bourdieu into the trap identified by Laclau and Mouffe as the 'closure' of the political field and the 'elision' of politics proper.

As we have already seen, for Bourdieu the fact that political struggles, symbolic struggles over the meaning of the social world, could take place reflected the essentially epistemological problem for each agent of finding 'within himself, the source of an infallible knowledge of the truth of his condition and his position in the social space'. There was a 'margin of uncertainty' between the objective positions occupied by agents and groups within the social field and the different symbolic representations of those same positions, so that the same groups could recognize themselves in different political discourses. It was within this 'margin of uncertainty' that any political debate or struggle would take place. The problem with such an account was that it reduced the political to a set of purely empirical and epistemological problems. In other words, this 'margin of uncertainty', and hence the very existence of politics itself, reflected first an empirical problem – the great number of different possible symbolic representations of the same social position – and secondly, an epistemological problem – the difficulty of ensuring any such representation was an accurate reflection or expression of that position. Here again, reference to the work of Laclau and Mouffe proves useful in revealing the limitations of this model of society and politics. They reject the notion that the open-endedness of the political process, the potential for 'discontinuity' between the 'truth' of any social group's position and the discourses attempting to articulate that 'truth', relates to a purely empirical and epistemological problem. As Laclau explains, according to one account, the difficulty of any single hegemonic project successfully 'suturing' the entire social field, attributing to it a single definitive meaning, represents a merely empirical problem, reflecting the immense complexity of that social field and the great number of possible meanings it generates. However, this account retains the notion that the social field is a closed totality, ideally, if not practically, susceptible to being rendered totally transparent to an adequate scientific gaze. As Laclau puts it:

> for this approach there cannot be a closed totality because it is not empirically possible for a social force to impose its hegemonic supremacy in such a complete way; but it is assumed that if such a supremacy ideally came about, the social would take on the character of a self-regulated and self-generated ensemble.
>
> (1990: 28)

It is this notion of a social field which, despite its immense complexity, might ideally prove itself to be entirely transparent to the social scientific gaze that we find in Bourdieu's work.

As we have noted, according to Bourdieu, any political change resulted from an attempt to 'impose a new vision and division of the social world', an attempt whose success was dependent on a number of factors. First, elaborating a coherent alternative vision of society and then imposing it demanded the possession of both the critical distance and the symbolic capital that was the preserve of intellectuals and/or the mandated delegates of dominated social groups. Second, the power of the 'critical discourse' elaborated by intellectuals or delegates depended on its adequacy to the truth, its ability to express the 'objectivity' of the group it sought to mobilize and the desires, emotions and aversions their position in social space expressed. Political analysis, for Bourdieu, thus became a matter of, to use his own terminology, 'objectifying the co-ordinates of the social field', to reveal the objective interests of certain social groups, the adequacy of a given political discourse to those objective interests and the amount of symbolic capital such groups or their delegates possessed. Hence Bourdieu understood neo-liberalism to be the expression of the objective interests of certain elite groups, successfully 'imposed' on French society by dint of the symbolic authority that such groups possessed on account of their elevated position in the French social and political fields, an authority bolstered by the global power of the US, of whose cultural and political traditions neo-liberalism was taken to be the ultimate expression. As we saw, the danger of such an analysis of neo-liberalism in terms of its 'objective' determinants and interests was that it elided the properly political processes at work here.

This is precisely Laclau and Mouffe's objection to any account of the socio-political that assumes the social field to be ideally, if not practically, transparent to an objectifying, scientific gaze. For them, the difficulty of any hegemonic project ever completely suturing the social field reflects not the empirical or epistemological problem of anyone ever completely grasping all of the objective interests at play in that field and hence offering a definitive account of its functioning. Rather, they argue that this difficulty represents the transcendental condition of possibility of politics itself, reflecting the fundamental open-endedness and undecidability of the socio-political. Any attempt to deny that open-endedness and undecidability, any assumption as to the ultimate transparency of the social field, implies, for them, a retreat into essentialism, a closure of the field of politics and an elision of politics proper. For Laclau and Mouffe, the Leninist assumption 'that there is a "for itself" of the class accessible only to the enlightened vanguard, whose attitude toward the working class is therefore purely pedagogical', involves an 'interweaving of science and politics' that risks evacuating the realm of political struggle proper (Laclau and Mouffe 1985: 59). As regards progressive politics, this is no longer seen as a *collective* struggle over social meanings and identities, since the revolutionary vanguard, the Party and its intelligentsia enjoy a privilege that is 'epistemological', a 'scientific monopoly', which guarantees, in advance, that theirs is the correct political interpretation and line (Laclau and Mouffe 1985: 60). Despite his shift from a Leninist to a more Socratic approach, Bourdieu retained this dual emphasis on the epistemological privilege of an intellectual vanguard and their subsequently pedagogic role, on politics as the uncovering and elevation of some essential social identity from the 'in itself' to the 'for itself'.

A 'social miracle'

One example of the elision of the political feared by Laclau and Mouffe might be found in Bourdieu's assumption that only social groups occupying a relatively elevated position in the social field possessed the critical capacities and the symbolic capital which could guarantee the symbolic effectiveness of a political act or utterance. This appeared to overlook the possibility of political movements emerging, unaided by bourgeois intellectuals, from the dominated classes themselves. Significantly, Bourdieu's own account of what he termed the 'social miracle' of the *Mouvement des chômeurs*, the unemployed movement that emerged in France in the late 1990s, seemed to provide evidence of at least one significant political movement that did not conform to the model of political action he had elaborated. In his address to the *Mouvement des chômeurs*, Bourdieu argued that their movement represented a 'social miracle', since it flew in the face of the evidence of their inherent political capacities that had been revealed in sociological studies such as those he had conducted among the Algerian sub-proletariat: 'all the scientific studies of unemployment have shown that it destroys its victims, wiping out their defences and subversive dispositions' (1998: 102 [88]). Thus, it might be argued that in forming a political movement France's unemployed had not merely confounded those reactionary commentators who might define them as idle or shiftless, they had also challenged the account of their inherent capacities contained in Bourdieu's ostensibly sympathetic, sociological analysis of their state. The unemployed had become active agents not by relying on an intellectual or delegate to express the shared truth of their collective ethos and habitus, as Bourdieu's model would presuppose. On the contrary, they had become agents by refusing to be constrained by that habitus and ethos, by refusing to keep to the role in society that sociology and statistical prediction had allotted them. Jacques Rancière has provided a useful model for this kind of political 'subjectification', as he calls it, a model, moreover, which implicitly defines itself in opposition to Bourdieu's account of politics.

Rancière argues that political 'subjectification', whereby groups and individuals gain political agency, is not a matter of the expression of the ethos of such groups as defined under an existing social division of roles, functions, estates or classes. Rather, political 'subjectification' involves a process of what he terms 'disidentification', or 'disincorporation', whereby groups, such as women and proletarians, refuse to accept their allotted, marginalized place in the existing division of social roles and functions, demanding equality, demanding to be 'counted' as equal members of the community and speaking for 'la part des sans-part', on behalf of those who have no share in the community as currently ordered. Such 'subjectification' is, at once, a political and an aesthetic process, since it redraws what Rancière terms 'le partage du sensible', 'the partition of the perceptible'. This 'partition of the perceptible' corresponds to the existing division of the sensible-intelligible world, a division which relates simultaneously to the realms of aesthetic representation and political discourse; it situates and attempts to fix groups and classes within their given roles. The concept of 'le partage du sensible' as a sensible-intelligible structuring of the socio-political world might be seen as comparable to what Bourdieu termed 'the dominant practical taxonomy', that 'vision and division of the social world' which defined correct modes of behaviour, thought and feeling. Drawing on Aristotle's distinction in the *Politics* between those who possess *phônè*, a voice capable merely of expressing inarticulate pain or complaint, and those who possess *logos*, speech or the capacity for reasoned argument, Rancière argues that politics is characterized by the struggle of those considered to possess only the former for the equality and dignity inherent to the latter. As Rancière puts it:

> Every subjectification is a disidentification, removal from the naturalness of a place, the opening up of a subject space where those of no account are counted, where a connection is made between having a part and having no part. 'Proletarian' political subjectification [...] isn't a matter of some form of 'culture' or collective *ethos* giving voice to itself. On the contrary, it presupposes a multiplicity of fractures separating the workers' bodies from their ethos and from the voice which is supposed to express the soul of this ethos, a multiplicity of speech events, that is to say of singular experiences of the dispute over voice and speech, over the partition of the perceptible [*le partage du sensible*]. 'Speaking out' is not awareness and expression of a self affirming what is proper to it. It is the occupation of a place in which the *logos* defines a nature other than the *phônè*. This occupation presupposes that the destinies of the 'workers' be, in one way or another, diverted from their given path [...]. A political subjectification is the product of those multiple

lines of fracture which allow individuals and networks of individuals to subjectify the gap between their condition as animals endowed with voice and the violent encounter with the equality of the *logos*.

(1995: 36–7, trans. modified)

The 'social miracle' Bourdieu found in the *Mouvement des chômeurs* might be best explained according to Rancière's terms of analysis as a moment of 'disidentification' or 'disincorporation' when the unemployed refused to accept the role they had been allotted, diverted themselves from the destiny which 'scientific studies' had predicted to be theirs, in order to speak and act for 'la part des sans-part'. For Rancière, statistical or sociological surveys, such as the ones on which Bourdieu relied, belong to the realm of 'police', to those forces seeking to attribute fixed roles and places to social groups and hence preserve the status quo. Politics proper is thus always defined against such a 'police logic', by producing 'a multiple that was not given in the police constitution of community, a multiple whose count poses itself as contradictory in terms of police logic' (Rancière 1995: 36). The *Mouvement des chômeurs* surely constituted one such 'multiple'.

In Rancière's work, moments of 'disidentification' from existing social identities are always assumed to be inherently progressive, while the kind of political agency they initiate appears still to be understood according to an implicit model of rational action or deliberative judgement. What this ignores is the possibility that such disidentifications might also work in politically regressive ways, while initiating political change that derives less from rational agency than from the investment of desire and affect in a new political direction. For example, neo-liberalism might be understood as provoking a 'disidentification' with the perceived rigidities of traditional class identities and hierarchies, channelling affects and desires into the possibilities for social mobility and betterment the market is claimed to offer. An example of this, in the British context, would be the Thatcherite policy of selling off social housing stock to its former tenants at favourable rates, hence encouraging council tenants to become property owners. A similar policy had been enacted in France in the late 1970s when Giscard d'Estaing introduced measures to replace state subsidy for the construction of social housing with subsidy to help individuals buy their own properties. For Bourdieu, this measure epitomized everything that was wrong with neo-liberal policy and he devoted a book-length study, *The Social Structures of the Economy*, to analysing the measure's genesis, passage into law and after-effects.

The Social Structures of the Economy thus represents the application of Bourdieu's fully worked out field theory to one particular neo-liberal reform. Thus far, we have only examined one side of that field theory in any detail, namely the concepts of habitus and practice as they relate to political analysis. This chapter, for example, has identified certain failings in the concepts of habitus and practice, arguing that such concepts could nonetheless become fruitful tools of political analysis on condition they be re-thought, that we insist upon the *constructed* nature of habitus and practical sense and on the fundamental *contingency* of their relations to the material conditions in which they are constructed. We have not, as yet, subjected Bourdieu's concept of 'field' to equally close scrutiny, much less suggested ways in which it too might require re-thinking. Nor have we examined how Bourdieu theorized the relations between the different semi-autonomous fields or what potential for political change might be contained in the contradictions or points of friction between those fields. Chapter 4 will thus examine Bourdieu's account of the genesis of one particular neo-liberal reform in *The Social Structures of the Economy* in some detail. This will allow for a more detailed critical analysis of the concept of 'field' than has yet proved possible. It will also enable us to test the validity of the hypotheses raised in this chapter regarding the apparent essentialism of Bourdieu's theory of politics.

4 Field theory and political analysis

In Chapter 3, it was suggested that Bourdieu had elaborated what might be termed an expressive model of politics. Political change was seen as a matter of 'imposing a new vision and division of the social world', a vision and division which was the expression of a set of unspoken values, tastes and aversions, an ethos, which reflected the position occupied by different agents or groups in the social field. Progressive political change was thus a matter of intellectuals helping dominated groups to objectify and express the values and feelings incorporated in their shared habitus and ethos, so that such values and feelings might become the basis for a political mobilization. Regressive politics involved an effort by the dominant class to stifle the expression of such feelings and values by re-establishing 'the silence of orginary doxa'. Alternatively, regressive politics might be read as the imposition of a vision and division of the social world which expressed the ethos and habitus, the values, assumptions and expectations, of the dominant class. The problem with such an account of politics was that the political risked being reduced to the status of a 'shadow theatre', to use Althusser's metaphor, a mere reflection or expression of objective interests and power struggles determined elsewhere, outside the political field itself, in the broader domain of economics or society as a whole. Such an account risked denying all autonomy to the political field; the realm of politics proper risked being elided, since politics would be read as simply the reflection or expression of a set of 'objective interests', which were themselves ultimately determined by the position agents and groups occupied in the social field as a whole.

It is, of course, precisely such an account of neo-liberalism that Bourdieu appeared to offer in the shorter, directly political pieces anthologized in the two volumes of *Contre-feux* and elsewhere. For there neo-liberalism appeared to be understood as the successful imposition by a political and economic elite of an ideology which expressed their ethos, interests and values. That ethos and those values and objective interests were, in turn, understood to be the expressions of that elite's position within the social field. Our analysis of the theoretical assumptions behind Bourdieu's fully fledged social theory in the preceding two chapters has suggested that the failings contained in this analysis of neo-liberalism cannot be attributed solely to the necessarily simplified and abbreviated form of his more directly political interventions. Rather such failings appeared to be inherent to

Bourdieu's fully worked out social theory. An opportunity to test this hypothesis further is provided by his late study, *The Social Structures of the Economy*, which saw Bourdieu deploy all the resources of his fully fledged field theory in his most detailed critique of a single neo-liberal policy.

The Social Structures of the Economy is an empirical analysis of the French housing market of the mid-to-late 1970s, which draws heavily on a series of articles that had already appeared in a special number of *Actes de la recherche en sciences sociales* in 1990. It pays particularly close attention to the passage, in 1977, of the Barrot Law, a reform to the system of state subsidy for social housing. This reform, passed under Giscard d'Estaing's presidency, signalled a shift away from state subsidy of the construction of homes (*l'aide à la pierre*) towards subsidy encouraging private property ownership (*l'aide personnalisée au logement* or APL). For Bourdieu, the reform of 1977 epitomized the negative effects of neo-liberal policy on French society, both exemplifying and anticipating a more general withdrawal of the state under neo-liberalism, while representing an important first step in 'the demolition of belief in the state and the destruction of the welfare state' (1998: 14 [6]). He argued that 'housing policy was one of the first arenas for the confrontation between the supporters of a "social" policy [...] and the defenders of a more or less radical liberalism' (2000: 148 [120]). Moreover, the reform had some disastrous social effects, being the 'major cause' of the problems subsequently faced by France's 'banlieues', the large, out-of-town housing estates, widely stigmatized in the French popular imaginary as places of rampant criminality, violence and ethnic tension. In *The Weight of the World*, he dedicated considerable space to documenting what he saw as the 'social costs' of this reform, costs born by the current inhabitants of the 'banlieue' (1993: 13–32, 81–99, 219–28 [6–23, 60–76, 181–8]). In *The Social Structures of the Economy* itself, Bourdieu made use of extensive ethnographic research to highlight the 'small-scale suffering' experienced by those who had been encouraged to buy their own homes and whose limited means had forced them to settle for poor quality housing, far from their workplaces or any cultural amenities.

Bourdieu was convinced that if these kinds of 'social cost' had not been anticipated, it was because of the dominance of neo-classical economics and supposedly neutral econometric models over public policy decision-making. A first chapter, in which Bourdieu applied his own concepts of 'field', 'practice' and 'habitus' to a detailed analysis of demand and supply in the housing market, was thus an attempt to refute the claims of neo-classical economics. The housing market was seen to be subject to a series of social determinants and public policy decisions seen to carry a series of social costs which economics and econometrics, with their assumptions about markets as self-regulating mechanisms, were unable to grasp. Reasserting the strengths of sociological analysis over econometric modelling thus became a way for Bourdieu to sketch out a role for progressive intellectuals in contributing to public policy debates. Such intellectuals, particularly sociologists, were equipped to anticipate the social costs of any reform, putting into practice the call Bourdieu had issued to intellectuals in *Firing back* 'to ensure the gains of science enter the realms of public debate, from which they are tragically absent' (2001: 9 [13]). A subsequent chapter saw Bourdieu attempting to explain how the 1977 housing reform came to be passed into law, deploying all of the resources of his 'field theory' to analyse the structure of the bureaucratic and political fields at the time of the passing of that reform.

The Social Structures of the Economy thus had a number of closely related aims and epitomized the symbiotic relationship between Bourdieu's typically succinct political interventions against neo-liberalism and his fully worked out sociological analyses. For the purposes of the current study, of most interest is the account Bourdieu offered of the passage of the 1977 housing reform. For this saw Bourdieu applying the theoretical framework we have examined in the two previous chapters, the particular conception of politics implicit in his concepts of practice, habitus and field, to the analysis of a single neo-liberal reform. A critical reading of Bourdieu's account of the 1977 housing reform will thus prove vital to any assessment of the contribution his sociology might have to make to political theory. Such an assessment will also necessitate looking in more detail at the way in which Bourdieu theorized the relations or forms of articulation among the different fields he identified in the course of his analysis, the bureaucratic field, the political field, the educational field and the broader social field.

Mapping the 'field of efficient agents'

In analysing the genesis of the 1977 housing reform, Bourdieu insisted on the need to map the coordinates of the field in which the provisions of that reform were elaborated (2000: 116 [92]). This was a matter of mapping the coordinates of what he termed 'the field of efficient agents in the matter of housing finance', a field composed of all those who had a hand in formulating the reform, notably by sitting on one of a series of parliamentary commissions charged with looking into the social housing sector. The 'field of efficient agents' thus included government ministers, civil servants from the French Treasury and Ministry of Works, representatives of the frequently wholly or partly state-owned banking and credit companies, local politicians and officials from those organizations which managed social housing, as well as representatives of tenants' associations (2000: 124–37 [99–110]).

Having identified those agents who qualified as 'efficient agents' in this context, Bourdieu collected a mass of biographical data about each of them, including social origin, education, career and social trajectory, before plotting that data by means of correspondence analysis. Correspondence analysis is a form of multivariate analysis which, given a sample of, in this case, individuals, defined by a number of different variables, first identifies which of those variables are the most distinctive. The two most distinctive variables typically serve as the horizontal and vertical axes of a graph which seeks to plot, spatially, the coordinates of the 'field' in question. These two axes bisect one another at their mid-points, giving a graph composed of four opposing quadrants, within which the relative positions of each individual are then plotted. Secondary characteristics, less distinctive variables, also influence the position of each individual since the analysis works by giving a 'profile' of attributes to individuals and 'clustering' those individuals with similar such profiles close to one another, while those with very different profiles are situated at some distance, clustered in a different quadrant of the graph. In the case of the 'field of efficient agents' that Bourdieu plotted in *The Social Structures of the Economy*, the most significant variable was age or length of career. By selecting age as one of the axes of his graph of the 'field of efficient agents', Bourdieu was able to uncover an affinity between a group of young, ambitious, 'innovators', as he called them, who were otherwise dispersed across the field, typically occupying posts on research bodies looking into the housing market.

This group of young, ambitious, well-educated civil servants, of similarly elevated social origin, enjoyed an 'affinity of habitus' with the 'young' and 'dynamic' new President, Giscard, which predisposed them to support a free-market reform of state housing subsidy. These young Turks or 'innovators' were typically recent graduates of one of the most prestigious *grandes écoles*. As such, they personified the technocratic branch of the 'state nobility' whose ascendancy in postwar France Bourdieu had traced in his earlier study of that name. Their shared habitus meant they were favourably disposed towards the particular technocratic form of neo-liberal discourse characteristic of the French administrative elite, the new 'dominant ideology' whose genesis and structure he had analysed in the 1976 article, co-written with Luc Boltanski, 'La Production de l'idéologie dominante'. Having been trained in the latest techniques in economics and econometrics, they were endowed with 'bureaucratic capital rooted in technical know-how', as Bourdieu put it. This contrasted with the 'bureaucratic capital rooted in experience' possessed by an older generation of civil servants (2000: 143 [117]).

This older generation was less disposed to support any outright assault on the role of the state in the name of the free market since they had a vested interest in supporting the state institutions for which they worked. Hence, they tended to defend the status quo in a defence of their own powers and privileges under the existing system that was also, Bourdieu argued, a defence of the 'social gains' inherent in state provision of social housing. As Bourdieu put it:

> Privileged, high-ranking civil servants, like those in the Ministry of Works, can thus find themselves, by the very logic of the defence of their own *corps* and its privileges, caught up in actions contributing to the defence of the social gains to which their own bureaucratic interests are linked.
>
> (2000: 140 [114])

In his earlier study *Practical Reason* (1994a), Bourdieu had offered a more general account of the way in which state bureaucrats could, in defending their own partial interests within the bureaucratic field, nevertheless contribute to the defence of the general public interest. He had argued that, historically, state bureaucracies had been founded by absolute rulers delegating some of their authority to a relatively autonomous 'bureaucratic field', to state institutions run by a *corps* of civil servants. In order to legitimize and strengthen the modicum of autonomy they had been delegated, the *corps* of civil servants had an objective interest in giving,

> a universal form to the expression of their particular interests, in elaborating a theory of public service and public order, and thus in working to autonomise the reason of state from dynastic reason, from the 'house of the king', and to invent thereby the *res publica* and later the republic as an instance transcendent to the agents (the king included) who are its temporary incarnations.
>
> (1994a: 130 [58])

Thus within such a relatively autonomous bureaucratic field, agents could only pursue their partial interests in career advancement and the accumulation of bureaucratic capital, 'at the cost of a submission (if only in appearance) to the universal' (Bourdieu 1994a: 131 [59]). As long as the bureaucratic field retained its relative autonomy from the fields of economic or political power, civil servants could only advance their own partial interests by respecting the 'universal' principles embodied in a public service ethos. According to the logic of what Bourdieu termed 'the corporatism of the universal', then, the older generation of civil servants resisting free-market reform and defending the status quo were, in defending their own narrowly corporatist interests, necessarily also contributing to the defence of the universal interests of French citizens, represented here by state provision of social housing. As Bourdieu's several calls to defend the 'hegelo-durkheimian vision of the state' demonstrated, this account of the subsumption of the particular interests of civil servants under the universal was greatly indebted to Hegel's *Philosophy of Right*. For Hegel, the 'executive civil servants' had a key role to play in 'the maintenance of the state's universal interest', by ensuring that the particular rights and interests of civil society, represented by the corporations, were 'brought back to the universal'. The modern state achieved this 'rooting of the particular in the universal' by ensuring that 'the corporation mind', in general, found 'in the state the means of maintaining its particular ends', while a civil servant, in particular, could only find 'in his office his livelihood and the assured satisfaction of his particular interests' provided he fulfilled his duties and acted in accordance with the universal interests of the state (Hegel 1821: 188–93).

If the older generation of French civil servants were thus safeguarding the universal even as they defended their own corporatist interests, the 'innovators', on the other hand, were doing the opposite. They were responsible for importing into the bureaucratic field the 'heteronomous' logics of politics and the market, through both their proximity to Giscard and their support for a measure of free-market reform. In their struggles to dominate the field in the face of the resistance of the old guard, they held a series of trump cards. Not only did they enjoy the benefits of youthful energy, their similar trajectories through the social and educational fields meant they formed a close-knit network. To use Bourdieu's terminology, they had a large stock of 'social capital' which they could profitably exploit in drawing alliances. Most importantly, their intellectual capital, the 'technical know-how' they had gained in one of the *grandes écoles*, notably their familiarity with the techniques of econometrics, gave them a key advantage over the older generation of civil servants, who lacked such technical expertise. The older generation of civil servants were thus ill-equipped to question the apparently scientific justifications for free-market reform put forward by the 'innovators', in the form of econometric models. As Bourdieu put it:

> If we add up the range of properties held by the innovators [...], we can see that these 'revolutionaries' are the most affluent participants in the field. And in fact, everything seems to indicate that, in the bureaucratic field as in many other fields, you have to possess a lot of capital to achieve a successful revolution.
>
> (2000: 145 [118])

Although they were pursuing their own partial economic and political agenda, these 'innovators' were able to exploit the form of the various commissions on housing reform on which they sat. These commissions consulted widely outside the narrowly political and bureaucratic fields and could thus claim to represent the considered opinion of French society at large. The very form of the commission, Bourdieu argued, thus gave the 'innovators' an apparent mandate for their reforms (2000: 146 [119]). By wisely investing their large stocks of social, intellectual and bureaucratic capital, by employing their almost instinctive 'sense of the bureaucratic game' to build alliances and formulate strategies, by exploiting the particular bureaucratic form of the commission, these 'innovators' were thus able to 'impose' their reform on the bureaucratic field and, by extension, on wider French society. Yet it was precisely these characteristics which predisposed the 'innovators' to ignore the long-term social costs of their reform. As Bourdieu put it:

> The French politicians and high-ranking civil servants, who, in the 1970s, imposed, doubtless in all good faith, a new policy of housing subsidy inspired by a neo-liberal vision of society and the economy, did not know that they were laying the ground for the long-lasting conflicts and dramas which were to set the inhabitants of high-rise council blocks, deserted by their better-off tenants, against the owners of suburban semis.
>
> (2000: 24 [12])

The account Bourdieu offered of the passage of the 1977 housing reform in *The Social Structures of the Economy* might be seen as a classic example of his field theory at work. The successful passage of this reform was understood not as reflecting the persuasive force of the ideology that lay behind it, the ability of its proponents to convince either politicians, civil servants or the French electorate at large of the attractions of private property ownership. Rather, the reform was understood to have been 'imposed' and the success of that 'imposition' to have been determined by the amount and forms of 'bureaucratic capital' possessed by the 'innovators'. As Bourdieu put it, 'you have to possess a lot of capital to achieve a successful revolution' and it was because they were 'the most affluent participants in the field', because they possessed the most 'bureaucratic capital rooted in technical know-how', that the 'innovators' had managed to get the reform passed (2000: 145 [118]). The form and volume of capital possessed by the innovators was, of course, a reflection or expression of the position they occupied within the 'field of efficient agents'. It was this position, Bourdieu argued, rather than any inherent characteristics of the 1977 reform, any capacity it might have to convince or garner popular support, that explained the victory of the 'innovators' over the older generation of civil servants. As Bourdieu put it:

> it would be pointless, at least in this case and doubtless more generally, to seek in discourse alone, as do certain adherents of 'discourse analysis', the laws of construction of discourse which in fact reside in the laws of construction of the space of production of discourse.
>
> (2000: 134 [106–7])

The reform of 1977 was thus to be seen as an expression of the struggles between agents occupying different positions within the bureaucratic field; it was these struggles which constituted 'the laws of construction of the space of production of discourse'. These struggles within the bureaucratic field were, in turn, to be understood as the expression of 'homologous' struggles in neighbouring and/or encompassing fields. Thus, the dominance the 'innovators' enjoyed, thanks to the educational capital they derived from studying at ENA or *Sciences-po*, reflected the shifts in the field of higher education which Bourdieu had traced in *The State Nobility*. These shifts, which had signalled the ascendancy of the more technocratically oriented *grandes écoles* at the expense of their more rigorously academic counterparts, were themselves the expression of the broader social shifts Bourdieu had traced in *Distinction*. These social shifts reflected the rise of the business and technocratically oriented fraction of the French dominant class over the liberal professions and progressive intelligentsia. On this basis, it appeared that Bourdieu's field theory did indeed risk denying any genuine autonomy to the realm of politics proper. For the political issues played out in the 'field of efficient agents in housing finance' were seen as merely a shadow theatre, a miniaturized reflection or expression of power struggles and social shifts determined elsewhere, in the neighbouring sub-field of higher education or in the broader encompassing social field. Two related questions are thus raised by Bourdieu's account of the genesis of the housing reform. First, it will be necessary to examine the possibility that Bourdieu's account overlooked a whole series of political issues raised by that reform. Among such issues might be possible failings in the state provision of social housing, which, in encouraging popular disaffection with statist solutions, might have paved the way for the reform of 1977. Second, on a more theoretical level, the notion of 'homology', which Bourdieu typically invoked to explain the relationship between different fields and sub-fields, needs to be subjected to more detailed critical scrutiny.

The elision of the political

As we have seen, Bourdieu saw the housing reform of 1977 to have been the result of an unequal struggle between a younger and an older generation of civil servants; the younger generation's victory was attributed to the greater volume and particular form of bureaucratic capital they possessed. What this account ignored was the possibility that the older generation of civil servants was unable to defend the status quo not merely because of lack of sufficient bureaucratic capital but also because of certain failings inherent in the existing system of social housing provision in France. As Christian Bachmann and Nicole Le Guennec have shown, in their seminal study of the subject, postwar French social housing policy epitomized the attempt to apply centralized statist solutions to France's social problems. They argue that if, by the mid-1970s, state provision of social housing had fallen into disrepute, this reflected the very real failings inherent in the way in which that policy was implemented. Bachmann and Le Guennec refer to 'the brutality of the policy of high-rise housing projects', according to which:

> Populations were not merely displaced; they were quite simply dumped, anywhere and anyhow. Those dispatched without further ado to the periphery of major cities, to La Corneuve or elsewhere, have not forgotten their treatment. This historical fact should be taken into account nowadays when the authorities deplore the fact that whole neighbourhoods live in a state of 'relegation'.
>
> (2002: 245)

It was these failings, Bachmann and Le Guennec argue, which led to the emergence, from the 1960s onwards, of a whole range of protest movements from tenants associations to professional bodies for town planners and architects. Such movements, which spanned the political spectrum from Left to Right, were united in their rejection of the kind of social housing France's state planners had thus far been providing. It was their justified opposition to the status quo, according to Bachmann and Le Guennec, which Giscard's reform sought to exploit and which, hence, provided the most important condition of possibility for its successful passage. Bachmann and Le Guennec argue that the strength of such protest movements meant that by the early 1970s the argument in favour of reform had already been won, before the various parliamentary commissions looking into the housing market had even been convened:

> From this moment on, neo-liberalism had virtually won. The political field was splitting and fragmenting. On one side were the fraternal enemies; those nostalgic for a 'good' interventionist state, split between the Communists and the former Gaullists. Their ideas were still around, but their social base, like their argument, was losing ground with every day that passed. On the other side, against statist imperialism, were ranged other social forces: the social

liberals and the liberal left, occupying spaces at once conflicting and complicit. In the confrontations of the end of the 1970s, it was the latter groups which came to the fore.

(2002: 301–2)

Once the extent of popular discontent with state provision of social housing is acknowledged, it becomes difficult to maintain that the housing reform of 1977 was 'imposed' by a particular fraction of France's political and administrative elite or that the success of that 'imposition' can be explained primarily by reference to the resources of bureaucratic capital that fraction possessed. Similarly, it becomes difficult to maintain that an older generation of civil servants failed to defend the status quo merely because they lacked the 'bureaucratic capital based in technical know-how' possessed by the 'innovators', the civil servants supporting the reform. Rather it would seem that their failure to defend their position reflected, to a significant degree, the fact that it had been fatally undermined by its own inherent failings, by the state's failure to provide decent, desirable social housing and by the popular frustrations and protest movements that had generated. Further, such failings mean that we must question Bourdieu's assumption that the older generation of civil servants were, in defending the status quo, unwittingly contributing to the defence of certain universal social gains, the universal ideals of public service. For those tenants housed in poor quality, isolated, high-rise French housing estates, lacking in the basic social and cultural amenities, it was surely by no means clear that the bureaucrats responsible for planning such estates were acting in the name of universal ideals. This is not to say that the provision of social housing does not constitute a desirable, even vital social role for the state to play. It does, however, mean that the manner in which the state seeks, in practice, to fulfil that role cannot be assumed a priori to represent the realization of the universal interest. It also means that the debates over housing reform in 1970s France are not reducible to a power struggle between opposing groups of bureaucrats and politicians located within the narrow confines of 'the field of efficient agents in the matter of housing finance' as Bourdieu defined it. Such debates extended far beyond that field proper and turned on the widely perceived failure of the state to fulfil its supposedly universal ideals.

Thus Bourdieu's use of field theory to explain the genesis of the 1977 housing reform seemed to elide a whole series of pressing political issues. These issues ranged from legitimate questions concerning the nature and possible failings of state housing provision to an analysis of how those pushing for reform might have been able to exploit popular disaffection at such failings, presenting private property ownership as their solution. It was significant in this light that Bourdieu could mention in passing that 'a certain number of ideas', such as 'the disengagement of the state', were 'in the (bureaucratic) air' in the years immediately preceding the reform (2000: 131 [104]). Yet he offered no account of either the origin or the possible popular appeal of such ideas, beyond seeing them as the expression of the social, educational and career trajectory of the 'innovators' who promoted them with greatest enthusiasm. Similarly, Bourdieu did point out that

Giscard's electoral victory played 'a decisive role in strengthening the hand of the reformers of a neo-liberal orientation' (2000: 122 [97]). However, he offered no explanation for Giscard's electoral victory, nor any detailed analysis either of the ability of his electoral programme to garner popular support or of the place of housing reform within that programme. In other words, the authority those pushing for reform derived from Giscard's electoral mandate was accorded only incidental importance in Bourdieu's account of how the 'innovators' came to 'impose' the 1977 housing reform on French society. A whole set of political issues thus appeared to have been elided in Bourdieu's analysis. It might be argued that this elision of the political was characteristic of the tendency of field theory to replace an evaluation of the inherent plausibility or persuasiveness of any political discourse with a calculation of the power or influence enjoyed by those groups or individuals promoting it.

To point to field theory's tendency to elide the properly political is not to deny all validity to the analysis of the workings of the bureaucratic field contained in *The Social Structures of the Economy*. Rather, it is to suggest that while the power struggles Bourdieu uncovered within the 'field of efficient agents' may have been permissive conditions for the passage of the 1977 housing reform, they did not, in isolation, constitute sufficient conditions. In other words, what seemed to be lacking from Bourdieu's analysis was any convincing account of the articulation between the power struggles within the confines of the bureaucratic field and the broader social and political movements taking place in French society at large. Interestingly, in the article he co-authored with Boltanski in 1976, 'La Production de l'idéologie dominante', Bourdieu did seem to offer an account, in general terms, of the way in which the form of technocratic neo-liberalism espoused by France's young administrative elite was articulated with broader popular discontent at the rigidities of French postwar statism.[1] Here Bourdieu and Boltanski had offered a detailed critique of the particular, technocratically inflected brand of neo-liberalism embraced by France's young administrative elite, pointing to the role played by the newly dominant *grandes écoles*, ENA, *Sciences-po* and others, in inculcating such values and ideas. Yet they had also emphasized the extent to which the new 'dominant ideology' attempted to tap into and exploit the desire for greater creativity and autonomy, the mass disaffection with the rigid hierarchies of the central state that had been so strikingly expressed in May 1968 (Bourdieu 1976: 44). This was a theme to which Bourdieu would return in *Distinction*, in his discussion of the way in which the lower middle class's embrace of some of the counter-cultural motifs of freedom, creativity and self-realization were being exploited by the forces of consumer capitalism to turn French citizens into depoliticized, isolated, atomized consumers, freed of all the old constraints of morality, class and community (1979: 431 [371]). The drive to personal property ownership might be seen as one striking example of this atomizing process.

It might be argued, then, that the political and social shifts Bourdieu had analysed in 'La Production de l'idéologie dominante' and *Distinction* were the key determinants behind the passing of a reform which aimed to encourage private property ownership. The upwardly mobile fraction of France's lower middle class, disaffected with the rigidities of a centralized state and inspired by a counter-cultural emphasis on creativity and autonomy, surely formed the very constituency to which the promoters of the 1977 housing reform could appeal. However, any detailed reference to these broader political and social shifts seemed to have fallen out of Bourdieu's analysis in *The Social Structures of the Economy* in a manner which appeared to reflect certain methodological and theoretical failings in his field theory. The methodological failings were implicit in Bourdieu's reliance on correspondence analysis as a means of plotting 'the field of efficient agents in housing finance'. As has been demonstrated, Bourdieu's use of correspondence analysis to map the coordinates of the field in question involved accumulating a range of biographical data about those 'efficient agents'. These data took the form of sociological variables such as age, social origin, education, career trajectory and so on, themselves taken to be expressed in both the habitus and the forms of social, cultural and bureaucratic capital possessed by each agent. It was on the basis of this positive set of attributes, of objective characteristics, as it were, that the opposing positions of each agent or group of agents could be plotted graphically, while the particular political agenda they embraced and the chances of that agenda meeting with success could be 'objectified', seen as a function of the relationship between their habitus and that field.

By their very nature, however, social variables such as the age or class of the agents in question could neither register nor represent the influence of broader shifts in public mood or in the ideological affiliations of the French citizenry on those agents and their capacity to effect policy change. According to the tenets of field theory, 'external factors', factors relating to developments occurring somewhere outside the field in question, only exerted an influence on that field inasmuch as they were 'refracted' through the differential structure of such a field; such 'external factors' were thus understood to be 'retranslated into the logic' of the particular field. The use of correspondence analysis to map the position of the different participants in a field meant, of course, that the only 'external factors' that could be taken into account were precisely those objective, statistically measurable variables relating to the education, class and career trajectory, in short to the personal biography of the individuals considered to be 'efficient agents' within that field. Such statistically measurable variables, which related to purely biographical data, were thus the only 'external factors' whose 'retranslation into the logic' of the 'field of efficient agents in housing finance' correspondence analysis could plot. Less tangible and hence less easily measurable factors, such as changes in public mood or opinion, could not, by definition, be registered by this kind of analysis and thus risked falling out of Bourdieu's account.

Popular desire and the pedagogic intellectual

This is not to say that Bourdieu simply ignored the popular appeal of private property ownership. As he argued in *The Social Structures of the Economy*, a personal home was, more than any other commodity, a 'product in which the symbolic component has an especially important share', and buying a house was 'the occasion of particularly significant *investments*, at once economic and affective' (2000: 33 [19]). *The Social Structures of the Economy* contained detailed and convincing analyses of the way in which advertisements for different house builders attempted to engage such affective investments, promising the freedom, prestige, warmth and security that the family home typically connoted to their potential clients. Such advertisements, Bourdieu argued, mobilized a series of 'poetic effects', which functioned analogously to the symbolic and social meanings he had identified at work in his much earlier analysis of the poetics of Kabyle domestic space (2000: 33–98 [19–88]). This, then, was Bourdieu's account of the role played by the aesthetic, affective structures of the habitus in the contemporary housing market. However, it was notable that he accorded such affective investments no legitimacy; government policies or advertisements for new houses which exploited this appeal were inherently demagogic, Bourdieu maintained:

> Advertising is only so effective because, like every form of demagogy, it flatters pre-existing dispositions the better to exploit them, enslaving consumers to their expectations and demands whilst appearing to serve them. (This is the opposite of a truly liberating politics that would make use of a realistic knowledge of those dispositions in order to work to transform them or shift them towards more authentic goals.)
>
> (1990e: 9)

Furthermore, the popular desire for home ownership did not appear to be historicized in any way in Bourdieu's account. There was no acknowledgment that the desire to own a home might have been rendered more urgent or acute precisely by the dehumanizing and alienating living conditions on offer in the high-rise housing estates provided by the state in the postwar period. Rather, such a desire appeared to be understood as somehow primary, primitive or even irrational, the expression of 'pre-existing' or 'primary dispositions', which were defined in opposition to the rational politics Bourdieu himself was advocating (2000: 78, 113 [55, 89]). Thus, the ability of the 1977 housing reform to exploit such a strong affective investment in home ownership was denounced as the manifestation of a demagogic politics which encouraged property ownership among social categories 'who would have offered a natural clientele for a policy aiming to encourage the construction of social housing for rent, whether flats or individual houses' (2000: 53 [34]). The latter policy presumably corresponded to the 'truly liberating politics' which Bourdieu argued should work to orient consumers' desires and affective investments towards 'more authentic goals' by drawing on the 'realistic knowledge' of the housing market, secured by a sociological enquiry such as *The Social Structures of the Economy* itself.

The role Bourdieu attributed here to sociologists in making use of 'realistic knowledge' to shift agents' dispositions towards 'more authentic goals' seemed to correspond to the Durkheimian component of his favoured 'hegelo-durkheimian vision' of the state. According to Durkheim, it was the role of the state

> Not to express and sum up the unreflective thought of the mass of the people but to superimpose on this unreflective thought a more considered thought [...] which ought to put the society in a position to conduct itself with greater intelligence than when it is swayed by vague sentiments.
>
> (1957: 92)

At the basis of this 'more considered thought' were to be the findings of statistical and sociological enquiries (Durkheim 1957: 92). The pedagogical role Bourdieu attributed both to the state and to those sociologists who influenced state policy, here, highlighted the differences between his conception of the role of the intellectual and Foucault's model of the 'specific intellectual'.

In a speech given in 2000 on Foucault's model of intellectual engagement, Bourdieu suggested that the Raisons d'agir collective he had founded represented 'a collective intellectual' composed of a group of ' "specific intellectuals" in Foucault's sense' (2002: 474–5). However, the inherently pedagogical role Bourdieu advocated for intellectuals in *The Social Structures of the Economy*, together with his assumption that the popular desire for home ownership was the expression of pre-reflexive or primary dispositions in need of correction or redirection to more rational ends by intellectuals and the state, appeared to contradict any such affinity. In a famous exchange with Deleuze, Foucault rejected any such pedagogic role for intellectuals, claiming that its inappropriateness had been revealed by the events of May 1968, during which, 'the intellectual discovered that the masses no longer need him [*sic*] to gain knowledge: they *know* perfectly well, without illusion; they know far better than he and they are certainly capable of expressing themselves' (Foucault 1977: 207). In his role as a 'specific intellectual' working with prisoners' groups, Foucault had learned that 'when the prisoners began to speak, they possessed an individual theory of prisons, the penal system and justice' (1977: 209). As a result, Foucault rejected the notion that the 'theorising intellectual' should serve as 'a subject, a representing or representative consciousness' for groups which could not represent themselves, concluding that the intellectual's role was 'no longer to place himself "somewhat ahead and to the side" in order to express the stifled truth of the collectivity' (1977: 206–8). In short, Foucault's notion of the 'specific intellectual' was the product of a radical questioning of all of the assumptions behind Bourdieu's conception of the intellectual's role as both pedagogue and mandated representative to the dominated classes.

Gayatri Spivak has provided a convincing critique of the idealism of Foucault's concept of the specific intellectual, of its romanticization of the desire of 'subaltern' groups as being transparent, self-knowing, even inherently transformative and progressive (Spivak 1988). However, it is not necessary to assume the affective investments of dominated groups to be inherently self-knowing and authentic in order either to acknowledge the potential significance of such investments as a political force or to interpret them as symptomatic of genuine political problems or contradictions requiring detailed analysis. It is here that the reconceptualization of the habitus, attempted in Chapter 3, can prove its worth. This implies understanding politics not as a struggle to express and impose dispositions already contained within the habitus but as a struggle to construct, elicit and mobilize those dispositions, desires and affective investments. Hence the attraction of property ownership might be seen not as the expression of a 'pre-existing', 'primary' disposition already inherent in the habitus, which advertisers and neo-liberal politicians then sought to exploit in a demagogic fashion. Rather, the disposition towards property ownership might be seen as something constructed in particular historical circumstances, a product of both popular disaffection with the failings of social housing and the ability of advertisers and politicians to construct the habitus in such a way as to elicit and mobilize popular desire for home ownership, itself presented as a plausible solution to such failings. At the political level, this would imply acknowledging the potentially valid criticisms of the failings of state housing provision contained in the desire to own one's own home. This, in turn, would necessitate the elaboration of political alternatives to both private property ownership and the form state housing policy had thus far taken. At the level of social or political theory, it would involve understanding the habitus to be not merely a determinant of but also a stake in political struggle. This, in its turn, might necessitate a rather broader conception than Bourdieu's of which agents or groups should be considered 'efficient agents' where the passage of the 1977 housing reform was concerned.

According to Bourdieu's definition, only those individuals who had an official role in housing policy were to be counted as 'efficient agents'. Yet this seemed to rule out in advance the influence the electorate as a whole might exert over such matters of public policy. At the very least, it was clear that the selection of those individuals or institutions considered to be the 'efficient agents' within a given field would always be a matter not only of great importance but also of considerable difficulty, and deciding where the boundaries of that field should be drawn would always risk a certain arbitrariness. In *Propos sur le champ politique*, Bourdieu responded to this question of how to decide where the boundaries of any field should be drawn as follows:

> People often ask me how I recognize that an institution or an agent forms part of a field. The reply is simple: you recognize the presence or existence of an agent in a field by the fact that he or she transforms the state of that field (or that a lot of things change if you take that agent away).

(2000a: 61)

Thus in order to define the boundaries of any field it was sufficient 'to include categories of agent for the simple reason that they produce effects in that field' (Bourdieu 2000a: 61). This was scarcely a convincing explanation, however, since it appeared to beg the question. In order to know which agents produce effects in a given field, it would be necessary to know in advance the boundaries of that field, otherwise it would not be possible to assess whether particular agents were producing effects within or beyond its boundaries. Bourdieu's assertion that drawing the boundaries of any given field was a 'simple' matter thus paradoxically revealed the genuine problems this question continued to pose for his field theory.

These difficulties in deciding, with any precision, where the boundaries of a given field might lie lead necessarily onto the question of the manner in which Bourdieu theorized the relationships between different fields. Did the boundaries of a given field render it relatively impervious to developments in neighbouring fields or was each field determined by or determining of developments in other fields, for example? Typically, Bourdieu invoked the notion of 'homology' to explain his understanding of the relations *between* a given field and its neighbouring or encompassing fields and sub-fields. He also employed the notion of homology to explain relations *within* any given field, pointing to the homology between 'position' and 'position-taking', between the position occupied in a field by agents and their 'position-takings' in that field, the political beliefs or ideologies they espoused. Clearly, the notion of homology was called upon to do rather a lot of important theoretical work in Bourdieu's field theory. It will be necessary to look in more detail at the role played by this notion of homology in order to shed more light on these questions regarding first the relationship between 'position' and 'position-taking' and second the forms of articulation between the different fields and sub-fields.

Homologies, positions, position-takings

When asked to clarify the nature of the relationship between the various semi-autonomous fields, Bourdieu would frequently seek, first of all, to distinguish his understanding of that relationship from Althusser's theory of economic determination 'in the last instance'. Thus, in *An Invitation to Reflexive Sociology* (1992b), Bourdieu explicitly rejected Althusser's notion of determination in the last instance by the economy, arguing there was no justification for claiming a set of 'invariant' relations between fields and insisting on the need to define such relations on a case by case basis, through empirical research (1992b: 84–5 [109]). In practice, Bourdieu would most frequently invoke the notion of 'homology' to explain the nature of the relationships between different fields, suggesting this was his preferred alternative to Althusser's theorization of such relationships.

According to Althusser's theory, the different ideological 'instances', educational, political, religious and so on, formed part of a 'structured totality' or 'structure in dominance'. In any given historical conjuncture, any one of those various 'instances' might find itself in the dominant position, yet ultimately, 'in the last instance', the play between the different elements of that structured totality would be determined by the economy. Each of those 'instances' was thus 'relatively autonomous' of the economic base, while being 'articulated' to it. Every product of such relatively autonomous instances, whether religious tract, political ideology or pedagogical theory, might thus be 'overdetermined', determined not merely by economic factors but simultaneously by a range of cultural, political and ideological determinants. Further, because of the relative autonomy enjoyed by these various superstructural instances, developments in the realms of culture, politics, education and so on could exert a significant influence on the economic base. In this way, Althusser sought to escape the form of 'expressive causality' he found in Hegelian Marxism according to which any cultural or political phenomenon was understood to be the expression of a transcendent Cause, of History or the Economy in its ineluctable dialectical development.

As early as his first book-length study of Kabyle anthropology, *Esquisse d'une théorie de la pratique* (1972), Bourdieu had sought to distance himself from Althusser's theory of structural determination. He argued that Althusser's model relied on an essentialist conception of the economy as an immanent substance, on Spinoza's model, or transcendent Spirit, on Hegel's, of which every social or historical development was merely the epiphenomenal expression. Having claimed to have broken with the Hegelian model of expressive causality, Althusserian theory had thus merely re-invented it in a more sophisticated form since it treated:

> the different instances as 'different translations of the same phrase', – according to a Spinozist metaphor which contains the truth of the objectivist language of 'articulation' –, hence reducing the relation between them to the logical formula which allows us to locate whichever of those instances from any single such instance. It is no surprise, then, to discover that the principle behind the evolution of the structures lies in a sort of theoretical parthenogenesis, which thus offers an unexpected revenge to the Hegel of the *Philosophy of History* and to his world Spirit which 'develops its unique nature' by always remaining identical to itself.
>
> (Bourdieu 1972: 278)

For Bourdieu, then, Althusser's Marxism remained tainted by the very economism it claimed to have rejected and, as such, was evidence of the economistic bias at the heart of all Marxism. His own field theory would thus seek to theorize the relationship between social class and politics, for example, between 'position' occupied in the social field and 'position-taking' within the field of ideology, without seeing the latter to be determined in the last instance by the economy, by position in the relations of production, as Marxism would have it.

Rather, Bourdieu sought to emphasize the 'multidimensional' nature of social space, insisting that agents simultaneously occupied various positions in different fields and that a range of different determinants, cultural, social, educational and not merely economic, thus affected their 'position-takings' in any of those different semi-autonomous fields. There were, nonetheless, 'homologies' between the ways in which each of those fields was structured, so that a fundamental opposition between a dominant group A and a dominated group B in the social field, as a whole, would be reproduced in homologous form in the oppositions between groups A1 and B1 in the more specialized fields of artistic production, higher education or politics, for example. Moreover, there were also homologies between the position occupied by any group in a given field and its position-takings within that field. Thus, for example, within the social field it was possible to distinguish between various fractions of the dominant class, a dominated fraction, the intelligentsia, who possessed relatively little economic capital but a large amount of cultural capital, and the dominant fraction, business leaders, industrialists and so on, who possessed more economic capital but less cultural capital. This basic opposition would then be reproduced, in homologous form, within the field of ideological production. Hence the dominated fraction of the dominant class would be disposed, through the dominated position they occupied with relation to the dominant fraction of the dominant class in the social field, to feel an affinity with the dominated classes within society and hence promote a progressive or libertarian politics. The dominant fraction of the dominant class, meanwhile, having no such affinity, would be disposed to promote a conservative or free-market politics. As Bourdieu put it in the 1977 article 'On symbolic power':

> The ideological systems that specialists produce in and for the struggle over the monopoly of legitimate ideological production reproduce in a misrecognizable form, through the intermediary of the homology between the field of ideological production and the field of social classes, the structure of the field of social classes.
>
> (1977c: 409 [1991: 168])

A first problem with this notion of homology related to Bourdieu's ambiguity as to whether the homology reflected a statistical correlation or a causal determination between position and position-taking. In 'Social space and the genesis of "classes"', Bourdieu was quite explicit in emphasizing that this was a matter of the strong statistical correlation between objective measurements of social position and the nature of the representations of the social world that different agents and groups possessed. Social position, 'adequately defined', he argued, was 'what gives the best prediction of practices and representations'. Nonetheless, it was important to 'avoid conferring on [...] social identity the place that "being" had in ancient metaphysics, namely, the function of an essence from which would spring all aspects of historical existence' (1984: 11 [1991: 248]). Hence Bourdieu emphasized that the 'relationship between the position occupied in social space and practices has nothing mechanical about it', as was evident in the 'observable differences between practices and opinions (especially political ones) amongst those occupying identical positions'. In order to account for such differences, it was necessary 'to take into account the practical or represented relationship to the position occupied' (1984: 14).[2] In other words, the position an agent occupied in any field could be represented in a number of different ways, so that the relationship between position and position-taking was not automatic and while the latter might be statistically correlated to the former it was not causally determined by it.

However, Bourdieu was not always so careful to emphasize this point, nor so circumspect in his use of language. For example, discussing the tenets of field theory in general terms in his 2000–1 lectures on the scientific field to the

Collège de France, Bourdieu talked of the '*law* of correspondence between positions and position-takings' (2001b: 185 [95], my emphasis). In *The Social Structures of the Economy*, meanwhile, he argued that it was the position occupied within 'the field of efficient agents', itself a reflection of position occupied within the broader social field, that both 'determined' and 'explained' the nature of the different positions taken by the participants in that field. As Bourdieu put it, it was 'the structure and distribution of powers and specific interests which determines and *explains* the strategies of agents and hence the history of the principal interventions which led to the elaboration and passage into law' of the 1977 housing reform (2000: 128–9 [102–3]). Bourdieu's language here – 'the law of correspondence', 'determines and explains' – contrasted strongly with his insistence in 'Social space and the genesis of "classes" ' that there was 'nothing mechanical' in the relationship between position and position-taking. Indeed, there appeared to be a constant slippage in Bourdieu's field theory from the language of statistical correlation to that of causal determination. This slippage was particularly evident in the following quotation from 'On symbolic power', in which Bourdieu described the 'structural homology' between the 'field of ideological production' and the broader social field:

> The properly ideological function of the field of ideological production is performed almost automatically on the basis of the structural homology between the field of ideological production and the field of class struggle. The homology between the two fields means that struggles over the specific objects of the autonomous field automatically produce *euphemised* forms of the economic and political struggles between classes.
>
> (1977c: 410 [1991: 169])

The slippage in this quotation from the phrase 'almost automatically' to 'automatically' is indicative of the more general tendency in Bourdieu's thinking to slippage from a language of probability and statistical correlation towards assertions of causal determination. At such moments, Bourdieu risked reproducing the very model of expressive causality whose persistence in Althusser's structural Marxism he had criticized. According to this account, struggles over politics and ideology 'automatically' produced 'euphemised forms' of the struggles between different classes and social fractions in the social field as a whole. The different ideological positions taken by agents appeared to be nothing more than the expression of the positions they occupied in the broader social field, the 'field of class struggle' as Bourdieu put it in 'On symbolic power'.

Position within the social field was, of course, the expression of each agent's, each class's or class fraction's habitus, itself measured by reference to a set of positive attributes – age, sex, class, education and so on. The habitus thus risked becoming an immanent substance, a kind of social essence whose various epiphenomenal expressions could then be read off in the different fields in which it was invested. This is not to argue that Bourdieu's field theory was a teleology, in which the habitus oriented all actions towards a predetermined goal or outcome.

Agents, who, thanks to their social origins and upbringing, shared effectively the same habitus, could invest that habitus in any number of different fields and hence follow any number of different trajectories. However, while field theory offered a sophisticated account of the various ways in which that habitus might be *mediated* through different fields, the habitus itself continued to be viewed as the immanent substance or logic ineluctably working itself out through those various mediations, albeit with no particular telos in view. While the different fields would 'retranslate' that immanent substance in accordance with their own logic, hence reproducing it in 'misrecognizable' or 'euphemised' forms, that substance would nonetheless remain the prime mover behind all social and political action. In this sense, we need to question Bourdieu's claim that his emphasis on the way in which external factors were always 'retranslated into the logic' of any given field, appearing only in 'misrecognizable' or 'euphemised' form, meant he avoided the 'short-circuit' between class position and political opinion he found at work in Marxism. For this notion of the mediating force exerted by any given field seemed indistinguishable from Althusser's understanding of the various instances as 'different translations of the same phrase'. Indeed, having rejected this notion of 'different translations of the same phrase' for its residual idealism in *Esquisse*, Bourdieu was to employ it twenty years later in *Invitation to a Reflexive Sociology* to explain the nature of the relationship between position and position-taking. As Bourdieu put it: 'Both spaces, that of objective positions and that of position-takings, must be analysed together, treated as "two translations of the same phrase" as Spinoza put it' (1992b: 81 [105]).

If position and position-taking were indeed to be understood as 'different translations of the same phrase' in this way and if the divisions structuring the social field were 'automatically' reproduced in euphemized form in the divisions of the political or ideological field, then there clearly was a powerful model of expressive causality at work behind Bourdieu's field theory. The danger of such a model was that politics truly would be understood as a mere 'shadow theatre', the euphemized expression of power struggles whose form and outcome was determined elsewhere, in the encompassing social field. According to such an account, it was within that broader social field that agents and groups acquired the habitus that disposed them to promote neo-liberal ideas, while equipping them with the kind and amount of capital that enabled them to 'impose' such ideas on society as a whole. Thus, in *The Social Structures of the Economy* Bourdieu identified the ascendancy gained by the neo-liberal 'innovators' over the older generation of civil servants as having been the key determinant in securing the successful passage of the 1977 housing reform. The ascendancy gained by the 'innovators' over the older civil servants merely reproduced or expressed the developments in the field of higher education Bourdieu had analysed in *The State Nobility*, namely the ascendancy gained by technocratically oriented *grandes écoles*, such as ENA or *Sciences-po*, over their more academically rigorous counterparts. These developments in the field of higher education, finally, themselves simply reproduced or expressed the social shifts Bourdieu had analysed in *Distinction*, namely the rise of a more business and technocratically oriented fraction of the French dominant class at the expense of the liberal professions and progressive intelligentsia. Developments in each of the two sub-fields in question here, the field of efficient agents in housing finance and the field of higher education, thus simply reproduced or expressed, in miniaturized, homologous, albeit euphemized form, the shifts that were taking place in the broader, encompassing social field. What happened in each sub-field was merely a 'different translation of the same phrase', a phrase originally written elsewhere, in the all-encompassing social field.

For Bourdieu, analysing questions of politics and ideology thus always risked becoming a matter of simply 'objectifying' the predetermined interests of the participants in the political field, interests seen as reproducing 'automatically', albeit in euphemized form, their position in the wider social field, itself taken to be the expression of that set of statistically measurable attributes contained in their habitus. Any political programme would then be understood as an expression of those same interests, while its success or failure would be attributed less to its plausibility or inherent force of persuasion than to the symbolic authority, again statistically measurable, of the individuals or groups promoting it. As this chapter has sought to demonstrate, such an understanding of politics risked eliding a set of specifically political questions in a manner which brought a number of damaging consequences to the potential efficacy of Bourdieu's field theory as a tool of political analysis.

A first such consequence was the inability of field theory to account for the popular appeal of political programmes that might appear inherently regressive or to run counter to the supposed interests of the groups to whom they appeal. It was at this point that field theory was forced to rely on a problematic of 'imposition', while relegating any such regressive desires or tendencies to the realm of a pre-reflexive 'primary disposition'. This led, in turn, to a failure either to acknowledge that such desires might be symptomatic of genuine flaws or contradictions in existing social or political arrangements or to engage in political debate about how such flaws or contradictions might best be addressed. It is of course true that neo-liberalism's supporters have exaggerated the extent of the state's failings in, for example, the provision of social housing; seeking to have the state's supposed incompetence in such domains acquire the status of an unquestionable truth. It is also true that the politics of the 'Third Way' favoured by Tony Blair and Anthony Giddens has taken that supposed incompetence as an article of faith, using it to justify barely euphemized forms of marketization and privatization. However, this merely underscores the urgency of engaging in these debates, acknowledging the failings of previous state policy, where these exist, while working to find genuine alternatives both to earlier failed policies and to the neo-liberal and Third Way promotion of the market as panacea for all ills. Bourdieu's use of field theory allowed him to elide such urgent political questions, however, and merely to oppose the 'universal' ideals realized in an interventionist state housing policy to the narrow particularism of the market. In the particular case of *The Social Structures of the Economy*, the bureaucrats defending existing state housing policy could thus be taken to be defending the universal interest, regardless of the well-documented failures of that policy to live up to such universal ideals. There was a clear parallel here with Bourdieu's reluctance to deal with the substantive political issues raised by the strikes of 1995 and Juppé's proposed social security reforms. In both cases, Bourdieu invoked an idealized vision of republican universalism in a manner which risked concealing the failings inherent to that republican tradition. Then he interpreted the position adopted by his political opponents as amounting purely to the expression of the objective interests and forms of symbolic capital they possessed, itself the expression of the position they occupied in the French social, political and intellectual fields. In each case, the invocation of republican universalism and the reduction of opposing political ideologies to the expression of power relations risked eliding a series of significant political questions.

To make such criticisms is to deny neither the questions of power and authority behind the ascendancy of neo-liberal ideas nor the genuine insights offered by Bourdieu's field theory into the operations of such power within the confines of the French bureaucratic field. Much less is it to promote private property ownership as a solution to all housing needs, justifying such a claim by a demagogic appeal to 'what the people themselves desire'. Rather, it is to argue that an analysis which explains the success of neo-liberalism solely by reference to power struggles, while denying any legitimacy to the popular desires that neo-liberalism exploits, risks eliding a series of important political questions. Field theory can prove a powerful tool for revealing the issues of power and authority at play in certain social universes. However, just as in Chapter 3 we argued that the concept of habitus could only be retained once it had been suitably reconceptualized, so the need to re-think the concept of 'field' has become evident in the course of this chapter.

The notion of homology has proved particularly troublesome in this respect. Our re-thinking of the concept of habitus in Chapter 3 resolved some of the problems inherent in Bourdieu's positing of a direct homology between position and position-taking. This process of re-thinking could now be extended to embrace Bourdieu's recourse to homology in explanation of the relationships between different fields. Thus, position-takings in the political field should no longer be assumed to be the straightforward expression of positions occupied in that field, which themselves reproduce, in homologous form, positions occupied in the wider social field. Emphasis on the contingent and constructed nature of any position-taking within any field would enable a greater awareness of potential contradictions between the positions occupied in different fields. Moreover, refusing to see position-takings in, say, the political field, as merely the homologous expression of position occupied in the social field, would allow for a more dynamic conception of the interactions between sub-fields and fields and of the contradictions they can throw up. Chapter 5 will turn to look at Bourdieu's contribution to the area of gender studies, a contribution that, like so much of his output, has been criticized for its alleged determinism and failure to acknowledge the capacity of ordinary agents to challenge normative definitions of gender roles and identities. Chapter 5 will examine such criticisms and question whether our reformulated conceptions of habitus and field might allow us to salvage significant elements of Bourdieu's account of gender politics.

5 Gender politics and the return of symbolic domination

In 1998, Bourdieu published *Masculine Domination*, a study of the production and reproduction of gender inequality both in pre-capitalist Kabylia and in advanced Western democracies. Indeed, Bourdieu used his ethnographic findings about gender inequalities in Kabylia to uncover certain continuities between the forms of patriarchy in Kabyle society and those at work in the West, highlighting what he termed the 'transhistorical constancy of the relation of male domination' (1998a: 110 [102]). This emphasis on 'the constancy' of gender inequality was Bourdieu's response to what he took to be the tendency among certain feminists, inspired by 'militant conviction' rather than 'scientific' scruple, to 'exaggerate' the changes to women's status in the West in the postwar period (1998a: 121–2 [113–14]). The work of Judith Butler, Bourdieu argued, with its emphasis on the 'performativity' of gender identities and their openness to 'subversive resignification', epitomized this kind of 'subversive voluntarism' (1998a: 110 [103]). *Masculine Domination* was published at the height of the controversy sparked by Bourdieu's more directly political interventions; the book's launch was widely covered in the French media, while its analysis was frequently held up as proof of the static, deterministic and outdated nature of Bourdieu's thinking as a whole.[1]

Such criticisms were not, however, limited to the mass media. Christine Delphy and several of her colleagues associated with the materialist feminist journal *Nouvelles questions féministes* had responded with understandable anger to the claim Bourdieu had made in the earlier article of 1990, 'La Domination masculine', that women's studies and women's history were 'unscientific' disciplines since their findings were necessarily distorted by their practitioners' political commitments to women's liberation (Bourdieu 1990b). For Delphy and her co-authors, such criticisms, along with Bourdieu's counter-claim to be speaking in the name of science, were not merely ignorant and unwarranted but formed part of a more general strategy adopted by a male-dominated French intellectual elite to silence and belittle the voices of feminists (Armengaud *et al*. 1995). In her study *Excitable Speech* (1997), Butler had undertaken a sustained critique of Bourdieu's account of political change, arguing that it rested on a 'conservative account of the speech act' which failed to acknowledge the inherent instability of normative definitions of gender identity. Some years earlier, the feminist philosopher Michèle Le Doeuff had criticized Bourdieu's analysis of Kabyle gender relations for uncritically reproducing gender stereotypes more appropriate to an 'inhabitant of the Latin Quarter' than to an anthropologist attempting 'to describe the idea of genders in a North African peasant community' (Le Doeuff 1987: 45). In a similar vein, Claire Michard-Marchal and Claudine Ribery had criticized Bourdieu's analysis of women's and men's respective levels of politicization in his 1977 article 'Questions de politique'. Here Bourdieu had used women's relatively high rate of non-response to opinion polls on political subjects as proof of their lower level of politicization. As Michard-Marchal and Ribery demonstrated, these conclusions rested on highly gendered assumptions about what counted as 'political' and on using men's responses to such polls as an 'objective' measure of politicization, in relation to which women were then found to be lacking (Michard-Marchal and Ribery 1982).

Some of the criticisms levelled against Bourdieu in this area were manifestly unjust. One example would be the claim, made both by Delphy and by Lisa Adkins in her Introduction to the recent collection *Feminism after Bourdieu* (Adkins and Skeggs eds 2004), that until the publication of *Masculine Domination* Bourdieu 'never spoke about gender' (Armengaud *et al.* 1995: 48) or 'had relatively little to say about women or gender' (Adkins and Skeggs eds 2004: 3). In fact, from some of his very earliest books and articles, Bourdieu had shown an interest in the importance of gender as a social determinant. His 1962 article 'Célibat et la condition paysanne', focused on the way in which the modernization and urbanization of postwar France was inflected by gender divisions. Bourdieu paid close attention to the role played by young women as agents of modernization, eager participants in the 'rural exodus' that took them away from their peasant roots to seek employment and autonomy in France's towns and cities. His famous article on the Kabyle house, originally written in the early 1960s, also focused on gender, identifying the division between men and women as representing the fundamental structuring principle of pre-capitalist Kabylia. In both *The Inheritors* (1964b) and *Reproduction* (1970a), Bourdieu had sought to challenge assumptions about the postwar 'democratization' of French universities by highlighting the continuing forms of discrimination to which female students were subject and examining the very different relationship female students had to their studies in comparison to their more self-assured and hence lackadaisical male counterparts. *Distinction* had contained detailed analyses of the mass entry of women into salaried employment in postwar France and of the forms of discrimination that governed their relationship to the labour market.

To point to Bourdieu's continuing interest in the question of gender throughout his career is not necessarily, of course, to invalidate the accusations of determinism that have been made against his account of gender relations. Indeed, even those feminists who have adopted some of Bourdieu's central concepts in their own studies have often voiced such criticisms. Thus, in her intellectual biography of Simone de Beauvoir, Toril Moi has demonstrated how productive Bourdieu's work on class, culture and education could prove in illuminating Beauvoir's position in the French intellectual field (Moi 1994). Yet this has not prevented her from suggesting that Bourdieu may have over-emphasized the stability of gender and sexual identities in postwar developed societies (Moi 1991). Similarly, Beverley Skeggs has demonstrated the usefulness of Bourdieu's theorization of the relationship between class and cultural capital in her study of young working-class British women training to be care assistants. Yet her findings lead her to reject Bourdieu's emphasis on the 'immediate' or unproblematic manner in which agents adhere to existing class and gender identities and to propose instead a more dynamic model that takes account of the potential for 'disidentification' or disaffection with such inherited social identities (Skeggs 1997). Thus even those who are most sympathetic to Bourdieu's work have sought to distance themselves from what they consider to be its tendency towards static and deterministic models of class and gender.

Bourdieu tended to attribute such criticisms to the risks inherent to his 'scientific' approach to the study of gender relations. His focus on the reality of the constancy of male domination was too often mistaken for a justification of the status quo (Bourdieu 1998a: 122 [114]). For Bourdieu, then, any dispute between feminists and himself was ultimately an expression of the difference between their idealism and his realism regarding the permanence or mutability of gender identities. This question of whether Bourdieu's work is overly pessimistic or deterministic, in this regard, or whether it might offer a useful corrective to the voluntarism of some feminist accounts has, in turn, tended to dominate much recent commentary on Bourdieu's contribution to gender studies (McNay 1999). Such debates have tended to contrast agents' capacity for reflexive or rational action to Bourdieu's emphasis on the pre-reflexive incorporation of gender identities. Hence they risk re-inscribing Bourdieu's work within the 'metaphysics of the *prise de conscience*' he attempted to escape, while overlooking the fact that social change need not always be thought on a model of deliberative judgement or rational action. Further, the assumption tends to be that any change or challenge to normative definitions of gender would necessarily have progressive effects. Finally, given that gender inequalities clearly do continue to exist in developed societies, the more pertinent question to ask of *Masculine Domination* may be not whether Bourdieu exaggerated the *extent to which that was so* but rather whether he offered a convincing explanation as to *why that might be so*. Thus this chapter will argue that the problem with *Masculine Domination* relates less to its emphasis on the constancy of male domination than to the nature of the explanation Bourdieu provided for this phenomenon. Indeed, it will be argued that the account of gender inequalities in *Masculine Domination* would seem to epitomize all of the problems with Bourdieu's social theory we have identified thus far. However, once we have both abandoned certain assumptions underpinning the concepts of field, habitus and homology and shifted our focus from *Masculine Domination* to the analysis of gender relations contained in *Distinction*, it will be possible to show that Bourdieu's social theory has much to contribute to the study of gender. For *Distinction* contains an account of the rapid changes which gender identities underwent in postwar France, understanding such changes in terms neither of rational agency nor of subversion of the status quo but rather of the new ways in which bodies, desires and affects were constructed, elicited and mobilized under late capitalism.

The androcentric unconscious

Bourdieu justified his use of data gleaned from his anthropological studies of Kabylia to elucidate the nature of gender relations in developed Western societies by positing the existence of an 'androcentric unconscious'. It was this androcentric unconscious that lay behind male domination, itself understood to represent 'the example par excellence' of symbolic domination, a form of domination that operated through the invisible, imperceptible, wholly naturalized forms of symbolic violence. To render this symbolic violence visible required a kind of critical estrangement from one's native social universe and everything one took for granted about it. Anthropology could provoke such a moment of critical estrangement, forcing both Bourdieu himself and his readers to suspend their pre-reflexive adherence to the apparent self-evidence of gender roles in their own social universe (Bourdieu 1998a: 9 [3]).

It was the existence of this collective 'androcentric unconscious' that explained the production and reproduction of homologous forms of gender inequality in societies as apparently different as pre-capitalist Kabylia and late twentieth-century France. This androcentric unconscious consisted of a set of gendered 'practical taxonomies', a gendered 'vision and division of the social world', which was incorporated at the pre-discursive, pre-reflexive level into agents' habitus. Moreover, it was because this gendered vision and division of the social world was incorporated at the pre-discursive or pre-reflexive level that it proved so difficult to challenge or overturn 'by a mere effort of will founded on a liberating *prise de conscience*' (Bourdieu 1998a: 45 [39]). Any account of change that relied on such a notion of a *prise de conscience* had ignored 'the opacity and inertia which results from the inscription of social structures in bodies' (Bourdieu 1998a: 46 [40]). This, then, according to Bourdieu, explained the striking 'transhistorical constancy of the relation of masculine domination', while justifying his emphasis on its 'transhistorically invariant' features. It was this emphasis, finally, that distinguished his analyses from those conducted by feminists, whose 'militant conviction' led them to underestimate the resilience of the androcentric unconscious (Bourdieu 1998a: 121 [114]).

Hence, despite the evident changes to women's educational opportunities, economic condition and legal and political status in the West, Bourdieu argued that these 'visible changes of *condition* in fact conceal permanent features in *relative position*' (1998a: 97 [90]). Thus, he argued that although women had gained increased access to higher education and the labour market, the disciplines they typically studied or the posts they occupied tended to be far less prestigious than male-dominated disciplines and professions. The persistence of such inequalities could be explained, according to Bourdieu, by the 'relative autonomy' of 'the economy of symbolic goods', which allowed 'masculine domination to perpetuate itself' in the symbolic realm, 'unaffected by the transformations of the economic mode of production' (1998a: 103–4 [96]). Thus any changes to women's social and economic position had been mediated through an older set of assumptions about their proper role and inherent abilities, assumptions belonging to the 'symbolic' realm: 'the changes in the condition of women always obey the logic of the traditional model of the division between the male and the female' (Bourdieu 1998a: 101 [93]). In Kabylia, the 'traditional model' was grounded in a fundamental opposition between the devalued private sphere of feminine domestic labour and the valued public sphere of masculine agricultural labour outside in the fields. In developed capitalist societies, this basic opposition was reproduced in homologous forms in the oppositions between feminized academic disciplines and professions, on the one hand, and their male-dominated equivalents, on the other. As Bourdieu put it:

> The fundamental opposition, of which Kabyle society offers the canonical form, is 'geared down' and, as it were, diffracted in a series of homologous oppositions, which reproduce that fundamental opposition, but in dispersed and often unrecognisable forms (such as the oppositions between the sciences and the arts, or between surgery and dermatology).
>
> (1998a: 113 [106])

In both *The Inheritors* and *Reproduction*, Bourdieu had shown how this fundamental opposition had expressed itself in the 'relegation' of female students into the least prestigious academic disciplines. In *Distinction*, this fundamental opposition had manifested itself in women's confinement in the labour market to the most stereotypically feminine and hence least lucrative positions within the burgeoning service sector. Bourdieu's analysis, in 'Questions de politique', of women's relative lack of engagement with the public realm of political debate might be taken as the manifestation or the expression of that fundamental opposition, in homologous form, in the political field or a developed Western society.

Bourdieu's account of the 'transhistorically invariant' nature of masculine domination would thus seem to epitomize many of the problems inherent to his social theory that we have identified in preceding chapters. His reliance on the notion of 'homology' to explain the relationship not only between different semi-autonomous fields – the educational, the political, the economic – in differentiated societies but also between different societies – pre-capitalist Kabylia and the developed West – seemed particularly problematic. For this indeed risked endowing the values and practical taxonomies incorporated into the gendered habitus with an essentialized and unchanging character. According to this account, these values and taxonomies were incorporated into the habitus of both men and women, in a process of pre-discursive inculcation whose archetypal form could be found in Kabylia, yet which was reproduced in homologous form in the developed West. Those practical taxonomies, based on a fundamental opposition between masculine and feminine values and incorporated into every agent's habitus, were then invested in, mediated or diffracted through a variety of different fields so as to produce within those fields homologous forms of that original or fundamental opposition. The gendered habitus and the fundamental opposition at its core would thus determine and be expressed in the oppositions structuring each of those fields. However, the fact of being mediated through those fields would not fundamentally affect the nature of the habitus and its gendered vision and division of the social world, since the relative autonomy of the symbolic would ensure that traditional vision and division endured regardless of changes in, for example, the economic mode of production. Moreover, it was because the fundamental opposition at the core of the gendered habitus was incorporated pre-reflexively or pre-discursively that, Bourdieu argued, it proved so resistant to change.

Ahistorical homologies

Bourdieu's account of gender relations in *Masculine Domination* would thus seem to provide further confirmation of our findings regarding the flaws of his social theory as a tool of political analysis. The affects, desires, tastes and aversions incorporated into the gendered habitus were assumed to be fundamentally in conformity with existing social structures, remaining 'opaque' and 'inert' until they were uncovered by a work of 'socio-analysis'. The determining force of the fundamental opposition structuring that gendered habitus was then understood to follow a logic of expressive causality; that fundamental opposition was expressed in a series of homologous oppositions structuring the wide variety of different fields in which it manifested itself as so many 'different translations of the same phrase'. The 'traditional model of relations between the sexes' was, finally, understood to represent some kind of survival of older, even primitive forms of symbolic classification which endured in the West despite shifts in the mode of economic production. As Christine Delphy has argued, there is something inherently ahistorical in this notion of patriarchy as a 'survival' either of historically earlier forms of social organization or of the alternative forms of social organization that anthropologists analyse in their studies of so-called pre-capitalist societies. Delphy explains:

> I do not believe in the theory of 'survivals' [. . .]. An institution which exists today cannot be explained by the simple fact that it existed in the past, even if this past is recent. I do not deny that certain elements of patriarchy today resemble elements of the 'patriarchy' of six thousand years ago or that of two hundred years ago; what I deny is that this continuation – insofar as it is a *continuation* (i.e. insofar as it really concerns the same thing) – in itself constitutes an explanation. Many people think that when they have found the birth of an institution in the past, they hold the key to its present existence. But they have in fact explained neither its present existence, nor even its birth (its past appearance), for they must explain its existence at each and every

moment in the context prevailing at that time; and its persistence today (if it really is persistence) must be explained by the present context.

(1984: 17)

Delphy's insistence on the need to explain a phenomenon's existence 'at each and every moment in the context prevailing at that time' proves a useful starting point from which to question some of the 'homologies' Bourdieu found between manifestations of masculine domination in Kabylia and those evident in the West. For example, Bourdieu noted the enclosure of Kabyle women within certain strictly defined spaces, activities and modes of behaviour, an enclosure whose 'most visible manifestation' was the imperative to wear the veil. This physical confinement was reproduced in homologous form, Bourdieu argued, in the 'symbolic confinement' of Western women – not only the constant injunctions that they adopt a submissive role in social exchanges, but also the physical limitations placed on them by clothing and fashion, 'as with those young women constantly pulling down a too-short skirt', so as to give the right impression of morality and restraint (1998a: 34–5 [28–9]). It could, of course, be argued that the veil and the miniskirt do indeed express an equivalent fetishization of the female body. However, this would not be the same as arguing, as Bourdieu appeared to, that the fashion for miniskirts was somehow caused by or represented the survival of the principles behind the imperative to wear the veil in an Islamic society. There seemed to be an illegitimate slippage here from noting a broad similarity between two phenomena to asserting that the second such phenomenon was caused by or was a homologous expression of the principles that determined the first.

The fashion for miniskirts surely reflects a striking feature of gender relations specific to advanced capitalist societies, namely the extraordinary fetishization of women's and increasingly men's bodies in the name of sexual liberation. This in turn might be seen as part of a more generalized commodification of intimacy and sexual desire since broadly the 1960s, as manifest, for example, in the normalization of pornography and the penetration of its imagery into mainstream culture, in advertising, popular music videos, and so on. As Rosemary Hennessy has argued, this ever 'deeper penetration and commodification of the body and identity' need to be related to the flexible modes of accumulation and the commodification of previously private spheres of life characteristic of late capitalism (Hennessy 2000: 106). If women who wear miniskirts can sometimes be observed pulling them down, as Bourdieu noted, it is by no means clear this equates to an expression of the traditional strictures on feminine modesty, strictures whose elementary or archetypal form can be found in pre-capitalist Islamic Kabylia. Rather such behaviour might be seen to express a fundamental contradiction between the allure of a garment marketed as a symbol of feminine autonomy and assertiveness and the sometimes awkward reality of wearing something that overtly objectifies and sexualizes the female body. It is surely questionable to what extent reference to the role of the veil in Islamic societies can illuminate the complex relationships between women's desire for sexual, social and political autonomy, the commodification of sexuality and the body, and the workings of late capitalism that are in play here.

Gender politics 105

The questionable nature of Bourdieu's claim that there was a homology between wearing the veil in Kabylia and the miniskirt in the West thus highlighted the importance of relating the gendered habitus to the particular historical conditions in which it is constructed. Further, his example of women pulling down their miniskirts suggested that the gendered habitus could not always be assumed to produce gender identities in an unproblematic way. Rather, assuming a gendered identity might often involve negotiating contradictions between, for example, the allure of dominant representations of liberated femininity and their lived reality. Similar problems emerged when Bourdieu used the notion of homology not transculturally, to suggest certain 'invariants' between Kabylia and the West, but within the same culture, to describe the relations between different fields in the same society at the same historical moment. As we have seen, Bourdieu argued that the predominance of female students in the least prestigious disciplines in the higher education field or in the least lucrative professions in the economic field reproduced, in homologous form, their dominated role in the social field, as a whole. Bourdieu seemed to employ a logic of all or nothing here, arguing that since women's entry into higher education and the workplace had not changed everything it had changed nothing, that since inequalities persisted in those domains, such inequalities manifested the reproduction of prior relations of domination, themselves fundamentally unchanged. This assumed that women's arrival in these spaces was itself smooth and unproblematic. It ignored the possibility that women's access to higher education and the workplace might itself have been the result of their own political struggles, struggles which themselves had challenged and eroded traditional definitions of women's roles in the symbolic realm. Similarly, it ignored the possibility that the very fact of women's greater presence in such domains, albeit in dominated disciplines and professions, may have itself significantly changed both the life chances of the individual women concerned and the nature of the institutions in which they now found themselves.

For example, in her study of gender and politics in inter-war France, Siân Reynolds has examined the process whereby bourgeois women's voluntary work in the charitable sector was gradually transformed into salaried labour in the institutions of the nascent welfare state. This was a process whose continuation in the postwar period Bourdieu would analyse in *Distinction*, understanding it to be the expression of women's socially determined disposition to work in the caring professions and the manifestation of the dominated positions women continued to occupy, despite increased involvement in the labour market. Reynolds makes a similar point when she refers to 'the "common-sense" ideology prevailing' in the inter-war years that social work 'was "natural" work for women' (Reynolds 1996: 139). However, she goes on to demonstrate that employment in the social services necessarily engaged the women involved in activities that, by their very nature, challenged those assumptions about a woman's 'natural' role or place in society. As Reynolds puts it:

> There was nothing obvious in the 1920s about sending young women from mostly sheltered backgrounds and with little 'street experience' into the

alien, sometimes hostile environments of the problem areas of large cities and suburbs (*la zone*). *They were expected to do something previously unthinkable for young unmarried women*, to travel out alone, with a bicycle as their only means of transport, a uniform as chief protection.

(1996: 142, my emphasis)

Reynolds draws similar conclusions about the increasing involvement of women in private-sector employment in the inter-war years. As she demonstrates, women were often prized by employers as a cheap and malleable labour force. Moreover, women's career advancement was frequently frustrated by the range of obstacles, formal and informal, men placed in their way. Hence, as Bourdieu would note for the postwar period, women's increased overall access to salaried employment in the inter-war years concealed the dominated positions they continued to occupy in the workplace. However, Reynolds shows that the very presence of women in the workplace, albeit in dominated positions, allowed them to participate in the labour movement, gaining a political autonomy and agency that otherwise would not have been available to them (Reynolds 1996: 118–29). The industries most affected by the 1936 strikes – strikes which have since acquired an iconic status in the history of French working class struggle on account of the gains they secured – were precisely 'those that employed women process workers or service staff' (Reynolds 1996: 105).

In short, while women's initial access to the workplace may have been achieved under conditions that seemed to reproduce older forms of gender inequality, the consequences of that increased access were neither entirely predictable nor wholly containable within those older structures of inequality. There was a danger of functionalism in Bourdieu's suggestion that the incorporation of women into education and the workplace was achieved in such a way as to reproduce earlier forms of gender inequality. The assumption seemed to be that a gendered system had been able to incorporate change in such a way as to or even in order to reproduce itself unproblematically. Not only did this risk ignoring the role played by women's own struggles to gain access to higher education and the workplace. It also risked flattening out any contradictions inherent in such transformations or seeing such contradictions, as the one Bourdieu noted between the symbolic order's traditional vision of gender roles and the economic field's demand for the best person for the job, as merely contributing to the reproduction of existing gender inequalities. However, the increasing access of women to the labour market was surely a more problematic process than Bourdieu implied, involving significant contradictions between the logics operative in different social fields, between the demand, in the economic field, for more labour, and those forces, in the social and political fields, seeking to defend more traditional definitions of gender. Twentieth-century France offers some striking examples of such contradictions and of the political and social effects they could produce.

For example, government policy during the Vichy regime was marked by a striking contradiction between the French economic field's need for female labour and that regime's ideological commitment to keeping women at home, in a subservient, domestic and maternal role. As Hanna Diamond has shown, the Vichy government's attempts in 1940, through both cajoling and legislation, to prevent public- and private-sector employers from employing married women came into direct conflict with the French economy's need for labour and had to be abandoned as a result (Diamond 1999: 32–6). This contradiction between ideology and economic necessity would recur in slightly different form in the postwar years, notably under the presidency of De Gaulle. De Gaulle was a politician wedded to an extremely conservative, Catholic vision of society, culture and morals. At the same time, however, he was committed to boosting France's *grandeur* by engaging in an accelerated programme of industrial modernization and urbanization which would transform France into an advanced consumer society. An inevitable consequence of such a rapid programme of urbanization and industrial modernization was, paradoxically, the erosion of the traditional morality, of the forms of sexual and social interaction, the rigid division of gender roles that De Gaulle himself sought to uphold. There was thus a fundamental contradiction between the economic, cultural and social consequences of De Gaulle's politics and the moral values he embodied. It is generally considered that the dramatic events of May 1968 were, in part at least, the product of this contradiction between the cultural, social and political forces De Gaulle's policies had unleashed and the conservatism he personified. The postwar French women's movement, of course, emerged from the events of 1968, reflecting both the politicization of a generation of feminists through their involvement in those events and their frustration at the sexism of their male counterparts.

The point here is not to posit some straightforward causal link between the contradictions of Vichy policy, the contradictions of Gaullism, and the emergence of the women's movement in the wake of May 1968. Rather it is to highlight the contradictions that have historically characterized the relations between the political, cultural and economic fields, contradictions which have not always served to secure the reproduction of gender domination unchanged, as Bourdieu claimed in the case of the contradiction between the economy's need for women's labour and the symbolic realm's adherence to a more conventionally gendered vision and division of the social world. As these several examples have demonstrated, the relative autonomy of the various fields cannot always be assumed to secure the reproduction of the same but can be sources of contradiction and instability. It is these contradictions and instabilities that Bourdieu's reliance on the notion of homologies between different fields, cultures and historical periods threatened to efface. This is not a matter of opposing a narrative of glorious and inherently liberating resistance to masculine domination to Bourdieu's apparently static and determinist model. Rather it is a case of emphasizing that historical change is always more contradictory and unpredictable than Bourdieu's ultimately functionalist account allowed. It is also to insist on the need to relate different forms of masculine domination to the particular historical, economic and political circumstances in which they manifest themselves rather than understanding the manifestation of such forms in different cultures at different historical moments or in different fields to be different expressions of the same essentialized androcentric unconscious.

Gender performativity

Bourdieu, however, theorized the possibilities for changing the existing system of male domination in rather different terms. Having attributed the constancy of male domination to the incorporation of the gendered taxonomies of the androcentric unconscious on the hither side of discourse, he argued that challenging existing gender inequalities would require a 'symbolic revolution' (Bourdieu 1998a: 47 [41]). As we have already seen, Bourdieu had already defined the conditions for any such 'symbolic revolution' as being first an 'objective crisis', which would disrupt agents' otherwise immediate adherence to the status quo, and second a 'critical discourse', elaborated by intellectuals, which would channel and direct the forces unleashed by that objective crisis. In order to be effective, any such critical discourse would have both to be adequate to social reality, revealing 'things which were already there', and to be underpinned by the symbolic authority, the cultural and intellectual capital, that intellectuals possessed on account of the position they occupied in social space.

In *Masculine Domination*, Bourdieu offered a significantly modified account of the symbolic revolution that would be required to overturn dominant definitions of gender relations. He noted that, unlike other dominated groups, those groups who were marginalized by the dominant definitions of gender – women, gays, lesbians – were not, as social groups, defined or characterized by their lack of cultural capital or symbolic authority. Since the categories of women, gays and lesbians cut across all the social classes, these dominated groups already contained within them 'relatively privileged' individuals possessing sufficient cultural capital and hence symbolic authority to speak on their own behalf, hence bypassing the need to delegate to an extraneous intellectual representative (Bourdieu 1998a: 134 [123]). Further, Bourdieu argued that the struggles of such groups for equal rights could not simply take the form of validating the objective reality of their condition, since this risked both falling into 'particularism' and 'organizing themselves as a category' constructed according to 'a socially imposed categorization', hence 'implementing' the very 'classifications' they were seeking 'to resist' (1998a: 131 [120]). Feminists, gays and lesbians could overcome the risks of particularism by taking cognizance of their unusual position, as stigmatized groups possessing 'the relatively improbable combination' of a 'strong subversive disposition' and 'strong cultural capital', and putting this 'at the service of the social movement as a whole', serving as its 'avant-garde' (Bourdieu 1998a: 134 [124]).

In *Masculine Domination*, then, the old Leninist vanguardism of Party and working class appeared to have given way to a somewhat improbable, avowedly 'utopian', vanguardism of the feminist, gay and lesbian movements. This account seemed to rely on a rather stereotyped notion of gay men as predominantly urban professionals, with an inherent capacity for creativity and symbolic subversion; on several occasions Bourdieu claimed that 'homosexuals' were 'particularly well-armed' to undertake such a symbolic revolution (1998a: 134 [123–4]). Moreover, this analysis continued to assume that political agency was the preserve of the 'relatively privileged', determined, a priori, by position occupied in the social field, contingent upon prior possession of sufficient cultural capital and symbolic authority. It is this assumption that leads Judith Butler to accuse Bourdieu of presenting a 'conservative account of the speech act' since he presumed that 'the conventions that will authorize the performative are already in place' (Butler 1997: 142). Butler questions Bourdieu's assumption that the performativity of any political utterance is always dependent upon the prior symbolic authority of its author, that language is 'a static and closed system whose utterances are functionally secured in advance by the "social positions" to which they are mimetically related' (Butler 1997: 145).

Butler draws on Jacques Derrida's deconstructive reading of speech-act theory to emphasize the 'iterability' of any utterance, the fact that any performative is always inhabited by the possibility of its going awry and not achieving its desired effect, and as such, is always open to 'subversion' and 'resignification'. Iterability and the possibility of performative failure or resignification are inherent to the structures of language; they are the very condition of possibility of language as such, she argues. Any social identity, whether defined in terms of ethnicity, sexuality, gender or class, is produced performatively both through discourse and through subjects' 'passionate attachment' to or libidinal investment in their identity. Yet that performative production does not take place at a single moment, in a definitive production of a fixed identity. Rather, according to the logic of iterability, it must be constantly reiterated, performatively re-enacted both in discourse and in embodied practice or ritual, in a performance. In this constant iteration and reiteration of social identity, its repeated performance, is contained the inherent possibility that its originally normative injunctions might go awry, the potential to 'appropriate those terms from the dominant discourse and rework or resignify those highly cathected terms to rally a political movement' (Butler 1997: 157–8). In their stylized performance of femininity, drag queens can thus subvert the dominant 'heterosexual matrix', re-iterating or performing femininity in a manner that de-naturalizes it and highlights its constructed nature (Butler 1990).

The typical critique of Butler's work is the one made by Bourdieu himself in *Masculine Domination*. He accused her of embracing a 'subversive voluntarism' which, in focusing on the construction and subversion of gender identities through discourse alone, conflated material with linguistic forms of domination and hence exaggerated the ability of dominated groups to challenge the normative definitions that constrain them (1998a: 110 [103]). However, to contrast Butler's alleged voluntarism with Bourdieu's apparently more realistic assessment of the material factors determining the capacity of different social groups to engage in a performative politics would be to miss the point. The fact is that both Bourdieu and Butler are wrong here, albeit for diametrically opposed reasons.

Butler is right to insist that, ontologically speaking, language and the performative are characterized by the inherent possibility of their going awry, so that any social identity is always, by definition, contingent, relatively unstable, open to resignification. She is wrong at the empirical level, however, to assume that any such resignification is necessarily intrinsically subversive and progressive and to underestimate the extent to which material and historical circumstance place limitations, if never absolutely determining the possibilities of such resignification achieving genuinely transformative results. Bourdieu committed the opposite error. He moved from making certain empirical observations to drawing unwarranted ontological conclusions about the very nature of the political itself. Bourdieu noted, at the empirical level, the greater symbolic authority and hence effectiveness of the speech acts of those occupying relatively privileged positions in social space. He then moved from this empirical observation to elaborate a theory of discourse and politics according to which the performative force of any speech act was taken a priori to be defined absolutely by position in the social field. The problem with Bourdieu's theory of politics was hence not that it overstated the difficulties for dominated groups of subverting or challenging existing social structures but that it failed to account for any such possibility at all, a possibility that, as Butler, echoing Laclau and Mouffe and Rancière in this, rightly points out, is a condition of possibility of the political itself.

In her study of young working-class women training to be care workers, *Formations of Class and Gender* (1997), Beverley Skeggs also takes issue with Bourdieu's assumption that there would be a straightforward relationship between the objective position occupied by her subjects in the social field, as working-class women, and the social identity with which they identified and in which they invested their desires and affects. In the behaviour of her subjects, Skeggs observed 'strenuous efforts to deny, disidentify, and dissimulate' their working-class identity (Skeggs 1997: 94). These were 'affective responses' motivated by a sense of injustice at their 'social and cultural positioning'. Yet such responses also revealed aspirations to 'social betterment', to the kind of middle-class respectability, femininity and material comfort embodied in the person and politics of Margaret Thatcher, in her form of market populism (Skeggs 1997: 76). Skeggs' analysis offers the possibility of thinking through the dispute between Butler and Bourdieu in a manner broadly consonant with the kind of reconceptualization of the notion of 'habitus' that we have attempted in earlier chapters. In Skeggs' work, the habitus remains a structure of expectations, of tastes, aversions and affects, but it is related to the objective realities of the social field in a purely contingent way; it is a construction rather than an expression of that reality. As such, the habitus contains within itself, as its very condition of possibility, the potential for disidentifications which constantly risk reconfiguring existing social and linguistic structures in new ways. A series of important theoretical consequences flows from this.

First, the incorporation of the norms of gender identity into the habitus cannot be assumed to be immediate or unproblematic since, as Butler rightly emphasizes, the iterability of such norms renders them, by definition, open to going awry and to potential resignification. Second, the nature of those norms themselves is affected by historical circumstance and cannot be taken to be the expression of an unchanging androcentric unconscious, as Bourdieu seemed to argue. Third, acknowledging the essential iterability of social norms and their consequent openness to resignification or to moments of disidentification need not lead to a theory of social or political change grounded in notions of rational agency, understood on the model of the *prise de conscience*, of the substitution of mute affective investment with rational political agency. Rather such disidentifications can themselves be affective in form, resulting from a disaffection with the status quo that unleashes new investments in possible alternatives. Finally, such disidentifications need not be assumed merely to correspond to those punctual moments of emancipation through 'subjectification', when dominated groups challenge the status quo in pursuit of intrinsically progressive alternatives, as Butler implicitly supposes. Rather, as Skeggs has shown, such disidentifications can be everyday affairs, processes or continuing attempts to change one's current position and the way others perceive that position in a manner that may be anything but progressive or subversive in its effects. Paradoxically, Bourdieu's account of the relationships between gender and the modernization of postwar France seemed to offer just such an account of changing gender identities as being related to a specific historical moment and involving the body and its affects more than any rational agency.

The return of symbolic domination

The premise behind Bourdieu's analysis of the social and cultural changes sweeping through postwar France in *Distinction* was that there had been a change in the mode of domination operative in developed capitalist societies. In *The Logic of Practice*, Bourdieu argued that such societies were witnessing a 'return' to the mode of symbolic domination characteristic of pre-capitalist societies such as Kabylia. In Kabylia, a society in which no institution had the monopoly of the legitimate use of violence, domination could only be exerted in its symbolic form, hidden behind a façade of disinterested gift exchange or personalized relations of honour and obligation. In its initial phases, the advent of capitalism had replaced these apparently gentle or masked forms of domination with straightforward coercion and the naked pursuit of profit. Yet, Bourdieu maintained, as capitalism developed and responded to the forces of opposition its coercion had unleashed, so the 'gentler' forms of symbolic domination began to return to take a central role once more (Bourdieu 1980a: 230–1 [133–4]). This return of symbolic domination was manifest, he argued, in the rise of public relations and advertising under mass consumerism, with their appeals to the emotions and affects of consumers, in the exploitation of the emotional and affective labour of workers in the new caring professions and the booming tertiary sector, and, finally, in the increasing importance to social reproduction of symbolic forms of capital, of educational and inherited social and cultural capital, rather than inherited economic capital.

Bourdieu's argument, in *The Logic of Practice*, was, then, that the *return* of symbolic domination needed to be related to the history of capitalist development. This contrasted with the assumption in *Masculine Domination* that symbolic domination, in its gendered manifestations, represented a *survival* of pre-capitalist symbolic forms and seemed to offer the possibility of relating particular forms of symbolic domination more closely to the particular historical circumstances in which they manifested themselves. Moreover, this return of symbolic domination had significant implications for gender since it corresponded to the rise of the caring professions and the expansion of the tertiary sector, which themselves coincided with the mass entry of women into the French postwar labour market and to the exploitation of supposedly typically feminine aptitudes. Further, the renewed emphasis on the 'gentler' forms of symbolic domination, on the exploitation of emotional labour in the realm of production and affective investments in the realm of consumption, challenged traditional masculine identities in the workplace, the home and the domain of sport and leisure. The implications of all of this were that Bourdieu's account of the modernization of French society in *Distinction* would focus on the transformation and reconstruction of the dispositions, affects, tastes and aversions incorporated within the habitus of all French citizens, in ways which had significant implications for gender and gender politics. This, in turn, might offer the possibility of developing that broadly Fourieriste 'politics of the passions' that Bourdieu himself promised but never delivered, an account which understood social and political change to be the result less of a 'liberating *prise de conscience*' than of a certain 'use of the passions' to 'unblock the [social] machinery' (Bourdieu 2002: 197).

For Bourdieu, the mass entry of women into the workforce was one striking manifestation of this return to a symbolic mode of domination, itself intimately related to France's transition to consumer capitalism in the postwar period. A key facet of mass consumerism is the need to manage and elicit an ever-growing range of new 'needs' and desires through the operations of the public relations and advertising industries, marketing and the mass media. It was in these industries, which placed such an emphasis on presentation and interpersonal skills, on charm and physical appearance, that the generation of women who had benefited from the postwar expansion of higher education were increasingly finding employment. As Bourdieu put it:

> Public and especially private bureaucracies are now obliged to perform representational and 'hosting' functions which are very different in both scale and style from those traditionally entrusted to men (diplomats, ministerial attachés and so on) [. . .]. The new requirements have determined the emergence of a whole set of female occupations and the establishment of a legitimate market in physical attributes. The fact that certain women derive occupational profit from their charm(s) and that beauty thus acquires a value on the labour market has doubtless helped determine not only a number of changes in the norms of clothing and cosmetics, but also a redefinition of the

legitimate image of femininity. Women's magazines and all the legitimate instances in terms of the definition of the legitimate image and use of the body transmit the image of femininity incarnated by those professionals in bureaucratic charm, who are rationally selected and trained, in accordance with a strictly programmed career structure (with specialized schools, beauty contests etc.) to fulfil the most traditional feminine functions in accordance with bureaucratic norms.

(1979: 169–70 [152–3])

This account seemed marked by an ambivalence concerning the extent to which these changes had redefined or merely reproduced 'traditional' gender identities. On the one hand, there was an emphasis on the 'transformation' and 'redefinition' of gender roles and identities, the concerted efforts at schooling minds and bodies involved here. On the other, the roles women played in the workplace were seen as conforming to 'the most traditional feminine functions'. This seemed to reflect a broader ambivalence in *Distinction* regarding both the consequences of these changes and the extent to which they required a wholesale re-shaping or merely the reproduction of a habitus constructed along 'traditionally' gendered lines.

In the course of his analyses, Bourdieu provided much evidence which seemed to underline the extent to which the gendered habitus was being reconstructed and re-shaped with the advent of mass consumerism. Thus, he pointed to the growing raft of specialists in beauty, health, diet and sexual relations, highlighting their role in shaping consumers' needs, desires and ethics in line with the demands of a consumer economy (Bourdieu 1979: 171–2 [153–4]). His text was illustrated with clippings advertising diet products or openings for female cabin crew and articles on schools where women could acquire the necessary skills of tact, deportment, taste and dress sense. As he pointed out, specialist schools for female flight attendants made their pupils undergo 'a radical transformation in their way of walking, sitting, laughing, smiling, talking, dressing, making-up etc.' (1979: 227 [206]). All of these suggested that women's place in the labour force of a developed economy like France's was not the expression of the 'survival' of a 'traditional' gendered habitus, such as might be found in Kabylia, but the product of a concerted and continuous process of training, of construction and of re-shaping of that habitus, a process specifically related to changes in the mode of production.

However, having noted the 'radical transformation' women underwent in flight attendant school, Bourdieu then went on to argue that such women accorded 'an unconditional recognition to the dominant representation of the body' that such schools sought to inculcate in their students (1979: 227 [206]). Evidence of this 'unconditional recognition' could be found, he maintained, in women's affective and material investment in their physical appearance, the fact that they 'accorded an equally unconditional adherence to all forms of cosmetic voluntarism (such as recourse to plastic surgery)' (1979: 228 [206]). The implication appeared to be that if women submitted so readily to the norms of behaviour and appearance dispensed by such institutions, this was because their gendered habitus had predisposed them to such 'unconditional recognition' of the 'dominant representation of the body'. It is perhaps worth remembering that prior to the expansion of the tertiary sector Bourdieu was describing, many women's career choices would have been limited to unpaid housework, domestic service, factory work or labouring on the family farm. Indeed, as Bourdieu himself had argued in the earlier article 'Célibat et condition paysanne', the susceptibility of young French peasant women to the images of femininity transmitted through the mass media, their eagerness to embrace an urban consumerist lifestyle and adopt a more sentimentalized vision of relations between the sexes all needed to be understood as an expression of their desire for emancipation from the servitude of the traditional peasant way of life (Bourdieu 1962). It would thus be possible to interpret the postwar exodus of young women from the French countryside as corresponding to a mass disaffection with the servitudes and rigidities of the traditional peasant way of life, a 'disidentification', to use Skegg's term, from the traditional role of the peasant wife, in favour of an affective investment in the possibilities for emancipation apparently offered by the new models of femininity promoted by mass consumerism and exploited in the burgeoning tertiary sector. This model might be extended to cover the mass entry of women into the tertiary sector as a whole. This might now be read less as the exploitation of pre-existing dispositions than the transformation and reconstruction of such dispositions, tastes, desires and affects, the channelling of women's desires for emancipation and their exploitation for commercial gain. The promises of emancipation held out by women's magazines, flight attendant schools or service sector employment might, of course, all too often prove to be false ones. This, finally, might suggest that, had Bourdieu undertaken ethnographic research among female employees in the service industries, he might have found such women to possess rather more ambivalent or contradictory attitudes to dominant gender norms than the 'unconditional recognition' he claimed they manifested.

Arlie Russell Hochschild's *The Managed Heart* (1983), a detailed ethnographic study of the 'management of emotion' in the service industries, provides a useful point of comparison and contrast here. Like Bourdieu, she argues that, since they are 'traditionally more accomplished managers of feeling in private life, women more than men have put emotional labour on the market' (Hochschild 1983: 17). Drawing on her studies of flight attendant training schools, she emphasizes the amount of explicit and codified inculcation involved in getting female cabin crew to conform to the required models of behaviour, deportment and personal appearance. However, far from noting women's 'unconditional recognition' of these models of behaviour and appearance, as Bourdieu would have it, Hochschild emphasizes the extent to which her flight attendants are conscious of their emotions being 'artificially created', as one of them puts it (Hochschild 1983: 4). As Hochschild concludes: 'a personality is not simply "sold"; people actively manage feelings in order to make their personalities fit for public-contact work' (1983: 219).

Drawing an analogy with Marx's account of workers' alienation from their bodies and the fruits of their labour in industrial capitalism, Hochschild argues that workers called upon to perform emotional labour can become alienated from their own sense of self. The conscious management of emotion demanded by emotional labour, along with the alienation this can engender, represents for Hochschild the locus of significant contradictions in the workplace. Such contradictions can be negotiated by the adoption of purely personal strategies, such as humour or irony, that enable one to 'salvage a sense of self-esteem' by defining 'the job as "illusion making"' and hence removing 'the self from the job' (Hochschild 1983: 135). At the extreme, such detachment from one's allotted role can form the basis of a kind of political agency, as in the so-called 'smile wars', when flight attendants protested about regulations regarding their body weight, personal appearance and behaviour by smiling and greeting passengers in a manner that was recognizably false and exaggeratedly 'polite' (Hochschild 1983: 127).

Hochschild's work on the 'management of emotions' in the service industries usefully highlights the extent to which what is involved is the construction and disciplining of emotions, affects and embodied practices more than the exploitation of a pre-existing 'traditionally' gendered habitus. Moreover, she convincingly demonstrates that such a process of construction is necessarily always provisional, contradictory and open to challenge. This is something that Bourdieu's assertion as to women's 'unconditional recognition' of the models of femininity promoted through women's magazines, the beauty industry, flight attendants schools and the panoply of advisors and counsellors seemed to ignore. Thus, on the one hand, he emphasized the extent of the transformations to gender relations in postwar French society. Yet, on the other, he always ultimately sought to domesticate such transformations by interpreting them as the expressions of the 'traditional' definition of women's role and aptitudes or as phenomena that had been unproblematically recuperated by a modernizing economy. For example, Bourdieu argued that the mass entry of bourgeois women, in particular, into higher education and salaried employment had led to 'the transformation of representations of the division of labour between the sexes' (1979: 149 [134]). The increased access of bourgeois women to higher education had 'determined [. . .] a modification of everything which, according to bourgeois morality, used to be the preserve of women, all the values that were once entrusted to women's care' (Bourdieu 1979: 358).[2] Moreover, increased access to higher education combined with the discourses of consumerism to encourage the petty bourgeoisie, particularly, to have much less limited aspirations than had their parents' generation, to refuse to be defined once and for all by their professional and social status, and to indulge in 'a sort of dream of social flying, a desperate effort to defy the gravity of the social field' (Bourdieu 1979: 429 [370]). These increased aspirations, the rejection of established hierarchy and dream of self-realization involved the production of social identities that were at once less rigid and more prone to psychological insecurity. Where previously, frustrations and disappointments could be made sense of in terms of a collective class identity, now they were read as symptoms of personal failure and tended to be experienced as psychological crisis:

> Whereas the old system tended to produce clearly demarcated social identities which left little room for social fantasy but were comfortable and reassuring even in the unconditional renunciation which they demanded, the sort of structural insecurity in the representation of social identity and its legitimate aspirations tends to shift agents from the terrain of social crisis and critique to the terrain of personal critique and crisis.
>
> (Bourdieu 1979: 176 [156])

However, Bourdieu did not see such fluid identities and disparities between aspiration and achievement as contradictions which might potentially disrupt the unproblematic reproduction of the status quo. Rather, he argued that to do so would be to ignore the fact that 'social contradictions and struggles are not always in contradiction with the perpetuation of the established order', that 'permanence can be ensured by change and the structure perpetuated by movement'. More specifically, Bourdieu maintained that

> the gap between the imposition of legitimate needs [...] and access to the means of satisfying them [...] does not necessarily and automatically threaten the survival of the system; the structural gap and the corresponding frustrations are the very source of the reproduction through displacement which ensures the perpetuation of the structure of positions through transforming the 'nature' of the conditions.
>
> (1979: 184 [164–5])

Here Bourdieu's analysis took on a functionalist tenor again, with the contradictions and fluid identities produced by the re-shaping of gender identities under mass consumerism being recuperated within the logic of the system's own reproduction. He pointed to 'the convergences between the routine themes of advertising – which has long been versed in the language of desire' – and certain popularized forms of 'postmodernist' theory, claiming both had conspired to 'supply the economy with the perfect consumer', freed from the old constraints of morality, class and community (1979: 431 [371]).

In the years which have followed the publication of *Distinction*, this notion that more fluid social, sexual and gender identities are simply the by-products of advanced consumerism has become more widespread. Frequently, this claim is accompanied by a stated allegiance to a materialist mode of analysis which distinguishes itself from so-called poststructuralist or postmodernist theory and its alleged 'celebration' of fluid identities or of the performative nature of gender and sexuality (Žižek 1999; Hennessy 2000). The problem with such analyses, a problem that Bourdieu shared, is their functionalism and economic determinism; they mistake the ability of certain capitalist enterprises to adapt and market to those more fluid identities for proof that those identities were created by capitalism in the first place, in pursuit of its own ends. This ignores the struggles individuals and groups have frequently engaged in to be allowed even to express such alternative identities. It also overlooks the inherently unpredictable and contradictory nature of any such change to established forms of social identity. In short, what such accounts fail to grasp is the properly *dialectical* nature of such changes, the extent to which they can simultaneously be politically enabling and susceptible to commercial exploitation.

As this chapter has attempted to show, throughout the course of his career Bourdieu proved sensitive to the gender dynamic of so many of the phenomena he sought to analyse. However, there was a tendency, most evident in *Masculine Domination*, to reduce any manifestation of gender inequality to be the expression of a 'transhistorically invariant' androcentric unconscious, an unconscious reproduced in homologous form in the various gender divisions structuring the different societies, historical periods and semi-autonomous fields he studied. Bourdieu's assumption that there were homologies between these different manifestations of masculine domination risked eliding any detailed analysis of the particular historical conditions in which gender identities were constructed and reconstructed, while smoothing over any contradictions between the various ways in which gender came into play in the different semi-autonomous fields. His notion that contemporary developed societies were marked by a return to forms of symbolic domination, however, seemed to offer the possibility of linking questions of gender more closely to the particular economic, historical and political circumstances prevailing in such societies. Indeed, Bourdieu's analyses of gender identities in a rapidly modernizing postwar France seemed to offer a more productive way of thinking about the relationships between historical circumstance and the shaping and re-shaping of such identities. Ultimately, a certain functionalism would creep back into Bourdieu's account, when he argued that the more fluid and unstable sexual and gender identities he described were themselves merely the means by which the 'established order' reproduced itself. However, once such functionalism was jettisoned; *Distinction* did seem to contain the germs of a more convincing account of the formation of gender identities under mass consumerism.

For what *Distinction* offered was a detailed analysis of the ways in which gender identities or gendered habituses are constructed through the incorporation both of changes in 'objective' circumstance and opportunity and of the explicit forms of inculcation and education contained in discourses of advertising, the mass media or training schools for emotional labour. Bourdieu demonstrated how such 'objective' factors were then incorporated into the habitus, so as to become a set of 'subjective' feelings, expectations, tastes, aversions and embodied practices. The habitus, in accordance with its aesthetic structure, became here the site where any rift between the abstract moral injunctions contained in women's magazines, etiquette guides or flight attendants' training manuals and subjective inclination, sensibility or affection might be healed. At this point, however, it would be necessary to question Bourdieu's assumption that this process of incorporation was necessarily smooth or unproblematic, that the recognition agents accorded the models of behaviour offered to them was necessarily 'unconditional'. Rather, it would be important to insist on the fact that this process of incorporation was always subject to failure; it could always go awry. Hence the constant need, amply attested to by Bourdieu's own evidence, to reiterate the values contained in the dominant representation of gender roles that emerged in the postwar period, a reiteration that took both a discursive form, in mass media representations of all kinds, and a practical, embodied form, in the shaping and re-shaping of women and men's bodies through education, sport and leisure practices.

To point to the necessarily contingent and potentially unstable nature of the gender identities produced by such means is not to embrace a naïve voluntarism. Rather, it is to insist on the inherently unpredictable and potentially contradictory nature of the formation of gender identities, as these alter in accordance with changing historical conditions. Such contradictions can be lived on a purely individual level, experienced on a continuum which ranges from a complete disidentification from dominant representations of gender to a contradictory mixture of rational awareness of the constructed, arbitrary, even absurd nature of dominant definitions of masculinity or femininity, combined with a residual attachment to such definitions, felt at the level of affective investment and manifested in embodied practice. These contradictions, moments of disidentification or disaffection can also, in certain circumstances, form the basis for more significant forms of social, cultural and political change. Grasping that potential for change, however, would demand abandoning Bourdieu's assumption as to the existence of straightforward homologies between the different fields. The notion of homology, as Bourdieu employed it, flattened out any contradictions between the different fields and hence overlooked the potentially transformative effects of tensions between the continuing adherence to traditional assumptions about gender at the political or symbolic level and the tendency of developments in the economic field to erase any such traditions, for example. A modified Bourdieusian framework, more attentive to the contradictions between different fields and alive to the provisional nature of the gendered habitus, might, however, offer important insights into gender politics, while escaping the dichotomy between voluntarism and determinism in this domain.

As we have seen, it is in their ambition to overcome the opposition between object and subject, to describe how objective structural law or abstract moral injunction is incorporated so as to become as one with subjective inclination, sensibility and affection, that Bourdieu's concepts of habitus and practice can be considered to possess an inherently aesthetic character. Thus far, however, we have only considered this aesthetic character in its most general sense, as it relates to the realm of social practice as a whole. Yet to endow all social practice with the characteristic features of the aesthetic is surely also to accord a very specific social and political role to the aesthetic in its more specialized sense, as it relates to the particular realms of artistic production and appreciation. In the last decades of his career, both in his political interventions and his more detailed theorizations of the artistic and literary fields, Bourdieu became increasingly preoccupied with the political implications of the aesthetic in this more specialized sense, arguing in favour of protecting certain 'universal' artistic and literary values from the incursions of the market. It is to a consideration of Bourdieu's theorization of the aesthetic in this more specialized sense and of his understanding of its potential political force that Chapter 6 will turn.

6 Aesthetics, politics and the market

Over the preceding chapters, we first established that Bourdieu's central concepts of habitus and practice were structured analogously to the aesthetic object. We then went on to examine some of the implications of the aesthetic characteristics of practice and habitus for social and political theory. However, this was to consider only one side of the coin, as it were, only one set of the potential implications of this analogy between social practice and the aesthetic. For, if the inculcation of social norms and appropriate social practices in Kabylia operated in a form analogous to a prose poem by Mallarmé, then poetry, and other cultural forms along with it, must be considered to possess a significant potential for transforming existing practices, for re-shaping the schemes of perception incorporated into the habitus. Indeed, in 'La Production de l'idéologie dominante' Bourdieu had attributed a key role to the cultural industries and cultural *animateurs* in channelling the subversive energies of May 1968 into an ethos and habitus better adapted to the consumerist lifestyles that accompanied the return to the 'gentler' forms of symbolic domination in postwar France (Bourdieu 1976: 51). While in this instance culture's transformative force had been exploited in the service of consumerism, Bourdieu's social theory nonetheless seemed to keep open the possibility of putting that transformative force to more progressive or liberating uses.

Such a possibility would appear to run counter to the received wisdom as regards Bourdieu's account of the objective function of the aesthetic and of legitimate culture in capitalist societies. To many commentators, Bourdieu appeared to deny any function to legitimate culture, any inherent value to the aesthetic, above or beyond their role in reproducing and naturalizing social divisions and distinctions (Wolff 1983; Bürger 1990). What seemed to be lacking from Bourdieu's work on culture was any clear distinction between culture in its *contingent function* as marker of social distinction, on the one hand, and the *inherent value* of any cultural artefact, on the other. The need for such a distinction had arguably become more acute in the later years of Bourdieu's career. For in both the punctual political interventions and the detailed theoretical studies of those years, he had become increasingly concerned with the need to defend the 'autonomy' of the 'field of artistic production' against the incursions of the market, in order to safeguard the 'universal value' of certain artistic and literary forms.

Bourdieu was, of course, far from alone in being troubled by the apparent loss of artistic autonomy in the face of so-called market imperatives. For example, in her study *Privatising Culture* (2002) Chin-tao Wu has subjected the increasing reliance of art galleries on commercial sponsorship to considerable critical scrutiny. In Britain, the role played by Charles Saatchi's patronage of a select group of 'Young British Artists' or 'YBAs' has frequently been criticized, held responsible for eroding the distinction between serious art and the degraded currency of sensationalist advertising campaigns (Stallabrass 1999; Hatton and Walker 2000). In the US, during the 'culture wars' of the 1980s and 1990s, concern at the increasing power of corporate sponsors over the art world became linked to campaigns against the attempts of right-Republicans like Jesse Helms to remove state support from challenging or controversial art and artists. For Helms was being funded by the very multinational corporations on whose sponsorship the art world had increasingly come to rely as state subsidies were reduced. It was these issues which were at the heart of the extended dialogue between Bourdieu and the artist Hans Haacke published in 1994 as *Free Exchange*. Haacke's own work typically takes the form of a series of polemical interventions in such debates, seeking to highlight the relationship between corporate art sponsorship and the *de facto* censorship of more controversial art forms or to lay bare the function of such sponsorship in allowing multinational corporations to conceal their exploitative practices behind a patina of disinterested philanthropy (Wallis 1986; Grasskamp *et al.* 2004).

In the course of his dialogue with Haacke, as in his shorter interventions on the topic, Bourdieu frequently invoked late nineteenth-century French artists and writers as personifications of his preferred model of artistic autonomy, a model he enjoined contemporary artists to follow. In their struggles against obscenity trials and *Salon* refusals, Charles Baudelaire, Gustave Flaubert and Edouard Manet had established the principle of artistic autonomy in the face of the state's attempts to determine what they could write about or represent artistically and how they could represent it. In producing work that struck contemporary audiences as difficult, contrary to accepted convention, or simply risible, these artists had simultaneously refused to give in to the 'temporal seductions' of worldly fame or wealth. In affirming their autonomy from the partial or particular interests of politics and the market, Baudelaire, Flaubert and Manet thus secured the 'universal value' of their work. When in 1896 Emile Zola published 'J'Accuse', condemning the wrongful imprisonment of Alfred Dreyfus, he provided, according to Bourdieu, 'the inaugural archetype of intellectual engagement' (1997b: 65); Zola intervened in the political field in the name of the 'universal values' cultivated and safeguarded in the autonomous field of artistic production within which he worked.

Bourdieu's account of both artistic autonomy and intellectual engagement appeared, then, to conform to a classically French republican model. However, his insistence that it was their distance from or refusal of the logic of the market that had secured the universal value of Manet, Flaubert, Baudelaire and Zola's work did seem to raise a number of potential problems. First, in studies such as

Distinction, Bourdieu had maintained that it was precisely the art world's claim to stand at a distance from the market that secured its role in reproducing and legitimizing class distinctions. In those earlier studies his argument had been that only those classes who possessed sufficient wealth had the time and leisure to indulge in artistic pleasures which defined themselves in opposition to the market. In a world increasingly dominated by market imperatives, to indulge in the apparently 'disinterested' pleasures afforded by the products of an autonomous field of artistic production had become a luxury, a signifier or marker of the dominant class's distance from the realm of brute material necessity inhabited by the dominated classes. Moreover, in promoting as 'universal' artworks which, according to his own account, occupied a rarefied sphere accessible only to the dominant class, Bourdieu seemed to have overlooked the possibility of developing forms of artistic practice that related in some way to the aestheticized structures of the habitus, to the schemes of perception and appreciation incorporated by ordinary agents in their everyday practice.

On a more pragmatic level, it was not immediately clear that the experiences of a range of canonical nineteenth-century French artists could provide a model of artistic autonomy that would prove adequate to the challenges faced by artists under late capitalism. The political constraints and market conditions under which contemporary artists work are clearly very different to those faced by Manet, Flaubert and Baudelaire. Thus, in citing these nineteenth-century artists as models of an artistic activity defined in opposition to the market, Bourdieu seemed to confirm the suggestion made by both Craig Calhoun and John Guillory that his theory lacked a detailed conception of capitalism and the market. Both Calhoun and Guillory have noted the paradox whereby Bourdieu, who did more than any other social theorist to extend the language of economics, of capitalism and the marketplace, to cover every form of social practice, nonetheless had very little to say about capitalism or the actual functioning of the marketplace as these evolved over different historical periods (in Calhoun *et al.* 1993: 61–88; in Brown and Szeman 2000: 31–2).

The market, in Bourdieu's theory, tended to remain un- or under-theorized, featuring only inasmuch as it was taken to correspond to a realm of 'naked economic interests'. The different forms of 'symbolic capital' and the various semi-autonomous fields in which those forms of capital were produced and accumulated were defined in terms of their distance from or proximity to the market, to that realm of naked economic interests. As such, the market figured in Bourdieu's social theory as the untheorized but nonetheless transcendent cause of all social practice; economic capital served as the universal general equivalent to which all other practices and forms of capital might ultimately be reduced, even if such practices represented mitigated or mediated, 'symbolic' and hence 'euphemized' forms of the 'naked economic interests' that held sway in the market itself. Indeed, throughout much of his career Bourdieu's efforts were devoted to effecting just such a reduction, to demonstrating that behind their mask of a universal or disinterested value defined in opposition to the market, culture, art and education performed a vital role in securing the material, hence ultimately economic interests of the dominant class. These forms of 'symbolic capital' represented, alternately, 'survivals of' or 'returns to' modes of symbolic domination for which Kabylia's pre-capitalist gift economy provided the archetype, rather as Franz Boas's studies of potlatch among native North Americans had provided Thorstein Veblen with the model for his analyses of 'conspicuous consumption' among the American ruling classes at the turn of the century (Veblen 1912). From, broadly, the mid-1980s Bourdieu shifted his emphasis to insist that their distance from the market was not only what endowed these forms of symbolic capital with their socially distinctive function, but it was also, paradoxically, what guaranteed their universal value. In both cases, the market as such remained strangely under-theorized, figured somewhat monolithically as merely a realm of naked economic interests against which symbolic forms of capital defined themselves.

This chapter will argue that the lack of an adequate theorization of the market or of the relationship between it and the field of cultural production manifested itself in certain flaws both in Bourdieu's account of the emergence, in nineteenth-century France, of an autonomous field of artistic production in *The Rules of Art* and in his analysis of current threats to artistic autonomy in *Free Exchange*. The various policy proposals Bourdieu made throughout the course of his career regarding cultural provision and education, however, pointed towards a rather different understanding of the relationship between art, the market and the realm of practice. Here, as in his unrealized contribution to the Daniel Buren retrospective at the Pompidou Centre in 2002, Bourdieu had begun to sketch possible ways of theorizing the political force of art and the aesthetic in a manner which related more closely to the aestheticized structures of habitus and practice. This chapter will therefore argue that these policy proposals and that unrealized contribution offer a series of more subtle and nuanced reflections on the relationships between the realms of art and everyday practice than those found either in *The Rules of Art* or in Bourdieu's more directly political interventions on such matters.

The struggle for artistic autonomy

In *Free Exchange* Bourdieu argued that the incursion of market forces into the field of artistic production, manifest in the withdrawal of state subsidies and the consequent rise of corporate sponsorship, represented a kind of historical reversal. The creative autonomy gained by artists and writers over the centuries was under threat and we were witnessing a return to a system of patronage comparable to that of fifteenth-century Florence: 'we're in a situation very similar to that of the painters of the *Quattrocento*, who had to struggle to gain the freedom to choose if not the subject, at least the "manner"' (Bourdieu 1994: 24–5 [15]). This analogy seemed something of a hostage to fortune. After all, the very rigid forms of courtly and church patronage obtaining in fifteenth-century Florence produced some of what are generally considered to be the greatest works of Western art. There would therefore seem to be little reason to worry about the re-emergence of such forms of patronage in the contemporary era, quite the contrary. Indeed, this is precisely the argument of Lisa Jardine, herself the author of 'new history of the Renaissance' (Jardine 1996). She has compared the benign influence of the Medicis on Florentine art to that of Charles Saatchi on the 'Young British Art' of the 1980s and 1990s, concluding that both are inherently positive phenomena (Jardine 1997).

Although they draw diametrically opposed conclusions about the current state of art, Bourdieu and Jardine make the same mistake here in drawing a too hasty analogy between the forms of patronage in fifteenth-century Florence and those at work in a highly developed late capitalist economy. For, despite superficial appearances to the contrary, Charles Saatchi does not occupy a role that is directly equivalent to that of, say, Cosimo Medici. To suggest otherwise is to conflate the role of an advertising executive operating in the global artistic and media marketplace of the late twentieth century with a banker operating within the very different constraints, religious, cultural, economic, political, of an Italian renaissance city state. Such a conflation rests on a failure to acknowledge the historical specificity of the market conditions in which artists work in each case or the complex interactions between those market conditions and other cultural, political and religious institutions. Granted, Bourdieu's reference to the *Quattrocento* might have been intended to have no more than a general illustrative value. On the other hand, however, it might be read as just one symptom of a more general tendency to pay insufficient attention to the specificities of the market and of its changing modes of operation. One further symptom of this tendency might be found in the frequency with which Bourdieu invoked, in *Free Exchange* as elsewhere, the examples of nineteenth-century writers and artists as models or personifications of an artistic autonomy now threatened by the encroaching market.

These invocations of Flaubert, Baudelaire, Manet and Zola linked the concerns of Bourdieu's dialogue with Haacke in *Free Exchange* to his earlier analysis of the nineteenth-century literary and artistic fields in *The Rules of Art*. This study of the emergence of autonomous fields of artistic and literary production in late nineteenth-century France was also, as Bourdieu put it, an attempt 'to rediscover the forgotten or repudiated principles of intellectual freedom' by staging a

> return to the 'heroic times' of the struggle for independence, when virtues of revolt and resistance had to assert themselves clearly in the face of a repression exercised in all its brutality (especially during the [obscenity] trials [brought by the French state against Flaubert and Baudelaire]).
> (1992a: 76 [48])

Yet here again, problems of historical specificity seemed to arise. For the obscenity trials and *Salon* refusals to which Manet's, Flaubert's and Baudelaire's work fell victim were all the result of state-sponsored institutions acting at the purely national level. The judiciary and the Académie sought to censure and censor the work of such artists in defence of national morality, of the political regime of the Second Empire, of a particular conception of the French nation and how it should be represented. The threats to artistic autonomy that Haacke's work seeks to spotlight and challenge, however, obey a rather different logic; these relate to the operations of multinational corporate sponsors, who have no moral values, other than those which best serve the accumulation of profit, and who subsidize art as part of their global marketing strategies. As Jane Mayo Roos points out, in the preface to her study of the conditions of artistic production in late nineteenth-century France, there are dangers inherent in returning to founding moments of modernist rupture with the aesthetic consensus as though they held the solution to the art world's contemporary problems:

> We seem to repeat over and over again key episodes of modernist failure – whether they be the difficulties of Courbet, Manet, or the Impressionists – each with a little feel-good lesson that plays well to a late twentieth-century audience. Confronted with the profound dislocations of the culture of the 1990s, we search through the past and, locating other moments when a public encountered the shock of revolutionary art, we offer ourselves the illusion of more courageous thought. The isolation of modernists as a failed avant-garde, engaged on a quest for 'pure' art, art for art's sake, seems nothing less than a solipsistically mythic inscription to free ourselves from the disturbing entanglements of money and painterly practice.
>
> (Roos 1996: xii)

Roos's comments are significant here because they imply that the temptation to idealize the era of Manet and the Impressionists reflects both a certain confusion in the face of the current relationship between art and the market and a failure to acknowledge the true nature of that relationship in nineteenth-century France. It will be necessary to keep these two possibilities in mind as we turn to examine in more detail Bourdieu's argument in *The Rules of Art*, questioning why he took artists like Manet, Flaubert and Baudelaire to personify artistic autonomy and to what extent they might offer practical models for current artistic production in an artistic field apparently dominated and distorted by commercial patrons and sponsors.

Bourdieu's argument in *The Rules of Art* can be summarized as follows: in their struggles against state censorship, in suffering obscenity trials or successive *Salon* refusals for refusing to meet the aesthetic criteria or conservative moral standards of the Second Empire, Manet, Flaubert and Baudelaire managed to establish the basis of artistic autonomy for all their fellow artists. Baudelaire famously published poems about drug-taking, lesbianism and prostitution. Flaubert scandalously wrote a novel about bourgeois adultery. Manet exhibited paintings that flaunted the academic conventions of painting, rejecting established hierarchies of subject matter and genre in favour of stark depictions of modern life. Collectively, they claimed the right of all artists to choose freely both the form and content of their work. In so doing, they refused what Bourdieu termed 'the temporal seductions' on offer to them. By refusing to conform to the existing tastes of the mass-market, they forewent immediate material reward. By challenging the moral and aesthetic standards upheld by the French state, they abandoned any prospect of immediate official recognition or state recompense.

Manet, Flaubert and Baudelaire hence acted as 'nomothetes'; they established the new *nomos* or law governing the operation of the field of artistic production, the new vision and division of that field. They were the catalysts behind the division of the artistic field into a 'field of restricted production', on the one hand, and a 'field of enlarged production', on the other. The field of restricted production represented 'an inverted economy' inasmuch as any writer or artist who experienced immediate commercial success would be subject to suspicion, accused of having compromised their artistic integrity to the unsophisticated demands of the mass-market, whose needs were catered to by the field of enlarged production. The more commercial success an artist enjoyed, the less specifically cultural capital he or she stood to accumulate. Commercial failure, in such circumstances, could paradoxically come to serve as proof of the artistic value of an artist's work. As Bourdieu put it: 'One is in fact in an economic world inverted: the artist can only triumph on the symbolic terrain by losing on the economic terrain (at least in the short run), and vice versa (at least in the long run)' (1992a: 123 [83]). Hence he argued that the 'symbolic revolution through which artists free themselves from bourgeois demand by refusing to recognize any master except their art produces the effect of making the market disappear' (1992a: 121 [81]).

If 'the market disappeared' in this field of restricted production, it was because success in that field, the ability to accumulate the specific form of symbolic capital on offer there, depended upon a collective refusal or denial of the naked economic interests that governed the operations of the market proper. In this, Bourdieu argued, the field of restricted production generated practices which belonged 'to the class of practices where the logic of the pre-capitalist society survives' (1992a: 211 [148]). Actual market imperatives or economic necessities came to bear on this restricted field only in a highly mediated and hence mitigated fashion. The expansion of formal education in the nineteenth century had produced an 'intellectual reserve army' of potential consumers of the new autonomous art forms. This educated *bohème*, unable to find posts in the state administration which reflected their educational qualifications, were drawn to the impoverished artistic milieus of Paris. Their expenditure on the products of the field of restricted production would have been insufficient to support the newly autonomous artists, had the latter not also been of bourgeois origin, able to rely on parental allowances and inherited rents to subsidize their art.

Finally, Bourdieu argued, in 'refusing' the 'temporal seductions' or immediate rewards offered either by the market or state institutions, Flaubert, Manet and Baudelaire refused to submit to any partial or particular financial or political interests. Thus their artistic practice and its products could lay claim to a universal value. When Zola published 'J'Accuse', intervening into directly political matters, he did so in the name of those universal values and with all the symbolic authority they conferred upon him (1992a: 464–5 [342]). Hence Bourdieu's call in *Free Exchange* for artists and intellectuals to resist any compromise with state or corporate sponsorship and follow 'the model invented by Zola' intervening in the world of politics with their 'own means and ends' and in the name of 'the autonomy of their universe' (1994: 38 [29]).

The first problem with this model of artistic autonomy and its relation to the political was its apparent tendency to efface the properly aesthetic force of artistic forms. What seemed to matter in Bourdieu's account was not *what artists produced*, the form or content of their paintings, poems or novels, but *the position within the artistic field from which they produced it*. Moreover, their artworks featured here as merely so many guarantees of their symbolic authority to intervene in the political field; any notion that those works might possess a political force related to their specifically aesthetic characteristics appeared to get lost here. This reflected a problem we have already identified in Bourdieu's field theory, namely the tendency to reduce any judgement regarding the inherent value of any product of a given field to a supposedly objective measurement of the position occupied within that field by the agent who produced it. The second problem related to Bourdieu's insistence that the universal value of an artist's work and, by extension, its potential political force were directly proportionate to his or her distance from the market. This account appeared peculiarly ill-suited to the particular case of Zola, a hugely successful novelist, who amassed a considerable fortune from book sales in the course of his career. What Bourdieu seemed to ignore was the possibility that an artist such as Zola might have gained his creative autonomy, in part at least, through the financial autonomy that large book sales brought. Further, it might be argued that 'J'Accuse' derived a considerable amount of its authority from Zola's status as successful novelist, his ability to address and speak in the name of his mass readership. In *The Rules of Art* Bourdieu did quote Zola's contention that 'money has emancipated the writer, money has created modern literature' (1992a: 136 [91]). Yet, as Ahearne notes, this was 'a rare concession', which could not easily be reconciled with Bourdieu's assertions elsewhere, that autonomy demanded artists adopt a principled distance from the market, that they work in a field of restricted production in which 'the market disappears'. As such, Bourdieu never adequately theorized the role that economic capital might play as a form of 'symbolic leverage' within an autonomous cultural field (Ahearne 2004: 75).

The market and the public sphere

A striking feature of Bourdieu's analyses in *The Rules of Art* was the absence of any detailed statistical information relating to the market for either novels, poetry or paintings in nineteenth-century France. Indeed, the only detailed statistics Bourdieu presented related to the sales figures between 1953 and 1969 of three postwar novels published by Editions de minuit (1992a: 204 [144]). As a result, the only definitions of the nineteenth-century market for cultural goods were negative ones; the restricted field of artistic production was defined merely in terms of what it was not, of its distance from or opposition to the nakedly economic logic of the market proper. This offered few insights into the actual functioning of the market for books and paintings in that period, of the income artists and authors derived from that market or of the contribution any such income might have made to their creative autonomy. This question of the relationship between income and autonomy was posed particularly acutely in the case of literature, in the struggles of authors from the late eighteenth into the nineteenth century to establish firm copyright laws, struggles which Bourdieu again did not analyse in detail. As Martha Woodmansee has demonstrated, in her analysis of the passing of copyright laws in late eighteenth-century Britain and Germany, authors could only lay claim to rights over their published work, and hence to a legally guaranteed share of the profits from book sales, by establishing the principle that they, as unique and autonomous creative geniuses, were the sole source of the ideas contained in their books. In the struggles over copyright law, the principle of artistic autonomy thus emerged not as the product of the *refusal* of the logic of the market, as Bourdieu would have it, but as the product of the desire to secure a share of the profits from that market (Woodmansee 1994).

Furthermore, as we have already indicated, for Zola too artistic autonomy was the result not of a refusal of the 'temporal seductions' of the market but of artists' increasing involvement in and control over the market and its financial rewards. For Zola, money was the key to artists gaining their autonomy from the patronage of state, church or aristocracy. As Zola put it in an essay on the relationship between art and money:

> And do you know what today should make us worthy and respected: it is money. It is foolish to declaim against money, which is a considerable social force [...]. And this dignity, this respect, and this extension of his [*sic*] person and his thoughts, to what does the writer owe it? To money, without any doubt. It is money, it is the gain legitimately realized through his works that has delivered him from all humiliating dependency, that has turned the former court jester, the former clown of the antechamber, into a free citizen, a man beholden to himself alone. With money he has dared to say everything, he has cast his critical eye everywhere, even on the king, without fearing the loss of his daily bread. Money has emancipated the writer, money has created modern literature.
>
> (1880: 200–1)

Journalism and the new mass media, identified by Bourdieu (1994: 28 [19]) as being primarily responsible for imposing a 'commercial logic' on previously autonomous artists and writers, played a vital role, according to Zola, in providing struggling writers with a source of income and hence autonomy. Zola had little time for those who bemoaned journalism's increasing influence: 'People cry out against journalism, accusing it of perverting literary youth, of distorting young talents. I have never been able to hear such complaints without smiling' (Zola 1880: 192). In the pamphlet he wrote in defence of his friend Manet, Zola drew an equivalent analogy between financial and creative autonomy, when, in his opening paragraph, he compared Manet to a respectable shopkeeper: 'The life of an artist, in our correct and civilised times, is that of a peaceful bourgeois, who paints pictures in the same way as others sell pepper behind their counter' (Zola 1866: 90).

Granted, in the case of Manet, there was a rhetorical element at play, as Zola employed this idealized image of bourgeois propriety to defend his friend against the accusations of depravity and immorality that paintings such as *Olympia* (1863) and *Déjeuner sur l'herbe* (1863) had elicited. Nonetheless, the choice of profession here, a shopkeeper or wholesaler selling a commodity, was surely not coincidental. For, as Michael Moriarty has shown, the attempts of Manet and the Impressionists to gain autonomy from the *Salon* and the Academy reflected less a refusal of the logic of the market than a renegotiation of their relations with that market. A state controlled system of patronage was replaced by what Moriarty terms the 'dealer-critic system'. Critics legitimated and publicized the work of new artists through their columns in the burgeoning mass-market press, while independent dealers served as the intermediaries between artists and the market. In both cases, artistic autonomy was secured by artists engaging with, rather than refusing, the logic of the market:

> the history of art in nineteenth-century France is thus the displacement of a hitherto dominant quasi-state institution from the centre of artistic production, which becomes regulated by a purer market structure, where the twofold mediation between painter and buyer is exercised by the dealer, operating on commercial principles, and the critic, who is inserted in the capitalist world of newspapers and periodicals.
>
> (Moriarty 1994: 20)

As we have already noted, in the course of *The Rules of Art* Bourdieu did make passing references both to the wealth Zola derived from his huge book sales and to his understanding of the interdependence of financial and creative autonomy. However, he never explained how this could be reconciled with his assertions that the field of restricted production was a realm in which 'the market disappeared' and that it was this distance from or refusal of the logic of the market that secured artistic autonomy. This prevented Bourdieu from grasping the relationships between artistic autonomy, the increasing commodification of cultural forms and the emergence of a 'public sphere', in the sense which Jürgen Habermas understands that term. Rather than refusing the logic of the market and retreating into a restricted field of production, as Bourdieu would have it, artists and writers at this period appear to have been attempting to address an emergent public sphere, bypassing older forms of patronage by recourse to the market. As Roos points out, the response of Manet and the Impressionists to the successive *Salon* refusals they suffered was to issue a series of pamphlets and petitions that appealed directly to the public as arbiters of artistic taste over the heads of the *Salon* jury. She suggests that this new relationship to the market and the burgeoning public sphere was mirrored in the specifically aesthetic characteristics of these painters' work, in their eschewal of consecrated subjects and styles in favour of the depiction of the public spaces of the street, the cabaret or the Seine outside Paris, the new spaces of conviviality and public leisure against the older subjects destined to glorify the established order of the Second Empire (Roos 1996: 83–132).

In *In Other Words*, Bourdieu did note that Manet's choice of subject matter, 'the representation of the contemporary world, men wearing top hats and carrying umbrellas, the urban landscape, in its ordinary triviality', represented 'a real symbolic revolution'. This 'symbolic revolution' might, moreover, be considered 'the revolution par excellence' since in flaunting all conventional intellectual and social hierarchies it had 'overturned mental structures' (1987: 177 [149]). However, this remark was never developed in *The Rules of Art* into an account of the symbolic force of the properly aesthetic characteristics of Manet's paintings. Rather the symbolic force Bourdieu attributed to artists in that study related not to the aesthetic characteristics of their work but to their position within the artistic field, to the autonomy artists gained by turning their backs on the broader public sphere. Against this account of a retreat into the rarefied field of restricted production, it might be argued that the artists and writers Bourdieu championed were involved in a series of attempts to engage with that burgeoning public sphere. Following Habermas's analysis of its emergence from the late eighteenth century on, that public sphere could be understood as comprising a number of related elements. First, the public sphere necessitated the elaboration of a shared sense of taste and aesthetic sensibility in the realm of arts and letters. Second, it rested on a new realm of rational–critical debate about political matters of the day, based on information circulated in a free, mass-market press. Third, it demanded the commodification of both that information and those artworks, their availability through the networks of the market, so that in the case of artworks, to quote Habermas, 'as commodities they became in principle generally accessible. They no longer remained components of the church's and court's publicity of representation' (Habermas 1962: 36). Hence, in Habermas's account the public sphere involves a particular articulation of aesthetics, reason and the market, the emergence of a space in which both what can be rationally justified and what conforms to a shared sensibility are publicized through the market to become a topic of public debate. It might be argued that the symbolic revolutions of Manet, Baudelaire and Flaubert conformed to just this pattern.

As Roos points out, when the Impressionists staged their first independent exhibition in 1874, they decided to group together into a 'société anonyme' or limited company, basing their founding charter on the bylaws of a bakers' organization. To quote Roos:

> The term 'société anonyme' is roughly equivalent to the American designation 'incorporated' or the British 'limited', and in its very nomenclature identified the group as something other than a circle of artistic 'friends'. The intent of the venture was commercial and selling artworks was the group's fundamental objective.
>
> (1996: 198)

Terry Eagleton has summarized this close and apparently paradoxical coincidence between creative autonomy and the commodification of art in the following terms:

> Art is now autonomous of the cognitive, ethical and political; but the way it came to be so is paradoxical. It became autonomous of them, curiously enough, by being *integrated* into the capitalist mode of production. When art

becomes a commodity, it is released from its traditional social functions within church, court and state into the anonymous freedom of the market place. [...] It is 'independent' because it has been swallowed up by commodity production.

(1990: 368)

Hence it would be possible to sketch an alternative account of the emergence of the figure of the autonomous artist in late nineteenth-century France, which did not rely on Bourdieu's notion of an 'ethical refusal' of the 'temporal seductions' of the market. Certainly, such an account would acknowledge that there was at this time a significant re-drawing of the relationships between art, the market and the forms of political or state power. However, this did not involve a straightforward refusal either of the market or of the judgement of the broader public. Rather this was a matter of the complex renegotiation of the relations between artists and the public sphere, which could involve appeals to the market as both a less partial arbiter of aesthetic taste and a source of economic autonomy from older forms of state, church or aristocratic patronage. This, in turn, might provide a new and better prism through which to consider current relations between artists and the market, to engage with the concerns expressed by Bourdieu in his dialogue with Haacke regarding the increasing reliance of the art world on corporate sponsorship.

For example, it might make us hesitate before rushing to condemn the so-called Young British Artists for their apparent accommodation with market forces, their alleged eagerness to curry favour with Charles Saatchi by producing sensationalist and superficial works. Such developments might be reinterpreted in less censorious terms as reflecting the attempts of a generation of artists to renegotiate their relationship with the market and the public sphere in the changed conditions of the 1980s and 1990s. Among the fundamental determinants of such changed conditions, we would have to include the massive postwar expansion in higher education and the consequently greatly enlarged potential audience for art, an audience for whom art appreciation is less a rarefied spiritual activity than a component part of the commodified realms of leisure and mass tourism. Second, it would be important to note the increased competition within the art world given the increased numbers of aspirant artists graduating from art schools, all competing for public recognition and scarce financial resources. Third, some account would have to be given of how such developments interacted with a more general aesthetic reaction against the high-minded seriousness of modernism or minimalism, which itself increasingly appeared to have been transformed into an academic canon as sterile and elitist as the Academicism of Second Empire France. All of these factors might finally be seen as having decisively influenced the Young British Artists' turn to the market and to techniques closer to the realms of the mass media and advertising than those of high art. Such a turn to the market and to sensationalist techniques could then be understood to have provided both a necessary source of financial autonomy and a riposte to the perceived elitism and sterility of high modernism, the market and an enlarged public again here being posited as less partial arbiters of aesthetic taste than an apparently hidebound art institution.

This alternative account of Young British Art in no way implies complacency in the face of the market's increasing dominance over the field of artistic production. As Habermas points out, the interrelationship between the market and the public sphere contains within it the seeds of that sphere's gradual decline, of the erosion of public debate in favour of the degraded currency of public relations, advertising and opinion polls (Habermas 1962). Yet it would surely be too hasty to take the rise of the Young British Artists, itself symptomatic of the more generalized incursion of the market into the art world, to be an unequivocal sign of the decline of a once vibrant, critical and autonomous artistic field. Rather these developments appear much more ambiguous than that and any assessment of their effects demands a properly dialectical grasp of their possibilities as well as their problems. For example, Saatchi's dominance of the British art scene in the 1980s and 1990s does appear to have allowed female artists such as Tracey Emin, Sam Taylor Wood and Rachel Whiteread to gain a prominence that the traditionally male-dominated institutions of the art world might otherwise have denied them. At a more general level, the transformation of art galleries into arms of the leisure and tourism industries has increased the size of the audience for art, even though that audience remains predominantly white, middle class and professional. In short, this is to follow Frederic Jameson in considering whether the erosion of the classically modernist distinction between the rarefied realm of art and the world of commerce, politics and everyday life might not contain the germs of a 'new radical cultural politics' (Jameson 1984: 85).

Grasping the potentially redemptive implications of any re-drawing of the boundary between art and commerce is surely particularly important in Bourdieu's case. Much of Bourdieu's work on art and culture had, of course, been devoted to uncovering the class interests that lay behind art's claim to occupy an autonomous or disinterested realm and to showing how it was precisely that claim to disinterested autonomy that allowed 'legitimate culture' to perform its function in reproducing and naturalizing class distinctions. Bourdieu's defence in his later career of those very values of autonomy and disinterest thus seemed problematic on two fronts. First, it appeared to overlook the contribution his earlier work might have made to creating a climate in which art's claim to autonomy was treated with suspicion and neo-liberal calls to 'open up' the art world to market forces appeared justifiable. Second, Bourdieu's attribution of a 'universal value' to art forms that, by his own definition, were accessible only to a privileged few seemed both inherently contradictory and unintentionally elitist. His preferred solution to this second problem was to call for 'the conditions of access to the universal' to be 'generalized', so that 'more and more people fulfil the necessary conditions for appropriating the universal for themselves'. This was to be achieved by means of a process of education, understood in classically French republican terms, inspired by the founders of the Third Republic (Bourdieu 1996c: 77 [66]).

Ultimately then, Bourdieu's solution to the incursion of the market into the artistic field was a reassertion of a classically modernist conception of autonomy, combined with a concerted programme of education to mitigate the socially distinctive effects of such autonomy. If 'legitimate culture' could be accumulated as 'cultural capital', it therefore appeared that this related less to the conditions in which its value was produced than to its unequal distribution. Hence Bourdieu did not call for a revolution in the mode of production of cultural value; he merely advocated a series of measures to help broaden access to such values. He did not advocate a revolution in the production of cultural value such that alternative cultural forms, produced by marginalized social groups and judged illegitimate as a result, might gain value and recognition. Nor did he attempt to imagine alternative modes of cultural production that might employ collaborative techniques and modern technologies to democratic or progressive effect. Rather he appeared to advocate the defence of both the most canonical art forms and a classically post-Romantic mode of autonomous artistic production.

One problem with Bourdieu's approach was his assumption that a defence of this classical notion of artistic autonomy necessarily ran counter to the interests of corporate art sponsors, whose increasing influence on the artistic field he bemoaned in *Free Exchange*. After all, it is only by virtue of art's claim to occupy an autonomous sphere, free of narrow political or economic interest, that corporate sponsors can profit by their association with the art world, passing off their pursuit of specific marketing goals as acts of disinterested philanthropy. Therefore, not only do corporate sponsors have a vested interest in promoting a certain conception of artistic autonomy, they also tend to withdraw their support from any more radical or overtly political art forms that might challenge that conception. This was a subject broached in *Free Exchange* by Haacke himself, in his discussion of Jesse Helms's attempts to have the American National Endowment for the Arts remove its support from controversial artists like Robert Mapplethorpe and Andres Serrano. As Haacke explained, Helms was supported by a group of East Coast neo-liberal intellectuals close to the journal *New Criterion*. Sharing neither the cultural nor the moral values of a Christian fundamentalist like Helms, these intellectuals supported his campaign by demanding that the universal values of the art world, its autonomy and disinterestedness, be preserved from the narrow political agendas they alleged left-wing artists like Mapplethorpe and Serrano were promoting (Bourdieu 1994: 55–6 [47–8]).

In this instance, a defence of artistic autonomy and disinterest enabled an unholy alliance to be forged between the Christian Right, neo-liberal intellectuals and corporate sponsors, an alliance which sought, sometimes tacitly, sometimes explicitly, to discourage the production of radical, innovative or challenging art forms. Haacke's awareness of the extraordinary ambivalence of the notion of artistic autonomy is evident in his own artistic practice. As Jameson points out, this involves the adoption of a 'homeopathic' strategy, the integration into Haacke's own works of 'the arms and weapons specific' to the worlds of commerce and advertising in a critique of those worlds that obeys a logic rather different to that of the principled, critical distance of modernist art (in Wallis ed. 1986: 38–50). Moreover, as Bourdieu noted in passing, Haacke's formal techniques bear a remarkable similarity to the kind of 'discursive montage', the mixture of text, photographs, graphs, newspaper clippings, he himself employed in his sociological studies, notably *Distinction*, a formal technique Bourdieu hoped might mitigate the exclusive or elitist character of his own work (1994: 110 [106]). This offered the possibility of relating the aesthetic efficacy of Haacke's work to the political implications contained in Bourdieu's sociological studies. Further, inasmuch as Bourdieu's discursive montages could be seen as attempts to capture that process whereby a range of discourses and practices were incorporated into the affective and aesthetic structures of the habitus, this might offer the possibility of thinking the relationship between aesthetics and politics at that more practical level, of elaborating a practical aesthetics and theorizing its political potential.

Towards a practical aesthetics

Although clearly sharing a concern at the influence of corporate sponsorship over the art world, Bourdieu and Haacke did seem to advocate rather different models of artistic practice in the course of their discussions in *Free Exchange*. Where Bourdieu invoked a nineteenth-century tradition of artistic autonomy personified by Flaubert, Manet, Baudelaire and Zola, Haacke himself cited representatives of the early twentieth-century avant-garde, Marcel Duchamp, John Heartfield and Alexander Rodchentko, as possible antecedents. According to Peter Bürger's definition, in his seminal study *Theory of the Avant-garde*, these latter artists formed part of the 'historical avant-garde'; their work distinguished itself from modernist painting and its claims to autonomy by employing techniques such as collage and photomontage to challenge the organicity of the work of art and the artist's claim to autonomous creation. The work of the 'historical avant-garde', according to Bürger, criticized the 'art institution' for the idealism of its pretension to stand at a distance from the everyday and the material, aiming finally to destroy that distance by reintegrating art into the praxis of life (Bürger 1984).

Haacke's own work typically employs the techniques of this 'historical avant-garde'. He uses collage and photomontage, incorporating the iconography and discourse of advertising, public relations and the literature of corporate sponsorship into the form and content of his pieces. By focusing on specific instances of corporate art sponsorship, he is able to highlight the cynical use to which art sponsorship is put, uncovering the exploitative commercial practices that corporate sponsors seek to conceal behind the appearance of disinterested philanthropy. In this sense, he could be seen as supplementing a classically avant-garde assault on the art institution with a critique of the increasing commercialization of the art world. Moreover, Haacke's work aims not merely to exert an effect on the solitary viewer. Rather, his most effective works have been widely reported in the mass media, so that the good PR corporate sponsors hoped to gain from their association with the art world is nullified by the publicity Haacke's work gives to their unscrupulous business practices. Hence Haacke's work does not stand at a principled distance from the commercialized domain of advertising, public relations and the mass media. On the contrary, he exploits the resources contained within that domain, using the mass media and the threat of bad public relations in an effort to shame corporate sponsors into changing their business practices. As Haacke put it in *Free Exchange*, it was important to 'learn a lot from advertising' and desirable to have one's work entirely recuperated by the mass media and PR industries: 'the most profound effect one can have is to be totally recuperated' (Bourdieu 1994: 111, 115 [107, 117]). This is what Jameson describes as the 'homeopathic' strategy adopted by Haacke.

Haacke's own artistic practice thus seems to obey a rather different logic from the strategy, advocated by Bourdieu, of standing at a principled distance from the market in an assertion of autonomy that guaranteed the universal value of an artist's work. Indeed, Haacke's works do not appear to lay claim to universality in the sense Bourdieu understood it. On the contrary, they seem to constitute a series of specific interventions with an explicitly polemical intent, each addressed to particular instances and abuses of corporate sponsorship. It is surely its specificity and particularity that explains Cynthia Freeland's negative assessment of Haacke's work as 'too preachy' and 'ephemeral', risking 'losing its punch when the context alters', and hence not qualifying as genuinely universal art (Freeland 2001: 113). If Haacke's pieces eschew conventional claims to universality, this does not prevent them from having an aesthetic force. His message is not communicated at the cognitive level alone, through the factual information about the art institution, corporate sponsorship and the practices of multinational corporations his pieces typically incorporate. Rather, these montages and installations, incorporating PR statements, press clippings, company reports and promotional material for commercially sponsored art exhibitions, work on the aesthetic level also; they jolt viewers out of their attitude of disinterested contemplation, forcing them to draw previously unconsidered connections between the gallery in which they find themselves, the art institution as a whole, its sources of revenue and the operations of multinational art sponsors. As Ahearne puts it, Haacke's works function by 'applying shock treatment' to the habitus of the art appreciating public (Ahearne 2004: 73).

It was this ability to deliver a jolt to the habitus, to intervene at the level of the symbolic and subvert the forms of symbolic domination employed by the advertising and PR industries, that Bourdieu singled out for special praise in *Free Exchange*. He argued that Haacke's work constituted a series of 'symbolic machines' which indicated 'the direction artists and intellectuals should look to give their critical actions a true symbolic efficacy' (Bourdieu 1994: 29–30 [20–1]). As we have noted, Bourdieu suggested there was a parallel between the techniques Haacke employed to achieve this symbolic effect and his own adoption of a style he termed 'discursive montage' in the articles published in his own journal, *Actes de la recherche en sciences humaines*, a style that had been employed most extensively in the text of *Distinction* (1994: 110 [106]). Unfortunately, the English translation of *Distinction* does not really do justice to this 'discursive montage' since the quality of the reproduced photographs and press clippings is poor and the range of colours and typefaces used in the original French text considerably reduced. However, in its original version *Distinction* combined the statistical analysis and textual commentary expected of a conventional sociological study with a collage of other texts, personal testimonies, excerpts from magazines and newspapers, advertisements and fragments of high literature or philosophical treatises. These diverse elements were set off from the main body of the text by being placed in distinct boxes and through the use of different shadings and typefaces. Like the artistic montage from which it took its name, this discursive montage worked to rupture and dislocate the smooth flow of Bourdieu's discourse by introducing a mass of heterogeneous material, fragments of the real as it were, into the main body of text.

One way of understanding the functioning of this discursive montage would be by analogy with Mikhail Bakhtin's concept of the 'polyphonic' novel. For Bakhtin, a polyphonic novel was a novel which incorporated into its narrative a variety of conflicting 'speech genres', of the different modes of speech and idiolects employed by different social classes. Fragments of these speech genres, integrated directly into the narrative, would become 'dialogized' by their interrelationships both with one another and with the authorial discourse that framed them. In this way, a typically bourgeois mode of speech would become, as Bakhtin put it, not 'the *primary means of representation*' but rather 'an *object* of representation' (Bakhtin 1981: 44). Torn from its original context and juxtaposed with fragments of working-class speech, an example of bourgeois speech would thus be relativized and dialogized, revealed to be merely one representative of a 'polyphony' of competing voices and speech genres, each expressing conflicting social, cultural and political values. The range of conflicting voices, discourses and images incorporated into the text of *Distinction* might be understood to function according to an analogous logic. These were not so much integrated directly into the main body of the text, as in Bakhtin's polyphonic novel, as framed off in clearly demarcated boxes. However, as Bourdieu pointed out, this device had the effect of 'changing completely the status of the text or document; what used to be the object of an ordinary somewhat distracted reading can suddenly take on an astonishing, even scandalous appearance' (Bourdieu 2002: 375). The process of framing-off thus necessarily achieved a kind of critical, even ironic, distance on the conflicting speech genres Bourdieu incorporated into the text of *Distinction*. Further, the reader's interpretation of these various speech genres was inevitably mediated by the rhetorical intention of Bourdieu's own commentary, around which they were placed and whose smooth flow they disrupted. For example, by being framed within an authorial discourse that sought to historicize the values contained in the legitimate discourse of aesthetics, fragments of that discourse intended by their authors to be taken at face value were thus parodied and relativized by being led back to the narrow social interests they were ultimately revealed to express.

The technique of discursive montage employed by Bourdieu, notably in *Distinction*, was thus clearly intended to work simultaneously at the practical and the theoretical, the aesthetic and the cognitive, levels. The heterogeneous materials he incorporated in his text reproduced, at the practical level, the discursive injunctions, patterns of speech and embodied practices incorporated into the class determined structures of the habitus. Yet the formal arrangement of those materials also worked to de-naturalize that process of incorporation, to make its socially arbitrary nature both understood and felt and to deliver a jolt to the habitus at both the practical and theoretical levels. In a telling comment in *Free Exchange*, Bourdieu compared both Haacke's work and his own use of discursive montage to Kabyle oral poetry, a poetry which worked on a number of levels, from the practical to the esoteric, to achieve effects at once aesthetic and cognitive (1994: 110 [106]).

As Ahearne has demonstrated, this attempt to combine the aesthetic with the cognitive, the practical with the theoretical, was mirrored in the proposals Bourdieu made regarding public policy on culture and education from the mid-1980s onwards. Moreover, as Ahearne argues, this emphasis on practical knowledge and education meant that Bourdieu was not advocating educational policies that would look 'simply to distribute more equitably the products of legitimate culture', rather he was promoting policies that 'would also work to reconfigure that culture itself', by recognizing previously devalued practical knowledge, tastes and aptitudes (Ahearne 2004: 61). In this context, Ahearne quotes the report on the future principles of French education that Bourdieu and his fellow professors at the Collège de France published at the request of François Mitterrand in 1985. In that report, Bourdieu and his co-authors called for a 'revocation of the prevailing hierarchies' in the domain of arts education through a style of teaching in which 'discourse' was 'subordinated to practice' and not only 'fine arts' but also 'the applied arts' would be valued, 'for example graphic arts, the arts associated with publishing and advertising, industrial aesthetics, audio-visual arts, and photography' (quoted in Ahearne 2004: 62). Ahearne goes on to show how Bourdieu pursued this attempt to mitigate the distance between formal and practical modes of education in the two petitions he published in 1988 and 1990, calling for French state TV channels to end their dependence on advertising revenue. At the core of Bourdieu's work on education had been his insistence that it was not so much the explicit content of formal education that was biased in favour of the dominant class as the implicit values and modes of knowledge that the education system recognized and rewarded; it was these values that were in accord with the practical dispositions picked up by the children of bourgeois parents through being brought up in a cultured, literate environment. In this sense, any reform to formal education could only have a limited effect in mitigating class distinctions since such a reform would not significantly reduce the determining force of that broader cultural and social environment. Bourdieu's calls to improve the quality of cultural and educational TV in France, by removing state TV's reliance on the advertising market, can be seen as an attempt to influence the broader cultural climate in which all French children grew up. Quality educational and cultural programming, broadcast through a mass medium, could form part of a policy that allied formal education to attempts to shape the practical dispositions, the habitus of all French citizens. Moreover, the details of the proposals put forward by Bourdieu and his co-signatories exemplified the role he saw the state playing in limiting the dominance of the market over the cultural field. The state was to provide public TV channels with an autonomous revenue stream by levying a tax on all media advertising revenues but was not to interfere directly in those channels' programming policies or broadcast output. Hence the state would establish the general financial and legislative framework within which cultural producers could then operate autonomously (Ahearne 2004: 64–6; Bourdieu 1988c, 1990d). This was an attempt to negotiate what Bourdieu identified as one of the 'antinomies of cultural policy', namely the fact that the most autonomous cultural forms were in most need of public subsidy, yet reliance on the state for such subsidy risked artists swapping subservience to market imperatives for subordination to the state's political agenda (Bourdieu 1994: 23 [13]).

These attempts to imagine forms of cultural practice and policy that would harness the properly aesthetic qualities or symbolic force of art, while seeking to relate that symbolic force to the aestheticized practical dispositions of the habitus, culminated in Bourdieu's unrealized project for an installation at the retrospective exhibition of Daniel Buren's work at the Pompidou Centre in 2002. Bourdieu proposed to arrange a selection of quotations regarding art, artists and Buren's work especially, on the facing walls of a room in the Pompidou. These quotations would be selected to exemplify three contrasting levels of interpretation of art and the art world. The first set of quotations would correspond to 'received ideas' about art; black text against a dark background on the room's western wall, these would represent what Bourdieu termed 'Beholder 1: *vox populi*'. The second set of quotations, inscribed on the grey-coloured north-western wall, would reproduce a series of 'glosses and glossalia', corresponding to 'Beholder 2: level of the critics'. A third set of quotations, on the light-coloured eastern wall, corresponded to the 'reflexive level' of 'Beholder 3', reproducing selected excerpts from the sociology of art. On the north-eastern wall would be projected footage of an actor reading a variety of quotations from 'Beholders' 1, 2 and 3. Finally, the ceiling would contain a painting by Errò, *The Background of Pollock* (1967), which attempted to represent Jackson Pollock's artistic habitus by juxtaposing an image of Pollock's head with reproductions of canonical modernist paintings by Van Gogh, Dali, Mondrian, Picasso and others. This would constitute a 'short-cut, in picture form', summarizing the prior knowledge of the history of art that appreciating Pollock's work demanded (Bourdieu 2002b: C85).

In his project for the Buren exhibit, Bourdieu thus appeared to be attempting to produce an installation that followed the same logic as the discursive montage he employed to such effect in *Distinction*. These different levels of discourse on art were to be set off one from another both by the different shades of the walls on which they were inscribed and by their different typefaces, in a manner which recalled the textual presentation of the heterogeneous texts incorporated in *Distinction*. Further, Bourdieu specified that 'the quotations on the three walls (of three levels: Beholders 1, 2, and 3), by means of techniques of graphics and presentation, should respond to one another: 2 responds to 1 and 3 responds to 2' (2002b: C85). Just as in *Distinction*, a Parisian advertising executive commenting on the required dress sense at his agency 'responded' to the Chevalier de Méré's 1677 discourse on manners, which themselves 'responded' to the Kantian discourse on aesthetics, so here the various levels of discourse on art would enter into dialogic relations with one another. Moreover, Bourdieu requested that 'the disposition of the walls' on which these discourses would be displayed should 'reproduce the disposition of the walls in the Kabyle house' (2002b: C85). The disposition of the walls in the Kabyle house had, of course, corresponded to a series of gendered oppositions between light and dark, masculinity and femininity, the worlds of work and of domesticity. In his famous essay on the Kabyle house, Bourdieu had argued that the Kabyles internalized the social and political imperatives contained in such overdetermined oppositions not through explicit or formal education but rather by picking them up, incorporating them into their habitus at the practical level, 'on the hither side of words and discourse'. His planned installation at the Buren retrospective could be seen as an attempt to harness these practical, aesthetic modes of learning to his own project in the sociology of art and culture, to combine the intellectual content of his sociological studies with the symbolic force proper to the realm of aesthetics in the name of a progressive or at least ameliorative cultural politics. As Bourdieu put it:

> Artists possess an extraordinary force, that which consists, amongst other things, of making intelligible things sensible. It seems to me – and this is very naïve – that for any liberating action an alliance of the genius specific to artists and [sociological] analysis could produce extraordinary effects.
> (2002b: C82)

It would indeed be naïve to suppose that Bourdieu's project for the Buren exhibit or his cultural policy proposals could solve at a single stroke all of the problems of class distinction and elitism in relation to art and culture. Bourdieu himself never made any such claim. However, in some of the undeveloped comments in his dialogue with Haacke in *Free Exchange*, as in the Buren project and his policy proposals, he did begin to open up some fruitful avenues of enquiry, suggesting ways of relating the symbolic force of art to the aesthetic structures of the habitus, of mitigating the cultural and social obstacles to forms of art appreciation more integrated into everyday practice. In this sense, these aspects of Bourdieu's work seem more productive than did his attempts in *The Rules of Art* to 'rediscover the forgotten or repudiated principles' of artistic autonomy personified by a range of nineteenth-century French artists. As this chapter has attempted to demonstrate, such invocations of a lost era of artistic and intellectual autonomy risked not only lapsing into nostalgia but also idealizing the extent of those artists' alleged 'refusal' of the logic of the market. Bourdieu's own use of discursive montage, his championing of the work of Haacke, his project for the Buren retrospective seemed, on the contrary, to offer the possibility of developing what Richard Shusterman terms a 'somaesthetics', provisionally defined as 'the critical, meliorative study of the experience and use of one's body as a locus of sensory-aesthetic appreciation and creative self-fashioning' (Shusterman 2000: 267).

Shusterman's 'somaesthetics' is the culmination of a 'pragmatist aesthetics' that takes from Bourdieu an attentiveness to the ways in which the body is aesthetically fashioned in society. It implies an increased openness to and education in the ethical, social and critical potential of high art. Yet it also demands an awareness of the aesthetic characteristics of everyday practice and a recognition of the aesthetic value of popular and mass cultural forms, 'an opening of the concept of art to include popular arts' like jazz, funk or rap (Shusterman 2000: 140). It was this final suggestion that provoked Bourdieu's criticism of Shusterman's *Pragmatist Aesthetics*, arguing that such a project amounted to a dangerous populism, which ignored the strength of those mechanisms that worked to deny popular art any legitimacy (see Shusterman 2000: 314 n.5). As we have shown, Bourdieu preferred to imagine ways to 'universalize access' to a realm of universal values elaborated in an artistic field defined by its opposition to the market and hence to the popular. This conception of the relationship between autonomy, distance from the market and the universal was by no means limited to Bourdieu's writings on art and culture. On the contrary, Bourdieu's political interventions were characterized by calls for the autonomy, and hence the universal values, of a whole range of semi-autonomous fields to be defended against the incursions of the market and the particular interests of neo-liberal politicians. Chapter 7 turns to look at this discourse of universalism in Bourdieu's work, examining in more detail its theoretical foundations as well as its potential strengths or weaknesses at the level of practical politics.

7 Universalism and the elusive public sphere

Bourdieu chose to illustrate the front cover of *Free Exchange* with a photograph of a piece by his co-author Hans Haacke, entitled *Calligraphy*. *Calligraphy* was Haacke's unsuccessful entry into a competition organized in 1989 to design a permanent sculpture to be placed in the courtyard of the Palais Bourbon, the home of the French National Assembly, the lower house of the French parliament. The sculpture was intended to commemorate the bicentenary of the French Revolution and hence of the Assembly's foundation. A central feature of Haacke's unsuccessful design was a large conical fountain, from whose apex water spilled down over the embossed legend 'Liberté, Egalité, Fraternité', translated and transcribed into Arabic script. The translation of the classically French republican slogan 'Liberté, Egalité, Fraternité' into Arabic was a clear act of provocation, inviting us to reflect on the relationship between such apparently universalist, egalitarian ideals and the status actually accorded Moslems within the French Republic, both in the past and now.

Calligraphy reminded us that during her colonial rule over North Africa, for example, France had systematically excluded Arabs and Moslems from its citizenry, all the while proclaiming adherence to those same universal, republican values. By extension, Haacke's piece raised the question of the status of France's current Moslem populations, of the discrimination, social exclusion and marginalization which a significant proportion of them continue to suffer. In short, *Calligraphy* raised the possibility that the egalitarian ideals of French republicanism might always have been based on a *false* universalism, a universalism which, historically, had functioned by excluding those social groups or categories it considered incapable of embodying the universal, a universalism which continued to this day to repeat that exclusionary gesture in its treatment of minority groups and cultures. To raise such a possibility was not necessarily to abandon all reference to universal ideals in favour of what, in a somewhat caricatural manner, might be termed a postmodern celebration of difference, a benevolent but ill-conceived multiculturalism or cultural relativism, according to which the most repressive of social practices would be justified in the name of respect for cultural difference.[1] Indeed, as Slavoj Žižek has pointed out, 'when we criticize the hidden bias and exclusion of universality, we should never forget that we are already doing so *within* the terrain opened up by universality'. In other words, any critique of *false* universalism necessarily involves an appeal to an ideal of the *genuinely universal* and should therefore lead not to a retreat to 'the standpoint of pre-universal particularism' but rather to a reconceptualization of the universal in more authentic, inclusive form (in Butler *et al.* 2000: 102). This, then, is the final provocation of Haacke's *Calligraphy*; it challenges us to imagine the possible forms that a more inclusive universalism might take.

All of the questions raised by Haacke's piece were, of course, of direct relevance to Bourdieu's own theory and practice of politics. As we have seen, in his political pronouncements Bourdieu frequently adopted a classically French republican rhetoric, identifying the French Third Republic as 'nearly an exact incarnation' of a state which embodied universal ideals (Bourdieu 1998b: 20), calling, in his petition in support of the strikers of 1995, for the defence of 'the universal gains of the Republic' (see Duval *et al.* 1998: 68), encouraging his fellow intellectuals to follow 'the model invented by Zola' in their political engagements (Bourdieu 1994: 38 [29]) and invoking the vision of education propounded by 'the founders of the French Republic in the late nineteenth century' as a means of generalizing access to the 'universal' achievements of science, art and culture (Bourdieu 1996c: 77 [66]). Such trenchant statements of allegiance to French republican universalism were not, however, unqualified. Thus, in *Acts of Resistance*, Bourdieu explicitly sought to distance himself from what he termed 'the false universalism of the West', an 'imperialism of the universal', of which France had been 'the supreme incarnation' (1998: 25 [19]). In *Pascalian Meditations*, meanwhile, he criticized the tendency to condemn all political demands made 'on the basis of a stigmatised particularity (women, gays, blacks, etc.)', in the name of an 'abstract universalism' which merely served 'to justify the established order, the prevailing distribution of powers and privileges – the domination of the bourgeois, white Euro-American heterosexual male'.[2] At the same time, he rejected what he termed 'the sceptical or cynical rejection of any form of belief in the universal', which he argued was merely another way 'in a sense a more dangerous one, because it can give itself an air of radicalism, of accepting things as they are' (Bourdieu 1997c: 86 [71]).

Hence Bourdieu set himself the task of elaborating a concept of the universal that would avoid reproducing the exclusions and disavowed particularisms of an older, false universalism, without lapsing into the cultural and moral relativism, which he feared, would necessarily follow from any straightforward repudiation of universalism. In *Pascalian Meditations*, he argued that this task could be achieved by overcoming the opposition between 'the two so-called "modern" and "postmodern" movements', personified by Jürgen Habermas and Michel Foucault, respectively. For Bourdieu, Habermas's notion of the 'ideal speech situation' rested on 'an irenic vision' of social communication, shorn of its constitutive antagonisms and differences of class position; Habermas's was thus a universalism which risked disavowing or effacing such differences. Foucault's analyses of power, on the other hand, while 'attentive to the microstructures of domination and to the strategies involved in the struggle for power', tended to 'exclude universals and, in particular, the search for any universally acceptable morality' (Bourdieu 1997c: 128–31 [106–11]). As an alternative to these opposing conceptions, Bourdieu elaborated his own notion of a 'corporatism of the universal', according to which universal ethical, aesthetic and rational values were understood as products of the historically determined conflicts and struggles between given agents and groups pursuing their own particular or corporate interests. In this way, the universal was seen to be produced by, rather than being antithetical to, the conflicts, contradictions and antagonisms which were constitutive elements of any polity and society.

For example, in Chapter 6, we saw that, for Bourdieu, artists and writers could produce work of universal value while pursuing their own particular or corporate interests in accumulating symbolic capital within the field of cultural production. This paradoxical situation, where pursuit of particular or corporate interests would contribute to 'the advance of the universal', could only happen as long as the autonomy of that field from political or economic interests was secured and maintained. Bourdieu extended this model to cover a range of other semi-autonomous fields: from the field of state bureaucracy to the intellectual field and the field of science. In each case, he argued that safeguarding the autonomy of those fields from the 'heteronomous' forces of politics and the market would ensure that their participants could only advance their own particular interests by acting in conformity with the universal ideals of, respectively, public service, intellectual enquiry or scientific experimentation and verification. However, Bourdieu's conviction that this account of the universal could escape the pitfalls of a false universalism, without lapsing into relativism, seemed to be belied by its unintended elitism.

By Bourdieu's own account, to produce art of universal value required that artists renounce immediate economic reward in favour of the symbolic profits on offer in the restricted field of cultural production. In *The Rules of Art*, he had argued that it was only those nineteenth-century artists blessed with sufficient inherited wealth who were able to subsidize their uneconomic artistic activities in this way, hence implying that only the relatively wealthy could produce art of universal value. Further, in *Distinction* and elsewhere, Bourdieu had argued that the capacity to appreciate the products of an autonomous field of artistic production required the adoption of 'the scholastic point of view,' and the leisurely attitude of contemplative distance on the world that enabled one to suspend all considerations of function and to appreciate an artwork as a thing of beauty in and of itself. This scholastic attitude, he had insisted, was the preserve and privilege of the bourgeoisie, contingent upon possession of sufficient wealth to suspend all question of practical utility and to secure one's distance from the realm of material necessity. By Bourdieu's own account, therefore, the capacity either to produce or to appreciate artwork of universal aesthetic value was contingent upon a certain material well-being. Indeed, this precondition would also apply to the ability to formulate and articulate universal truths in the intellectual and scientific fields. As Bourdieu put it in *Pascalian Meditations*, 'the suspension of economic and social necessity is what allows the emergence of autonomous fields'; a certain distance from material necessity was thus the precondition for the emergence of any autonomous field in which universal values could then be elaborated. Hence such universal values were understood to be 'universal acquisitions made available by an exclusive privilege'. Therein, Bourdieu concluded, lay 'the fundamental ambiguity of scholastic universes and all of their productions' (Bourdieu 1997c: 27 [15]).

Bourdieu's 'corporatism of the universal' thus risked proving just as exclusive as the false universalism it sought to replace. He had located the universal within a specific and avowedly 'exclusive' realm, one or other of the series of autonomous fields. He had then argued that possession of sufficient material resources was the precondition for contributing to or appreciating the universal values produced there. The possibility that universal values might be elaborated anywhere outside these, by Bourdieu's own definition, 'exclusive' and 'privileged' realms, in the discussions, debates and activities of ordinary citizens, seemed to be overlooked here. Rather, in his lectures on the sociology of science, Bourdieu argued that it was the very 'self-enclosure of the autonomous field' which constituted 'the historical principle of the genesis of reason and of the exercise of its normativity' (Bourdieu 2001b: 108 [54]). This appeared to ignore the possibility that ordinary citizens who were not scientists, intellectuals or artists, who did not participate in a self-enclosed autonomous field, might be capable of expressing opinions that laid legitimate claim to rationality, universality and normativity. As we noted in Chapter 6, what seemed to be missing from Bourdieu's conception of the universal was any notion of a public sphere, any theorization of a democratic arena in which the opinions and wishes of ordinary citizens might be expressed and debated, feeding in to decisions regarding the values and policies to be pursued in a given society and polity.

Bourdieu's notion of the universal thus raised important questions concerning the level of rationality he attributed to the opinions of ordinary agents and, as a consequence, the extent to which his social theory allowed for some kind of public sphere or democratic arena in which those opinions could be voiced and taken into account. These questions were raised in concrete form by two of Bourdieu's later and most explicitly political works, *The Weight of the World* and *On Television and Journalism*. The main body of *The Weight of the World* was taken up with transcriptions of interviews Bourdieu and his team of sociologists carried out with a range of informants whose personal experience was taken to epitomize the destructive social effects of the neo-liberal policies of French and US governments alike. These testimonies were explicitly intended to have a political effect; 'able to touch and to move the reader, to speak to their emotions', they aimed to politicize the reader by rendering 'tangible [*sensibles*]' the 'objective structures that scientific work strives to expose' (Bourdieu 1993: 922 [623]). The testimonies also raised the question of the level of validity or rationality Bourdieu was prepared to accord to the opinions of ordinary agents, as against specialized scientists, artists or intellectuals.

Some of the interviewees in *The Weight of the World* were supporters of the racist FN or expressed racist views, while others belonged to France's Moslem minority. This meant that at certain points, the question of the apparent *social* exclusivity of Bourdieu's universalism intersected with the question of that universalism's openness to the specificities of race and ethnicity, specificities which French universalism has traditionally had difficulties accommodating. *The Weight of the World* can thus serve as a useful test case for examining Bourdieu's claims to have avoided the pitfalls of a false universalism. Finally, the testimonies contained in *The Weight of the World* can be read as expressions of Bourdieu's desire to give a voice to groups too often marginalized or ignored by professional politicians and the mass media and hence to extend and revivify the realm of democratic debate. Such a desire was also evident in his critique, in *On Television*, of the way French television treated representatives of striking workers in autumn 1995. Read alongside *The Weight of the World*, *On Television* will prove important in any assessment of how Bourdieu reconciled this desire to allow marginalized groups to have a voice with a theory of universalism that appeared, a priori, to deny any universal validity to their thoughts and opinions. This chapter will therefore start by examining in more detail Bourdieu's theorization of the universal in later texts such as *Practical Reason* and *Pascalian Meditations*. It will then move on to examine how that theory of the universal was worked out in practice in both *The Weight of the World* and *On Television*, focusing on the questions of the apparent exclusivity of Bourdieu's universalism, the seemingly under-theorized role of democratic debate in his social theory, and his openness to questions of race and ethnicity.

The two universals

Haacke's piece *Calligraphy* did not merely appear on the front cover of *Free Exchange*. It was also reproduced within the text itself at a point in their dialogue where Haacke and Bourdieu were discussing the way in which various neo-conservative groups in the US had sought to combat attempts to bring a measure of multicultural awareness into the domains of art and education by invoking the necessity to defend certain 'universal' values of Western civilization. Bourdieu suggested that a similar phenomenon could be observed in France in 'the much more disguised form of a critique of cultural relativism', typified by studies such as Alain Finkielkraut's *La Défaite de la pensée* (1987) or by Alain Renaut and Luc Ferry's 1985 book *La Pensée 68: essai sur l'anti-humanisme contemporain*. Both these books have been criticized for their nostalgic, even reactionary, laments for the passing of an age of more certain, 'universal' French republican values in the face of an increasingly multi-ethnic French society (Forbes and Kelly, eds 1995: 258–63; Lyotard and Rogozinski 1986).

Rejecting the kind of universalism advocated by Finkielkraut, Ferry and Renaut for being based on 'the absolutization and naturalization of a historical culture', Bourdieu sketched out his own conception of the universal, a universal understood as being based in some way on the particular:

> I will only say that there is no absolute, universal point of view, either in the universe of different societies, contemporary or from different epochs, or

even within a single society. There are, however, people who fight to impose their particular point of view as the universal point of view, and who, to that end, attempt to universalise their particular point of view (through which is affirmed, moreover, their recognition of the universal, quite often within the logic of the tribute that vice renders to virtue, but which really does contribute to the progress of the universal).

(Bourdieu 1994: 68 [62])[3]

This brief sketch of the principles behind the notion of the 'corporatism of the universal' was expanded upon in the section of *Practical Reason* devoted to an analysis of the bureaucratic field and the sections of *Pascalian Meditations* which examined 'the historicity of reason'. As we have already noted, Bourdieu's analysis of this issue rested on the assumption that the participants in each of the semi-autonomous fields of any differentiated society were necessarily involved in struggles to preserve or accumulate the particular forms of 'capital' on offer in those fields. Thus participants in a given field necessarily pursued their own particular interests, seeking to accumulate or conserve their stock of capital, whether 'bureaucratic', 'scientific', 'cultural', 'political' or other. However, in order for scientists, for example, to accumulate scientific capital, it would be necessary for their work to conform to certain epistemological criteria guaranteeing the universal validity of their experimental procedures and systems of verification. Hence, in pursuing their particular interests in the preservation or accumulation of scientific capital, scientists had paradoxically to contribute to the progress of universal scientific truth. Similarly, Bourdieu argued, civil servants working in the bureaucratic field could only accumulate bureaucratic capital, that is could only pursue their particular career interests, by conforming to the universal ethical criteria of public service. An analogous process was at work in the fields of intellectual and artistic production also.

Bourdieu insisted that this process, whereby agents pursuing their particular interests within a specific field could nonetheless contribute to the progress of the universal, could only operate as long as each field retained its relative autonomy from, most notably, the fields of politics and the market. As soon as intellectuals, for instance, could pursue their particular interests by seeking the immediate 'temporal' rewards of celebrity and wealth that, say, the mass media might offer, the universal value of their work was threatened. The value of their work was no longer submitted to the autonomous criteria of judgement employed by their peers within the intellectual field but was legitimized in relation to the heteronomous criteria of fashion, accessibility or political acceptability that ruled over the field of the mass media. Hence, according to Bourdieu, the universal value of intellectual or artistic work was contingent upon securing a certain distance from the urgencies, both temporal and economic, of the market. The 'scholastic point of view', the attitude of leisurely distance on the social world whose distortions and social exclusivity Bourdieu had criticized in his work in anthropology and the sociology of culture, was nonetheless the precondition for contributing to the 'advance of the universal'. Hence his insistence in

Pascalian Meditations that highlighting 'the social conditions of the formation of the scholastic disposition' should not lead us to 'denigrate or condemn the mode of thought it makes possible', since this was 'at the origin of the rarest conquests of humanity' (Bourdieu 1997c: 63 [49]). As Bourdieu openly acknowledged, the fundamental ambiguity of his theory of the universal was that it located the universal in social fields to which access was both exclusive and privileged:

> If the universal advances, it is because there exist social microcosms which, despite their intrinsic ambiguity, linked to their enclosure in the privilege and the satisfied egotism of a separation by status, are the site of struggles in which the universal is at stake and in which agents having [. . .] *a particular interest in the universal*, in reason, in truth, in virtue, take up arms and fight with weapons which are nothing other than the most universal conquests of prior struggles.
>
> (1997c: 146 [123])

As we have already indicated, the fact that, by his own account, access to the universal was contingent upon privilege and social distinction represented a first major difficulty with Bourdieu's conception of the corporatism of the universal. His notion that certain professionals, working within enclosed autonomous fields, could contribute to universal values while pursuing their particular interests was clearly indebted to Hegel's description of the state bureaucracy in *The Philosophy of Right*. Hegel attributed to a state bureaucracy, composed of middle-class civil servants, the responsibility for enacting 'the absolutely universal interest of the state proper'. Civil servants, however, had, both individually and collectively, an interest in 'the assured satisfaction' of their 'particular interests', in securing their 'livelihood'. By ensuring that continued tenure of any post was 'conditional' on a civil servant 'fulfilling his [*sic*] duties', the state could guarantee that civil servants should 'forgo the selfish and capricious satisfaction of their subjective ends', finding 'their satisfaction in, but only in, the dutiful discharge of their public functions'. A tenured post in the state bureaucracy not only prevented civil servants from giving in to their own particular interests, it also provided 'the protection they need against another subjective phenomenon, namely the personal passions of the governed'. In this way, Hegel maintained, 'the particular' could be subsumed 'under the universal' (Hegel 1821: 188–93).

It might be argued that Bourdieu's 'corporatism of the universal' was an attempt to extend and generalize Hegel's definition of the universal role and proper functioning of the civil service, applying it to a range of other fields, the artistic, the intellectual, the scientific and so on. Certainly, the young Marx's critique of the elitism and 'pseudo-universalism' of Hegel's *Philosophy of Right* would seem equally applicable to Bourdieu here. As Marx pointed out, Hegel started 'with the assumption of a pseudo-universal, [. . .] of universality fixed in a particular class', the class of bourgeois civil servants (Marx 1975: 112). As such, Hegel assumed that the 'universal forms no part of the character of civil society or the class of private citizens' (Marx 1975: 142). Hence Hegel ignored the potential for any democratic forum to oversee the supposedly universal functions performed by the state bureaucracy:

> The knowledge and good will of the Estates are, therefore, partly superfluous and partly suspect. The people does not know what it wants. The Estates do not possess the same degree of knowledge of state affairs as the civil servants who have a monopoly of it. In the task of dealing with 'matters of universal concern' the Estates are quite superfluous. The civil servants *are able* to do what is best without the Estates, and indeed they *must* do what is best despite the Estates.
>
> (Marx 1975: 127)[4]

The mature Marx would, of course, conclude that the universal was located not in the particular class of civil servants but in the universal class that was the proletariat, and that the universal was borne not by the elite but by the workers. However, it is not necessary to subscribe to Marx's assumption that the proletariat are the universal class to acknowledge the applicability of his critique of Hegel to Bourdieu's theory of the universal. Indeed, following Marx, we might ask a series of questions concerning the kinds of democratic control Bourdieu anticipated being exerted over the elaboration of universal truths and values. We might also question whether Bourdieu's universalism allowed of the possibility that ordinary citizens, rather than the specialist participants in particular fields, might at times themselves be the bearers of universal values.

Its evident social exclusivity was not, however, the only difficulty with Bourdieu's universalism. For in the interim between Bourdieu's discussion of *Calligraphy* with Haacke and his full-blown elaboration of a corporatism of the universal in *Practical Reason* and *Pascalian Meditations*, the terms of his argument had undergone a significant shift. For his account of the way in which agents pursuing their own particular interests could contribute to the universal presupposed that those interests were reducible to competitions over prestige and status, to struggles for capital within a given field between dominant and dominated groups, struggles which reproduced, in 'refracted' form, the hierarchies of class and status in society at large. What was at issue in Haacke's *Calligraphy* and the discussions contained in *Free Exchange* was the particular interests that come to the fore in a multi-ethnic society, the particular interests of France's ethnic minorities and immigrant populations. Bourdieu's theory of the corporatism of the universal, however, seemed to risk effacing or at the very least reducing those particular ethnic interests to differences between class or status groups defined in terms of a more traditional logic of class distinction.[5] Moreover, that older logic of class distinction was itself implicitly accorded the status of a universal in Bourdieu's work.

As Alain Caillé has pointed out, there was an anthropological assumption underpinning Bourdieu's field theory, the assumption that all agents were driven by the need to accumulate or preserve the different forms of capital on offer in the various fields and, further, that it was the possession or lack of such capital that formed the primary axis of discrimination in society (Caillé 1986: 55–172). There were thus two universals underpinning Bourdieu's universalism. The first, largely unacknowledged, was the assumption that agents were driven by the universal imperative to accumulate and preserve their stocks of capital. The second related to the universal values of truth and morality that could be safeguarded provided the universal compunction to accumulate capital was contained within autonomous fields, so that the universal drive to pursue one's particular interests might be subsumed under the necessity to respect universal intellectual or ethical criteria as one did so. Each of these universals was problematic. The first risked effacing or reducing all differences and particularisms to differences of class or status. The second appeared to make the universal the preserve of relatively privileged or specialist groups in society. These hypotheses are perhaps best tested against Bourdieu's treatment of his informants' testimonies in *The Weight of the World*. For in transcribing and interpreting these testimonies, Bourdieu and his co-authors necessarily confronted the question of their validity, of their relationship to the universal scientific truths to which the sociologist might lay claim. Moreover, since several of the informants either belonged to ethnic minorities, expressed casual racism, or were FN activists, questions of race and ethnicity were posed in a particularly dramatic way.

The Socratic model and its limits

Bourdieu compared the research interviews whose transcriptions formed the major part of *The Weight of the World* to a series of Socratic dialogues. He saw his role and that of his team as having been to help 'create the conditions for the appearance of an extraordinary discourse, which might never have been spoken, but which was already there, merely awaiting the conditions for its actualization' (1993: 914 [614]). Publishing transcriptions of the interviews with his research subjects had enabled the latter 'to bear witness, to make themselves heard, to bring their experience from the private into the public sphere' (1993: 915 [627]). In this way *The Weight of the World* aimed to challenge the complicit silence of professional politicians and mainstream media concerning the social effects of the neo-liberal policies whose inevitability they proclaimed. Here, then, Bourdieu was attempting to give practical form to the theoretical role he had elaborated for intellectuals as early as 'Questions de politique' in 1977. The intellectual was to adopt a Socratic role, helping dominated groups to articulate a 'heterodox' discourse, which expressed the truth of a marginalized experience that the 'orthodox' discourse of the dominant class tried to silence and naturalize. It would be quite wrong to conclude, however, that this implied Bourdieu was attributing an absolute or universal truth to the unmediated expression of his informants' experiences.

As we have already noted, the Socratic dialogue is based on a fundamental structural inequality which is at once social and epistemological, an inequality of status and consequently knowledge. Socrates always possesses the knowledge or truths he seeks to help his interlocutors recognize, articulate and understand; he always enjoys a position of social superiority over those interlocutors, his students or the 'little slave' in the *Meno*. In Bourdieu's case, this meant that the adoption of the Socratic method left open the possibility of his rejecting or dismissing the interpretation his research subjects offered of their experiences if that interpretation contradicted his own 'scientific' analysis of their case. As Bourdieu explained:

> social agents do not innately possess a science of what they are and what they do. More precisely, they do not necessarily have access to the principle behind their discontent or their malaise, and, without aiming to mislead, their most spontaneous declarations can express something quite different from what they appear to say.
>
> (1993: 918–19 [620])

Hence it was necessary to keep in mind 'the difference between the "voice of the person" and the "voice of science"', refusing any 'unconscious slippages from one to the other' (1993: 925 [625]).

Bourdieu's adoption of the Socratic method and his claim to speak the 'voice of science' as against 'the voice of the person' thus left open the possibility that he might simply reject the validity of any given testimony in the name of the universal scientific truth to which his status as sociologist gave him access. As he put it in a section entitled 'Resistance to objectification', sociologists needed to be on their guard against any informants who mistakenly assumed that 'they are capable of taking in hand their own objectification and of adopting towards themselves the reflexive point of view'. As an example of such a 'false objectification', Bourdieu reproduced the testimony of a female university student, the daughter of Moroccan immigrants, whose parents had separated, one living in Morocco, the other in France. The student explained her personal difficulties and malaise as resulting from her sense of being torn between her Moroccan and French cultural identities, personified by her mother and father, respectively. Bourdieu rejected this explanation, claiming it to be typical of 'the false, collusive objectification, a half-baked and therefore doubly mystificatory demystification'. The student's literary studies had given her the tools to construct an apparently persuasive narrative of her situation, in which she played the stereotypical role of the immigrant: 'the respondent pretends to be the character who is expected in this encounter, the (female) Immigrant'. The problem with this narrative, Bourdieu argued, was that it excluded 'de facto any investigation of the objective facts of her trajectory other than those which enter into the project of self-portraiture as she conceives it' (1993: 912–14 [615–17]).

Bourdieu's chosen example of 'false objectification' did not only demonstrate how his claim to speak in the name of a universal scientific truth not accessible to ordinary agents could serve to dismiss or silence voices with which he disagreed. His rejection of the student's own interpretation of her situation on the grounds that this concealed the 'objective facts of her trajectory' strongly implied that he was rejecting any explanation based on ethnic criteria in favour of the more 'objective' criteria of social class, status and trajectory. This hypothesis would seem confirmed by his treatment of questions of both ethnicity and racism in the interpretations he offered of his interviews with a range of other informants. For example, at one point in *The Weight of the World*, Bourdieu offered his interpretation of his interview with two young inhabitants of one of France's *banlieues*, the economically depressed housing estates on the edge of her major cities. One of the young men, François, was of European origin, the other, Ali, of North African ethnic origin. Remarking on their friendship and sense of solidarity, Bourdieu sought to generalize from their case, claiming it demonstrated 'the patent absurdity of those who introduce into the political discourse, and into the minds of citizens, the dichotomy between immigrant and French'. Any stigma experienced by Ali because of his ethnicity merely served to 'redouble or, better, *radicalize* the handicap linked to the lack of degree certificates and qualifications, itself linked to the lack of cultural and particularly linguistic capital' (1993: 83 [62]). There can be little doubt that Bourdieu was motivated by the best of intentions here, seeking to counter the claims of those in France who would point to any friction between 'native' and 'immigrant' populations as evidence of a fundamental incompatibility between the Christian and Moslem traditions. However, in his eagerness to refute such claims, Bourdieu surely risked denying any specificity to ethnic identity as a social determinant, reducing it to the status of a sub-category of a more general or universal dynamic of social distinction and class division determined by the amount of linguistic or cultural capital possessed by agents. Indeed, Gérard Grunberg and Etienne Schweisguth take such episodes in *The weight of the world* as evidence of

> the persistence in Bourdieu's work of a narrow conception of the social world, in which, for example, notions of identity or feelings of belonging to a group defined in national, religious or ethnic terms have no place and must be effaced in favour of the only explanations considered pertinent, namely determinisms linked to dominant or dominated positions in social space.
>
> (1996: 149)

Bourdieu's interpretation of the testimonies both of François and Ali and of the student of Moroccan parents thus demonstrates the manner in which the two universals that underpin his universalism could intersect at certain moments to deny or at least play down the significance of any determinants other than those of class and status. In the name of the sociologist's privileged access to universal scientific truths, the student's testimony could be dismissed as a false objectification. In the name of a fundamental dynamic of class distinction, taken to be a universal facet of social action, the specificity of ethnicity as a social determinant risked being effaced. A similar dynamic was evident in Bourdieu's treatment of the question of racism as it emerged in several of the testimonies in *The Weight of the World*. The original French version of the text contained two interviews with members of the extreme right-wing FN, only one of which was retained in the abridged English translation. The positioning of these interviews within the text was, in itself, significant. Both were placed alongside other testimonies of

152 *Universalism and the elusive public sphere*

social malaise by subjects who had nonetheless not turned to the xenophobic, nationalistic and racist FN in search of a solution. Thus the interview with a female FN activist appeared in a section entitled 'Social decline', while the testimony of an adolescent male FN supporter was included in the section 'The contradictions of inheritance'. This strongly implied that support for the FN was to be understood as an expression of socio-economic decline and social malaise equivalent to any other; that FN supporters were just as much victims of the current socio-economic conjuncture as were the homeless, the young unemployed, the handicapped, alongside whose testimonies their opinions were reproduced. What this seemed to ignore was the possibility that support for the FN might reflect racist or xenophobic sentiments which obeyed a specific logic not reducible to the expression of a generalized social malaise or economic decline. This hypothesis seemed confirmed by the interpretations of the testimonies of FN supporters offered by Bourdieu and his co-authors.

For example, in her commentary on her interview with Marie, whom she met distributing FN literature, Frédérique Matonti notes Marie's reluctance to reveal any details of her career before she became unemployed. For Matonti, this represented another case of 'resistance to objectification' since what Marie wanted to avoid was that 'her political life might cease being a little corner of freedom, a moment of madness, and appear instead like a necessary outcome'. There was, according to Matonti, 'a necessity' in her political 'engagement' that lay in her declining social trajectory, her unemployment and consequent socio-economic decline (in Bourdieu 1993: 572). Bourdieu seemed to apply a similar interpretative strategy in his comments on the testimony of Frédéric, an adolescent FN supporter, the son of a former Socialist Party militant. Frédéric's testimony was presented as merely one case of the more general phenomenon of 'the contradictions of inheritance' and, as such, Bourdieu interpreted his support for the FN in terms of a familial and social drama inherent to such contradictions. Frédéric's support for the FN, Bourdieu argued, was the result of a failed identification with his father, resulting in part from his difficulties at school, which seemed to provide objective proof of his inability to assume his father's social and symbolic inheritance, by following the social trajectory his father had laid out for him. This had left Frédéric with 'no other choice' than 'symbolically to kill the parental "project" in its very principle by rebelling against everything the family stands for' by engaging 'in the lowliest tasks of extreme right-wing activism' (Bourdieu 1993: 713–14 [509]). The commentaries of both Bourdieu and Matonti were thus characterized by a marked reluctance to acknowledge, engage with or theorize the specificities of the racism, nationalism and xenophobia that support for the FN surely betrays. Rather, support for the FN was interpreted as being merely the expression of a more generalized social malaise, whose objective determinants could be found in unemployment, declining social trajectories, educational failure, familial tensions and economic deprivation. It was these purely socio-economic factors, according to Bourdieu and Matonti, which meant their informants 'had no other choice' than to join the FN; allegiance to the FN was the 'necessary outcome' of such socio-economic deprivation.

In his concluding remarks to *The Weight of the World*, Bourdieu argued that the hostility towards foreigners expressed by farmers and small shopkeepers who had no direct experience of immigrants should be interpreted as 'a form of displacement', offering 'a solution to the contradictions specific to these sorts of capitalist with proletarian incomes and to their experience of the state, which they hold responsible for an unacceptable form of wealth distribution'. He suggested that through the interview process such individuals could be made to express such feelings, while being forced to articulate and hence recognize their 'real foundations' (Bourdieu 1993: 919 [621]). Again, Bourdieu clearly had the best of intentions here, yet his reluctance to acknowledge that racism might be anything more than the displaced expression of an objective socio-economic situation surely risked undermining those good intentions. This is not to deny any correlation between economic deprivation and the prevalence of racism, rather it is to emphasize, as Angela McRobbie has insisted in her critique of *The Weight of the World*, that racism is not reducible to economic or social deprivation alone (McRobbie 2002: 131–2). Indeed, Bourdieu's interpretation of racism in *The Weight of the World* seemed to obey the logic of expressive causality we have already located elsewhere in his work. Racism was understood as the straightforward *expression* of agents' declining or dominated position in the social field rather than being grasped as a complex of tastes, aversions, prejudices and ideas with its own autonomous logic which, as such, required its own specific tools of analysis. Ironically, the concepts of habitus and practice, with their emphasis on the central role of affective investments, tastes and aversions to social action, might have proved peculiarly well-suited to the analysis of racism. For racism is a phenomenon that clearly relates to the realm of affect more than to that of discourse or ideology, the latter so often serving as merely a 'secondary rationalization' of an initial affective reaction to the presence or perceived threat of the Other.

The two forms of exclusion that we identified as being inherent to Bourdieu's universalism would thus appear to be in evidence in *The Weight of the World*. First, Bourdieu's assumption that he and his co-authors had access to a universal scientific truth about the social world not available to ordinary agents enabled him to exclude the testimony of the student of Moroccan parents as a 'false objectification'. Second, the assumption that distinctions of class and status represented the most fundamental and universal determinants of social action led to the exclusion or effacement of any other social factors, of ethnicity, nationalism or racism, as specific determinants in their own right. This is by no means to argue that Bourdieu was indifferent to racism. On the contrary, he unequivocally denounced the racism inherent in French immigration policy and the discrimination faced by France's ethnic minorities in their dealings with the state bureaucracy (Bourdieu 1998: 21–42 [15–18]; 93–4 [78–80]). It is, however, to point to an unwillingness to theorize the specificities of either racism or ethnicity, an unwillingness that sometimes manifested itself as an overt hostility to any theoretical approaches that did attempt to grasp those specificities. Such overt hostility was particularly evident in both the tone and content of an article co-authored with Loïc Wacquant, entitled 'On the cunning of imperialist reason' (Bourdieu 1999).

Here Bourdieu and Wacquant juxtaposed a certain discourse on race relations and ethnicity with Cultural Studies and the theory and practice of neo-liberal globalization, arguing that they all constituted interrelated examples of US intellectual imperialism, of the illegitimate imposition of problematics drawn from the North American experience onto societies to which they were not applicable. It was in this context that they attacked Michel Wieviorka's careful sociological study of different forms of racism in France, *La France raciste* (1992). Despite providing no evidence to substantiate their accusation, Bourdieu and Wacquant savaged Wieviorka's book for being a 'scientifically scandalous' study, 'more attentive to the expectations of the field of journalism than to the complexities of social reality' (Bourdieu 1999: 53 n.10).[6] Earlier in the article, they had mockingly speculated on the possibility of soon finding 'in bookstores a handbook of *French-Arab Cultural Studies* to match its cross-channel cousin, *Black British Cultural Studies* which appeared in 1997', as though the prospect were self-evidently absurd (Bourdieu 1999: 47).

Of course, it would not be necessary either to adhere to a US-inspired model of race relations or to attribute some irreducibly 'other' identity to France's ethnic minority citizens to acknowledge certain specificities in the nature of those citizens' social, cultural and political experiences. The work of both Paul Gilroy and Stuart Hall demonstrates that it is entirely possible to theorize the importance of ethnicity in European societies in a manner that remains distinct from US experience and analysis. Indeed, McRobbie (2002) has argued that the work of such thinkers might have helped Bourdieu to make sense of the questions of ethnicity and racism he encountered in the course of researching *The Weight of the World*. As both Pnina Werbner (2000) and John D. French (2000) have pointed out, in their responses to Bourdieu and Wacquant's article, what seemed to lie behind the authors' hostility to theories of race and ethnicity was their investment in the myths of French republican universalism, in 'their own country's mythic national construction of itself as universalistic and, by definition, non- if not anti-racist' (French 2000: 122).

In both its tone and content, then, 'On the cunning of imperialist reason' pointed to a strong reluctance on Bourdieu's part to engage with the specificities of ethnicity and racism, a reluctance evident also in his treatment of these issues in *The Weight of the World*. As we have seen, in that study the refusal to engage with the specificities of ethnicity and racism was justified in relation to an explicit claim to the sociologist's privileged possession of universal scientific truth and an implicit assumption that distinctions of class and status represented the primary, even universal, axes of discrimination in society. Bourdieu's rejection of certain testimonies as 'false objectifications', however, co-existed with a more generous, democratic impulse to enable marginalized and dominated groups to have a voice, to gain access to the public sphere. The potential contradiction between the exclusivity of the autonomous intellectual's claim to universal truth and Bourdieu's evident desire to open up the sphere of democratic debate was also manifest in *On Television*. For here Bourdieu emphasized the need for intellectuals to strengthen their autonomy from the media and the market, to construct a 'sort of ivory tower' in which intellectuals' work would only be submitted to the judgement of their suitably qualified peers. This call for greater intellectual autonomy co-existed with a cogent critique of the media's failure to provide a genuinely democratic space in which oppositional or marginalized voices might be heard. *On Television* thus posed in particularly acute form the question of the relationship between an avowedly exclusive intellectual field and the broader public sphere of democratic debate.

The media, intellectuals and democratic debate

One of Bourdieu's central concerns in *On Television* was the threat posed by the media and the market to intellectual autonomy. Once intellectuals could accumulate prestige or capital by appearing on the mass media, their output was no longer subject to the judgement of their suitably qualified peers; its universal value was hence threatened by the influence of heteronomous forces and criteria of judgement. This concern was also manifest in Bourdieu's lectures in the sociology of science, published as *Science of Science and Reflexivity* (2001b), where he bemoaned the increasing reliance of scientific research on commercial funding and its potentially distorting effects. It was against this background that Bourdieu called for the autonomy of the intellectual field to be strengthened, so that rather than being subject to the dictates of fashion, accessibility or commercial gain, the work of a mathematician would only be judged by the community of suitably qualified mathematicians, of a historian by other historians, of a scientist by other scientists. This then was 'that sort of ivory tower inside of which one can judge, criticize, even fight one another, but from a position of knowledge' (Bourdieu 1996c: 71 [61]). Inside these autonomous intellectual fields, Bourdieu argued, 'Habermas's theory is true', a kind of ideal speech situation might be created in which 'the force of the best argument would win out'. However, Habermas had wrongly attributed to language certain inherently universal properties, overlooking 'the question of the social conditions of possibility' of autonomous fields in which the universal could progress, hence ignoring the fact that only those suitably qualified could participate in such fields (Bourdieu 2001b: 161–2 [82]).

Anticipating the accusations of elitism that such an account of intellectual autonomy might provoke, Bourdieu harked back to 'the founders of the French Republic in the late nineteenth century', to their ideals of free, obligatory and universal education as the means of educating every citizen and hence 'universalizing the conditions of access to the universal' (1996c: 77 [66]). More generally, he insisted that while the intellectual field demanded high 'entrance fees' from its participants, it imposed upon them in return an 'exit duty'; it was incumbent on intellectuals to communicate the products of the autonomous intellectual field to the widest possible audience. Hence, Bourdieu maintained, had it not fallen sway to commercial forces, television 'could have become an extraordinary instrument of direct democracy', through which intellectuals could have communicated their knowledge (1996c: 8 [12]). Hence also his decision to deliver the content of the major part of *On Television* as two televised lectures on the cable channel Paris Première in May 1996. Indeed, Bourdieu's establishment and editorship of the Liber-Raisons d'agir series, as well as his decision to participate in Pierre Carles's documentary *La Sociologie est un sport de combat*, could be seen as further examples of his attempts to realize this 'exit duty'. Bourdieu was evidently sincere in his insistence that 'we must generalize the conditions of access to the universal, in order that more and more people fulfil the necessary conditions for appropriating the universal for themselves' (1996c: 77 [66]). However, his concrete proposals for how this might be achieved posed a number of problems.

First, on the purely pragmatic level, it was surely impractical to imagine that any citizen, however well-educated, would ever be able to fully master all the developments in the fields of sociology, political science, theoretical physics, genetics, biochemistry and so on. What becomes important in such circumstances, beyond ensuring as high a level as possible of general education, is inventing effective forms of democratic control over the kinds of research that are pursued, the ethical conditions under which such research is conducted and the uses to which its findings are put. In his justifiable emphasis on the need to safeguard the intellectual field from the influence of heteronomous political and economic forces, Bourdieu left unanswered the question of the form of democratic control that might legitimately be exercised over that field. More problematically, at times he appeared to consider any such democratic control to represent a risk to intellectual autonomy. For example, in *On Television* he identified as one of the primary obstacles to sociology achieving its autonomy the fact that 'everyone sticks their oar in', everyone thought they had the right to pronounce on the social world (1996c: 71 [61]). In *Science of Science and Reflexivity*, he repeated this point, arguing that if sociology had difficulties imposing 'the monopoly of truth', this was because of, 'among other things, a contamination of the scientific order by the principles of the political order and of democracy', which meant that 'different symbolic powers, notably political and religious, and above all journalistic', were 'socially armed to claim, with some chance of success, the right to pronounce the truth about the social world' (2001b: 144–5 [73]). It might, of course, be argued that the founding assumption of any democracy is that no-one has an a priori 'monopoly of truth' about society, that every citizen has a fundamental 'right to speak the truth on the social world', to have their opinions on society heard and taken into account. At the very least, in figuring groups attempting to exercise that right as representing a 'contamination of the scientific order', Bourdieu highlighted his failure adequately to theorize the relationship between those autonomous fields in which universal values were apparently produced and the broader democratic realm.

However sincere Bourdieu's desire to 'generalize the conditions of access to the universal' through education, the project, as defined, remained decidedly top-down. The universal would still be exclusively located in the autonomous intellectual field and intellectuals would still have the 'monopoly of truth', deciding whether or not ordinary citizens' education had progressed far enough that their opinions might qualify as universal. There seemed little place for genuine dialogue in Bourdieu's account, little opportunity for ordinary citizens to challenge, question or hold intellectuals to account, for citizens to denounce the allegedly universal values of the intellectual field as false universals, to express alternative opinions that themselves laid legitimate claim to the universal. That, on one level, Bourdieu was committed to providing opportunities for such dialogue was evident in his critique of the falsity of staged television debates on topical issues. The solutions he offered to this situation, however, again indicated the difficulty of reconciling this stated commitment to democratic debate with a theory that located the universal in an avowedly self-enclosed and exclusive intellectual field.

Bourdieu's critique of the falsity of staged TV debates was perhaps one of the most convincing sections of *On Television*. Much of his analysis suffered from being overly generalized, from lacking nuance and hence being exclusively negative in its assessment of the role of the mass media. Bourdieu's criticisms of TV debates, on the other hand, related to a specific case. They summarized arguments he had voiced during his own appearance on the programme *Arrêt sur images* in January 1996, in which he had successfully demonstrated that a trade unionist invited onto an earlier television debate to discuss the strikes of autumn 1995 had received much less respectful treatment than that accorded an intellectual and a government minister, who had been hostile to the strikes.[7] Bourdieu generalized from this specific case to question the manner in which the panels of such TV debates were pre-selected, so as to limit the range of possible opinions expressed, and to criticize the differential treatment accorded panel members, depending upon their intellectual and social status. Such factors conspired to allow TV channels to be seen to be fulfilling their democratic obligations, while in fact they were curtailing genuine democratic debate (1996c: 32–9 [30–6]). As a solution to this problem, Bourdieu argued that journalists should take into account the differences in intellectual and linguistic capital of their various interviewees. TV presenters should 'help those who are, relatively speaking, the most deprived' to express themselves; they should 'put themselves in the service of people whose thoughts and opinions we want to know, whose words are important, by helping them give birth to what they have to say'. TV presenters should thus pursue the same 'Socratic mission' as Bourdieu and his team had followed in *The Weight of the World* (1996c: 36 [33]).

As we have already seen, this apparently generous and open model of Socratic dialogue would reach its limit when an interviewee offered an interpretation of their situation that did not accord with the sociologist's 'scientific' analysis of that situation. How, for example, should a TV presenter have reacted to the student of Moroccan parents whose testimony, according to Bourdieu, needed to be rejected as a 'mystifying', 'complacent' instance of 'false objectification'? What would happen if that interviewee challenged the interpretation of the social world offered by the presenter or sociologist, rejecting Bourdieu's assumption that their dialogue was defined by a structural inequality of status and knowledge and thereby demanding that the dialogue be both open and equal? The problem here was not that TV presenters or sociologists did not have the right to question others' interpretations of the social world, offering alternative interpretations in their place. The problem arose when such questioning rested on a claim to scientific authority, to a priori possession of a universal truth to which, by definition, one's interlocutor had no access, since they had not paid the necessary 'entry fees' to gain access to the autonomous field of sociology. From this moment, no further dialogue or democratic debate was possible. Bourdieu's assumption that a structural inequality of status and hence knowledge was written into every exchange thus paradoxically removed the possibility of democratic debate at very moment he claimed to be protecting it.

Beyond false universalism

There is no reason to assume that Bourdieu was anything but sincere in his commitment to generalizing access to the universal and in his concern at the curtailment of democratic debate in the mass media. However, his own brand of universalism seemed to fall victim to the same mistake as previous false universalisms. Typically, such universalisms are based on a logic of inclusion/exclusion. They locate the universal within a particular geographic or cultural space, most often Europe, while making the universal the preserve of a particular social or ethnic caste or class, white bourgeois men. Access to the universal then becomes dependent on fulfilling a set of epistemological criteria, on excluded groups 'evolving' to a sufficient cultural or intellectual level through a programme of education. The philosophy behind the 'civilizing mission', as it applied to the indigenous populations of France's colonies, would typify such a conception of the universal. Bourdieu's corporatism of the universal fell into a similar trap; having located the universal exclusively in the privileged spaces of the autonomous intellectual and artistic fields, he then advocated education as the means to bring that universal to the wider population. An analogous process of inclusion/exclusion was at work here; a set of hierarchized distinctions was established between those groups considered capable of embodying the universal and those groups who, by definition, fell outside its ambit. A programme of education was then envisaged as the necessary means of closing the gap between the first and second groups. Of course, it is vital to distinguish between the tradition of French universalism in which those distinctions were made on the basis of race or ethnicity and Bourdieu's universalism in which such distinctions were social and epistemological, with the first criterion taken to determine the second. Bourdieu was certainly not guilty of merely rehearsing the ethnic exclusions characteristic of French imperial ideology. Nonetheless, as we have demonstrated, the exclusions underpinning Bourdieu's universalism did make it difficult for him to allow for the possibility of genuinely democratic debate and dialogue about the social world, since he implicitly delegated all decisions about society to those suitably qualified experts who enjoyed privileged access to the universal.

In order to avoid the pitfalls of earlier false universalisms, a number of thinkers have insisted on the need to resist the temptation to locate the universal in a predetermined social, cultural or geographic space. Such thinkers have sought to conceive of the universal as an 'empty' or 'floating' signifier, shorn of all determinant content and thus itself open to being 'filled in' by any number of social groups who lay claim to the universal in the course of political struggle (Laclau 1996). For example in the Introduction to *Contingency, hegemony, universality* (2000), Butler, Laclau and Žižek, before proceeding to argue over the precise manner in which the universal should be theorized, state as the founding assumption guiding their debates that 'universality is not a static phenomenon, not an a priori given, and that it ought instead to be understood as a process or condition irreducible to any of its determinate modes of appearance' (Butler *et al.* 2000: 3). An analogous assumption underpins Rancière's recent work, in which he insists that the universal is not the property of an intellectual or social elite but rather lies on the side precisely of those excluded from existing definitions of the universal. Historically, he argues, it is those groups excluded from dominant definitions of universal rights – the working class, women, gays, lesbians, immigrants – who have been the bearers of genuinely universal values. The universal is thus articulated by those who speak for 'la part des sans-part', on the part of those who have no part or share in existing definitions of the universal, of the current distribution of social roles and political rights. It is such excluded groups, according to Rancière, who are the true bearers of universal values; in denouncing the falsity of existing universalisms and laying claim to a genuine universalism as they do so, they reconfigure the political field in an inherently progressive, inclusive manner (Rancière 1995). Rancière, Butler, Laclau and Žižek might all be seen as attempting to adapt and extend upon Marx's critique of the social exclusivity of Hegel's false universalism, so that it is not merely the proletariat who are seen as the universal class but rather, potentially, any excluded or marginalized social group.

Rancière's thinking on this subject should be understood, in part at least, to reflect specific political developments in 1990s France, his category of the 'sans-part' having both a general and a more specific referent. As Sarah Waters has pointed out, the most significant political and social movements in France from the 1990s onwards were typically driven by

> groups who are absent from mainstream structures of representation, finding themselves in a position of exclusion in relation to the rest of society. They are the 'sans', literally 'those without', and include groups such as the *sans-papiers* (undocumented immigrants), the *sans-emploi* (unemployed) or *sans-abri* (homeless).
>
> (2003: 41)

According to Etienne Balibar (2002: 23–5), the French owe a debt of gratitude to groups such as the *sans-papiers* who, by protesting at their exclusion from the domain of supposedly universal rights, have forced a debate on what form a genuine universalism might take. As we have already seen, Bourdieu welcomed and supported the movement of the unemployed (the *sans-emploi*). Yet he could only understand it as a 'miracle' since it defied both his own theory of political agency and his assumptions about which social groups were capable of articulating universal values. Similarly, Bourdieu supported undocumented immigrants (the *sans-papiers*) in their struggles for political recognition. Yet his social theory seemed to imply that any claim such groups might make to the universal would be an illegitimate 'contamination' of the field of universal scientific truth by the logic of democracy. The attempts of thinkers such as Rancière, Butler, Laclau and Žižek to conceive of the universal as empty of any predetermined content, a floating signifier able to be filled, temporarily, by excluded groups fighting for recognition, might offer a solution here, a way of locating the universal firmly within the field of democratic struggle rather than outside it, in the 'privileged' or 'exclusive' realm of an autonomous field.

As Laclau has pointed out, there are dangers in assuming that the universal is always located on the side of the 'sans-part', of 'the uncounted', of those groups excluded or marginalized within the dominant definition of universal rights. As he argues, Rancière overlooks the possibility that 'the uncounted might construct their uncountability' in politically regressive ways, 'in a Fascist direction, for instance' (Laclau 2005: 246). Thus the universal can never be entirely shorn of normative judgements, and the challenge is to conceive of the most democratic forums possible, in which such norms would be the subject of constant debate and struggle by all, rather than being assumed to be the preserve of suitably qualified intellectuals. It might prove necessary, at this point, to draw a distinction between epistemological norms, on the one hand, and ethical, political and aesthetic norms, on the other. While the epistemological norms operative in the field of the hard sciences are doubtless less 'pure' than their advocates might claim, there is surely some merit to the argument that only the suitably qualified can reasonably lay claim to advancing universal truths in theoretical physics or genetics, for example. In such cases, the challenge becomes that of putting in place the best possible forms of democratic control over the manner in which research in the hard sciences is conducted and exploited.[8] As regards the representation, functioning and governance of the social world, areas corresponding broadly to the social sciences and the humanities, it is surely a founding assumption of democracy that no particular individual or group can claim a priori exclusive possession of universal criteria of judgement in these domains. On the contrary, any genuine democracy must start from the assumption that everyone has the right to claim a universal status for their opinions or their chosen mode of aesthetic representation.

Chantal Mouffe's distinction between the Enlightenment project's political aspects (universal human rights) and its epistemological aspects (the 'grand narrative of Science and reason') may prove useful here. Retaining a commitment to the first, she rejects the applicability of universal epistemological criteria of scientific reason to the realm of human praxis, since this is 'a region not characterized by apodictic statements, where the reasonable prevails over the demonstrable' (Mouffe 1993: 14). If the realm of human praxis is conceived not as explicable in terms of the universal criteria of scientific truth but rather as the site of struggles over what is just and reasonable in terms of universal human rights, then intellectuals can no longer be assumed to be the privileged bearers of the universal. As this chapter has demonstrated, in insisting on the scientific status of his sociological findings and in asserting that universal values could only be articulated in autonomous fields of qualified experts, Bourdieu linked the epistemological to the political, moral and aesthetic in an inextricable fashion. His universalism was thus founded on the constitutive exclusion of those groups in society considered unqualified to articulate universal values, those groups who had not yet paid the necessary 'entry fees' to gain access to one of the autonomous fields in which the universal progressed. Bourdieu's universalism was thus ultimately a false universalism and the exclusions on which it was founded undermined his doubtless genuine desire to give a voice to the marginalized and excluded, to open up the realm of democratic debate. As this chapter has argued, the attempts of Rancière, Laclau, Mouffe and others to conceive of the universal as an empty or floating signifier seemed to offer one way out of the impasse into which Bourdieu's universalism had led him.

Conclusion

In *Firing back*, Bourdieu criticized the 'double standard' at work behind the efforts of the WTO to liberalize global trade, a double standard that enabled 'the dominant, and in particular the United States, to have recourse to the protectionism and subsidies they forbid to developing countries' (2001: 100 [91]). Having figured neo-liberal globalization as an 'invasion', the 'imposition of the American model' on Continental Europe and the rest of the globe, it was unsurprising that Bourdieu should single out the US for special mention here. Symptomatically, this allowed Bourdieu to bypass any analysis of the extent to which the EU, and France itself, were massive beneficiaries and enthusiastic sponsors of these iniquitous processes of global trade liberalization and market deregulation. Indeed, according to OECD estimates, it was the EU, and not the US, which was destined to reap the greatest benefits from global trade liberalization in the years from 1993 to 2000. The US was forecast to be the fourth greatest beneficiary, behind the EU, China and Japan (Ellwood 2001: 33). Indeed, the dumping of protected EU food surpluses on developing economies forbidden access to Western markets would arguably have offered Bourdieu a more striking example of the double standard he had identified, particularly as under the Common Agricultural Policy (CAP) EU farmers receive higher average subsidies than do their American counterparts – 36% of the value of their products, as against a figure of 23% for the US (Smith 2004: 82). France, of course, remains one of the staunchest defenders of the current system of EU farm subsidy. Moreover, the benefits which France, in common with other developed nations, derives from globalization are not limited to the agricultural sector. French based multinationals, often those which had initially developed under the protection of the French state as either wholly nationalized or part-public part-private enterprises, have proved to be some of the most aggressive and predatory operators in the global market, extending their reach precisely by exploiting the deregulation of markets abroad.

Acknowledging the extent to which the EU and France were both culprits and beneficiaries of unequal global trade regulations would, of course, have obliged Bourdieu to question his eagerness to characterize neo-liberalism as an 'invasion', something inherently foreign, originally American, 'imposed' on France and other nations throughout the world. This, in turn, would have necessitated an acknowledgement of the extent to which France and 'the French model' he opposed to that 'neo-liberal invasion' were themselves fully implicated in the injustices of globalization. Furthermore, any such acknowledgement might have required Bourdieu to conduct a more sophisticated political analysis of the problems faced by some of the marginalized social groups to whom he sought to restore a voice in *The Weight of the World*. For example, Bourdieu reproduced the testimonies of several farmers from his home region of the Béarn, who bemoaned the decline of French agriculture and the indifference of political elites to their plight. Bourdieu sympathized with their situation, while reinforcing their assertions that the aloofness of state bureaucrats and politicians, their adherence to the dogmas of neo-liberalism were to blame (1993: 433–45, 519–31 [381–91]). Given that such farmers have historically been some of the most determined defenders of the CAP, there was a potential contradiction here between Bourdieu's critique of the protectionism of the developed world and his sympathy for the farmers in whose name such protectionism continues to be defended. This is not to argue that this contradiction is irresolvable, that the only way to render trade between developed and developing world more equal would be to abandon farmers in the developed economies to their fate at the hands of unrestrained market forces. It is to argue, however, that there are complex political questions here, questions to which Bourdieu notably failed to provide any answers. Indeed, attributing iniquitous global trade regulations to a US-led process of neo-liberal globalization and blaming the plight of French farmers on distant, unresponsive indigenous elites allowed Bourdieu precisely to elide such complex political questions.

Bourdieu's remarks on the injustice of current global trade regulations in *Firing back* thus epitomized the problematic nature of the political interventions that characterized his later years. His critique of the injustices of globalization, like his concern at the plight of farmers in declining French rural communities, was entirely justified and laudable. However, his eagerness to attribute such phenomena to external forces, to a US-led 'neo-liberal invasion' or to complicit indigenous elites, allowed him both to overlook the extent to which his own society, like every developed society, was implicated in the injustices against which he rightly protested and to elide the thorny political questions this necessarily raised. This is not to argue that Bourdieu was simply wrong to identify the role played by supranational organizations like the WTO or indigenous think tanks in elaborating and spreading the neo-liberal creed. Indeed, as we have noted, Bourdieu showed considerable prescience in anticipating the way in which certain sections of the French 'Second Left' of the 1960s would gradually adopt positions sympathetic to the kind of technocratic neo-liberal discourse that came to predominate in French government circles from the mid-1980s onwards. However, he seemed reluctant to accept that such positions, however ideological, might have represented answers to real problems or contradictions in French society. As a result, he offered no convincing account of the articulation between neo-liberal ideas at the elite level and the beliefs, hopes and aspirations of the mass of French citizens. Rather, he tended to reduce the efficacy of such ideas to the expression of power relations, to the amount and forms of 'capital' that had enabled governing elites to 'impose' neo-liberalism on the populations of the world.

As this study has sought to demonstrate, there are particular historical and political factors specific to France that have encouraged Bourdieu and other French critics of globalization to interpret neo-liberalism as resulting from the 'imposition' of ideas and policies by self-serving elites. Ultimately, however, as the example of Bourdieu's silence on the issue of the CAP demonstrated, such interpretations prove both inadequate and politically disabling. Moreover, Bourdieu's tendency to interpret neo-liberalism as an 'imposition' related less to the specifically French experience of neo-liberal globalization than to certain founding assumptions behind his broader social theory, assumptions which underpinned his concepts of habitus, practice and field. It was a fundamental premise of Bourdieu's field theory that the 'symbolic power' of any utterance, ideology or political programme could not be located in its inherent characteristics or force of persuasion. Indeed, in *Pascalian Meditations*, he maintained that it was this premise that distinguished his own approach from Marxist inspired theories of ideology, 'Marxist thought', in this context, representing 'more of a hindrance than a help'. In preference to Marxism, Bourdieu turned to Weber's focus on 'the specific interests' of and 'the interactions' between the different participants in 'the religious field', the various producers of religious doctrine and interpretation. What Weber had shown, according to Bourdieu, was the necessity of analysing those interests and interactions, rather than the inherent characteristics of any given religious message, in order to understand such a message's genesis and symbolic force (Bourdieu 1997c: 212 [177]).[1] Messages or utterances of whatever kind, religious, political, artistic, were always produced by agents positioned somewhere within a force-field of differentially defined positions. A purely 'internal reading', which attended solely to the form or content of any given utterance, would overlook the question of the specific interests of the agent or group responsible for producing that utterance. These specific interests were related to the position occupied by those agents or groups within such a field of production and exerted a decisive influence over their various 'position-takings' in that field, over which doctrines or ideas they advocated and which they rejected. Further, the efficacy or symbolic power of such utterances was not to be seen as dependent merely on their inherent force of persuasion but rather as reflecting the power conferred upon those agents or groups by dint of the position they occupied within the field in question.

The problem with this kind of analysis was that it risked reducing all signifying relations to power relations. The power political ideas gained either through rational persuasion or through engaging the hopes and desires of agents risked being overlooked in favour of an allegedly objective, scientific calculation of the amount and forms of capital possessed by those individuals and groups promoting such ideas. Political analysis thus became a matter of 'objectifying the coordinates of the field' in which various political agents operated, of attributing their various political 'position-takings' to the 'specific interests' their 'objective position' in that field expressed, interests that only the objectifying gaze of the sociologist could uncover. As Laclau and Mouffe have argued, the assumption that the social field is entirely transparent to the social scientific gaze, that agents' political positions are merely the expressions of their objective interests, risks denying all genuine autonomy to the political realm and hence eliding the political proper (Laclau and Mouffe 1985). As this study has shown, such an elision of the political was manifest in Bourdieu's interpretation both of the strikes of autumn 1995, in his shorter political speeches and articles, and of Giscard's housing reforms, in the more detailed study *The Social Structures of the Economy*. In each case, the position taken by those favourable to neo-liberal reforms was interpreted as the expression of the objective position they occupied in the social field, consequently of their 'specific interests' and of the forms and amount of capital they possessed. The substantive political issues relating to possible flaws inherent to the existing system of social welfare or to state provision of social housing were elided, as was the possibility of suggesting alternative reforms to address those flaws. Indeed, evocation of the French republican tradition as supposed guarantor of the universal interest against neo-liberalism seemed to close off any possibility of examining the flaws inherent to that tradition or proposing more progressive alternatives.

As this study has argued, Bourdieu's field theory was marked by his tendency to reduce every agent's 'position-taking' in a particular field to a straightforward, 'homologous' expression of that agent's position in that field, itself merely a mediated expression of their position within the social field as a whole. Field theory thus relied on a model of expressive causality and the habitus risked becoming a kind of social essence whose inherent characteristics would then be expressed in any of the different fields in which it was invested. To argue that the concept of habitus risked taking on the characteristics of an essence may seem self-evidently nonsensical, given Bourdieu's constant emphasis on the social and historical conditions determining the habitus's formation. However, society, history and culture can all too easily take on the character of metaphysical principles when they are invoked as determinants of an agent's social identity and praxis; as the organic metaphor of *culture* itself suggests, the dividing line between explanations of social action that appeal to cultural factors and those that appeal to essence is not as absolute as many social scientists seem to believe.[2] A striking example of the tendency of the habitus to take on the character of an essence was provided by *Masculine Domination*. Here an unchanging 'androcentric unconscious', incorporated into the habitus of both men and women, was taken to express itself in phenomena as diverse as the wearing of the veil in a pre-capitalist Islamic society, the fashion for miniskirts in the developed world, the role of women in Kabylia, and the limitations on women's opportunities in education and the job market in postwar France.

The tendency of the habitus to take on the character of an essence was also evident in Bourdieu's account of progressive political change. As we have seen, he argued that such change resulted from intellectuals elaborating a 'critical discourse' which rendered explicit feelings and experiences contained within the dominated habitus, encouraging dominated groups to mobilize into a political force based on the collective assumption and assertion of a hitherto marginalized or repressed identity. Bourdieu maintained that the 'symbolic power' of any such critical discourse corresponded to a 'determined principle of pertinence', to its capacity to 'reveal things which are already there' and to its adequation to the objective reality that was contained in a dominated habitus. As we argued, the assumption that the symbolic power of any political utterance was dependent on its adequation to objective reality seemed to rely on the notion that the dominated habitus contained a unitary core of shared feeling and experience, a fixed identity or essence that pre-existed any discourse that might seek to publicize and validate it. What this seemed to ignore was the possibility that political discourses work less by *expressing* a pre-existing reality or giving voice to objective interests hitherto repressed than by *constructing* that reality and those interests in different ways.

The limits of Bourdieu's model of political change were amply demonstrated by the rise of *Front national* (FN) in France, a party whose successes clearly cannot be attributed to the extent to which its discourse reveals 'things which are already there'. Similarly, Bourdieu's call for intellectuals to perform a 'Socratic mission', by helping dominated groups to give voice to the truths they already held within themselves, would demonstrate its limitations when, in *The Weight of the World*, he encountered dominated agents who gave voice to their support or sympathy for the FN. His argument that support for the FN was merely a 'displacement', the displaced expression of the objective realities of socio-economic decline, unemployment, educational failure and familial conflict appeared once again to rest on an elision of the properly political issues in play here, on a reluctance to accord any autonomy to racism, xenophobia or nationalism as political phenomena. If up to 15% of the French electorate regularly vote for a party which attributes mass unemployment to the presence of immigrants on French soil this surely does not reflect the extent to which such claims 'reveal things which are already there' or are 'founded in reality'. Such claims derive their power not from their ability to express a pre-existing objective reality but from their capacity to construct reality in a way that seems plausible, on the rational or cognitive level, while appealing to, mobilizing, eliciting and constructing tastes, aversions and dispositions at the affective level.

As this study has argued, many of the problems encountered by Bourdieu's political theory can be resolved by jettisoning his assumption that political discourse *expresses* the values and assumptions contained in the habitus, itself a structure of dispositions which *expresses* the objective position agents occupy in social space. This notion of expression and expressive causality needs to be replaced by an emphasis on *construction*, on the ways in which political discourses, historical and social factors combine to construct, elicit and mobilize the affects, practical taxonomies and dispositions incorporated into the habitus. The habitus can then be understood as a provisional and contingent construction on, rather than the expression of, social reality. It is here that Bourdieu's theory of practice has genuine insights to offer in comparison to more conventional forms of political analysis or theories of ideology. As we demonstrated in Chapter 5, Bourdieu's analysis of postwar French society in *Distinction* can be read as an account of the ways in which the gendered habitus was constructed and re-shaped in response both to changing economic circumstances and to women's desire for political and social emancipation. In this way, the advent of consumerism in postwar France, the modernization of the economy and the mass entry of women into higher education and the workplace can be seen to have involved an effort to construct and shape the habitus of both men and women, eliciting, mobilizing and channelling their desires and dispositions towards the new models of the dynamic young business executive, the stereotypically feminine new occupations in the service sector and the promise of self-realization offered by consumer products and leisure practices.

The habitus, then, can become a powerful tool for understanding social and political change. As we have seen, in modelling the habitus on the aesthetic, Bourdieu was attempting to theorize the manner in which any rift between abstract duty and embodied habit, sentiment and affect might be healed. The model could be extended to embrace objective historical or social change also, so that, as Bourdieu argued in *Pascalian Meditations*, the very dichotomy between subjective agency and objective change itself breaks down. As he put it: 'one should not say that a historical event determined a behaviour but that it had this determining effect because a habitus capable of being affected by that event conferred that efficacy upon it' (Bourdieu 1997c: 177 [149]). However, in distinction to Bourdieu himself, we would wish to emphasize that this process whereby objective event or abstract duty is incorporated into subjective sentiment and habit is always inhabited by the possibility of going awry, of producing unexpected, unpredictable outcomes. This, then, is to agree with Judith Butler that social identities are always performances characterized by an iterability that leaves them open to the possibility of a performative resignification. This is not however, as Bourdieu and others have charged, to embrace a 'subversive voluntarism'. Indeed, in her most recent work, Butler has focused on the discursive, institutional and legal limitations placed on any performative resignification of given gender identities. As she shows, transsexuals, whose very existence challenges given or essentialized notions of gender or sexual identity, are nonetheless obliged to conform to those essentialized notions; they must prove they are 'really' men trapped inside a woman's body, or vice versa, if they are to have their desire for gender realignment surgery recognized by the medical profession and covered by social insurance (Butler 2004). To assert that all social identities are marked by an iterability that renders them inherently provisional and open to resignification is by no means to claim that there are no limits placed on the possibilities for such a performative resignification. Rather, it is to maintain that social identities are never determined absolutely by material circumstance.

This distinction between limitation and determination can also prove useful in relation to Bourdieu's use of the concept of field. As Butler rightly points out, Bourdieu's version of speech-act theory is ultimately a conservative one because he assumes that the performative force of any utterance is determined in advance by the symbolic authority of the agent making such an utterance, an authority which, in turn, reflects their position in the field in question. To question this assumption is not, however, necessarily to abandon the concept of field altogether, to deny it all explanatory force. Rather it is to note and regret Bourdieu's constant slippage from observing statistical correlations between position and position-taking within a given field to arguing that position in a field 'determines and explains' such position-taking, as he put it in *The Social Structures of the Economy*. Conceiving of society as being composed of a series of interrelated force fields in which agents occupy positions of power and prestige in varying amounts can prove illuminating, provided such fields as seen not as determining practice absolutely but merely as representing the set of limitations within which agents must operate. Bourdieu's assumption of a homology between position and position-taking therefore needs to be challenged, as does his assumption that relations within each field reproduce, in homologous form, the relations obtaining in neighbouring or encompassing fields. This would necessitate a greater attentiveness to the possibility for disparity between position and position-taking, as well as the potential contradictions between the logics of the different fields. Further, the use of correspondence analysis to map a given field should be acknowledged to be a purely heuristic device rather than a scientific objectification of its coordinates, as Bourdieu claimed. As we have demonstrated, correspondence analysis depends upon making a series of prior choices about which agents or institutions to include in the field and which social factors will be considered pertinent, objective determinants of the practices undertaken in that field. Not only does such a process of pre-selection involve a measure of arbitrariness, it can also only encompass statistically measurable criteria, such as age, class, education and so on, which typically relate purely to the personal biography of the individuals concerned. Less tangible factors, such as psychological motivations or broader shifts in pubic mood, fashion or opinion, simply cannot be registered by correspondence analysis; as such its usefulness as a tool of political analysis is somewhat limited.

The results of Bourdieu's tendency to assume that practices or position-takings were absolutely determined by position occupied in the field could be seen in the problems encountered by his particular brand of universalism. As we saw, he argued that universal aesthetic, scientific or intellectual values could only be elaborated by agents located within autonomous fields that were defined by their social privilege and exclusivity. In the case of aesthetics this seemed particularly perplexing, first because he had spent so much of his early career debunking the claims of autonomous art to universal value and second because, having modelled the habitus on the aesthetic, his own social theory seemed to offer the possibility of imagining an aesthetic that related directly to the everyday practices of ordinary agents. As we noted in Chapter 6, Bourdieu's decision to base his installation for the Buren exhibition on the structure of the Kabyle house, as well as his proposals on reforming state education, pointed to an attempt to relate his projects in aesthetics and education to the practical aesthetic sense he had located at the core of the habitus. However, such attempts were never fully developed by Bourdieu, and his major efforts seemed directed to defending the autonomy and exclusivity of the field of cultural production in order to safeguard the universal values elaborated there. Bourdieu may have been quite justified in his concern at the incursion of market forces into the field of art, as into the fields of science and intellectual activity more generally. However, in his eagerness to defend such fields from the market, he neglected to specify the forms of democratic control that ordinary citizens might reasonably expect to exert over the participants in such self-enclosed, privileged fields of activity. At the extreme, this would lead to Bourdieu figuring the pretensions of non-sociologists to have their say about the social world as a 'contamination' of the world of science by 'democracy' and 'the political order'. What such remarks demonstrated was the striking absence of any developed theory of democracy or of the public sphere, however defined, in Bourdieu's work.

There is no reason to suppose that Bourdieu was anything but sincere in his stated desire to 'generalize the conditions of access to the universal', through a programme of education that took its inspiration from the founding values of free, obligatory and secular education under the Third Republic. Nor is there a reason to question the genuineness of his belief that such a programme of education might hold the key to a more democratic future society. Similarly, his call for intellectuals to engage in a 'Socratic mission', helping dominated groups in society to express and assume the truth of a social experience they already possessed at the practical level, was surely motivated by the most generous of sentiments. However, in each case Bourdieu's political understanding rested on the interweaving of science and politics, on an a priori assumption as to the social and hence intellectual inferiority of certain groups and a consequent belief that their emancipation would necessarily depend on the intercession of intellectuals as their mandated delegates. Having located the universal exclusively in the privileged spaces of one or other of the autonomous fields, Bourdieu overlooked the possibility that ordinary agents, marginalized or dominated groups, might themselves be the bearers of universal political or aesthetic values. Although he advocated a programme of education to generalize the conditions of access to the universal, to achieve the universal would still demand meeting certain epistemological criteria ultimately determined by intellectuals. Despite his best democratic intentions, therefore, Bourdieu's universalism would remain marked by an unintended elitism.

The problems encountered by Bourdieu's elitism would seem to confirm Rancière's claim that any genuine theory of democracy must start from the premise that all individuals are equal and that the emancipation of minorities or dominated groups can only ever come from within; no third party can emancipate an individual or group on their behalf or in their name. As he explains, a political theory that starts from the presumption of social inequality can only, whatever its good intentions, end up reproducing such inequalities:

> It is a matter of starting out from the point of view of equality, of affirming it, of working from its presupposition in order to see everything it can produce, in order to maximize everything that is given of freedom and equality.

Anyone who starts from the opposite position of mistrust, who starts from inequality, proposing to reduce it, ends up hierachizing inequalities, hierarchizing priorities, hierarchizing intelligences, and reproducing inequality indefinitely.

(Rancière 1998: 95)

Rancière's presumption of equality might best be seen as an enabling fiction, the necessary price to be paid if political theory is not to end up assuming the existence of inequalities it claims merely to be registering and hence locating the universal in a privileged space to which access is then conditional. It is this presumption of equality, moreover, that allows Rancière to grasp that the universal is not the preserve of certain privileged social groups but the property of any marginalized social group protesting at its exclusion from existing definitions of the universal. It is surely on this kind of presupposition, rather than on Bourdieu's regrettable scientism, that any genuinely progressive politics might be built.

Notes

Introduction

1 For a detailed account and critical analysis of Bourdieu's contributions to these public policy debates, see Ahearne (2004).
2 This explanatory rubric or statement of intent appears on the inside front cover of several, although not all, of the books published in the series. See, for example, ARESER (1997).
3 Le Goff acknowledges these similarities. However, he criticizes Boltanski and Chiapello's claim that the forces of capital were able to 'recuperate' the themes of the progressive political movements of the 1960s and 1970s, appropriating them to a neo-liberal agenda. For Le Goff, this notion of 'recuperation' remains hostage to exactly the form of economism on which neo-liberalism itself relies (2002: 118–28).

1 Neo-liberalism as 'imposition' and 'invasion'?

1 Loïc Wacquant's decision to translate the title of the second volume of *Contre-feux* as *Firing Back* reflects the fact that the French noun 'le contre-feu' can also mean 'returning fire'. The fact that, in the Preface to the first *Contre-feux*, Bourdieu referred to 'les dangers contre lesquels ont été allumés les contre-feux [the dangers against which the *contre-feux* were lit]' suggests that he was using the term in its sense as a tool of the fire-fighter (Bourdieu 1998: 7).
2 Keith Dixon's *Les Evangélistes du marché: les intellectuels britanniques et le néo-libéralisme* (1998), published in the 'Liber-Raisons d'agir' series, places a similarly exclusive emphasis on the role of such think tanks in the rise of Thatcherism.
3 For detailed analyses of this range of factors, see Desai (2002); Harvey (2003).
4 Granted, it could be argued that the first neo-liberal policies enacted in Britain resulted from the financial strictures imposed by the IMF in 1976 on the Labour government of James Callaghan. The skill of Thatcher lay in her ability to adopt such externally imposed strictures and transform them into tokens of the moral and financial rectitude necessary to 'put the "great" back into Great Britain'.
5 'Europe: Schröder et Chirac s'unissent pour sauver le oui', *Le Monde*, 27 April 2005, p. 1; 'Chirac, l'ultime leçon de constitution', *Libération*, 27 May 2005, pp. 2–3.
6 For a more detailed analysis of the manner in which so-called globalization theory involves a slippage from 'globalization' as *explanandum* to 'globalization' as *explanans*, see Rosenberg (2000).
7 Bourdieu was not personally a member of ATTAC (Association pour la taxation des transactions financières pour l'aide aux citoyens), the group campaigning for the levying of a Tobin tax. He was, however, closely allied to many of its leading members, themselves members of the 'Raisons d'agir' collective founded by Bourdieu, which, in turn, had organizational membership of ATTAC. He believed the Tobin tax to be

a necessary measure but one that would prove insufficient in itself if it were not accompanied by the establishment of global institutions charged with controlling global financial flows (Bourdieu 2002: 457–8).

2 The poetics and politics of practice

1 This debt was acknowledged in Bourdieu's earlier study *Le Déracinement* (see Bourdieu 1964: 152 n.1).
2 Lévi-Strauss's allusions to the poems of Rimbaud, the novels of Proust and Western classical music were clearly important precedents for Bourdieu's evocations of music and poetry. In insisting on the 'improvized', 'non-written musical scores' orchestrating Kabyle practice, however, Bourdieu was attempting to distance himself from what he saw as the formal closure of Lévi-Strauss's accounts of agency.
3 Bourdieu's notion of 'amor fati', of the love of one's socially determined fate, was presumably taken from Nietzsche's *Ecce homo*:

> My formula for greatness in a human being is *amor fati*: that one wants nothing to be different, not forward, not backward, not in all eternity. Not merely bear what is necessary, still less conceal it – all idealism is mendaciousness in the face of what is necessary – but *love* it.
>
> (Nietzsche 1969: 258)

4 For a more detailed analysis of Pascal, inflected by a reading of Bourdieu, see Moriarty (2003: 100–50).

3 From practical sense to performative politics

1 Bourdieu's allusion to 'serial existence' and to the formation of groups, combined with his rejection of the 'mythology of the *prise de conscience*', suggested he was engaging in a critique of Sartre's theorization of the emergence of 'groups in fusion' in the *Critique of Dialectical Reason*. According to Sartre, at certain historical moments agents or groups would 'discover' a unity of objective condition and purpose through their 'collective praxis' and hence move from a purely 'serial existence' to form a 'group in fusion'. This collective praxis itself represented an attempt to 'negate' and 'transcend' a shared 'alienated' condition that had previously existed solely at the level of the 'practico-inert' (Sartre 1960).
2 When questioned about the political role of intellectuals in an interview of 1981, Bourdieu rejected what he termed 'the Leninist dream of the intellectual disciplining a working-class apparatus' (in Bourdieu 2002: 168).

4 Field theory and political analysis

1 In a footnote to *The Social Structures of the Economy*, Bourdieu referred back to 'La Production de l'idéologie dominante' as offering a more detailed account of the structure and genesis of the values espoused by the 'innovators' who were behind the 1977 housing reform (2000c: 149 n.10 [243 n.30]).
2 This passage does not appear in the abridged English translation.

5 Gender politics and the return of symbolic domination

1 See, for example, Geneviève Brissac, 'Bourdieu, l'ami des femmes', *L'Express*, 20 août 1998, pp. 56–7.
2 The passage from which this quotation is taken does not appear in the English translation.

7 Universalism and the elusive public sphere

1 For a more detailed critique of the contradictions inherent to what he has termed 'elitist multiculturalist liberalism', see Žižek (1999: 215–21).
2 Bourdieu's comments here should be read in the context of his own involvement in the campaign to have same sex relationships accorded legal recognition in France (see Bourdieu 1997d).
3 The 'tribute that vice renders virtue [l'hommage que le vice rend à la vertu]' was, of course, La Rochefoucauld's definition of hypocrisy.
4 It is of course true that Bourdieu supported the 'Estates General of the Social Movement' that emerged from the 1995 strikes, figuring his role as the modest one of providing the sociological expertise that might help trade unionists and workers better formulate their own demands and policies (1998: 58–65 [34–9]). However, as soon as Bourdieu disapproved of the wishes expressed by ordinary agents, as in the case of the popular desire for home ownership he criticized in *The social structures of the economy*, his approach changed radically. At such moments, he adopted a less modest, more pedagogical role, invoking the 'universal' values safeguarded by a privileged caste of sociologists and state bureaucrats *against* ordinary agents, whose susceptibility to the 'demagogy' of advertisements for new homes he disparaged. Bourdieu's political analyses thus oscillated between championing the wisdom of ordinary agents against a corrupt political elite and, as soon as such wisdom ran counter to his own opinions, invoking the scientific, universal knowledge available only to the privileged few to deprecate ordinary agents' inherent inability to grasp the objective logic of their own social universe.
5 For example, in 'Social space and genesis of "Classes"', Bourdieu argued that 'ethnic affiliation' represented a 'principle of division' which 'reinforced' the 'principles of division which, like the volume and structure of capital, determine the structure of social space' (1984: 4 n.4 [1991: 289 n.3]). The possibility that ethnicity might have specific effects other than reinforcing existing forms of social distinction seemed to be overlooked here.
6 Following the article's publication in *Theory, Culture, and Society*, Wieviorka demanded and received the right to have his book reviewed by an impartial commentator. Bourdieu and Wacquant's disparaging comments about *La France raciste* were removed from the revised version of the article included in the recent volume *Pierre Bourdieu and Democratic Politics* (see Wacquant ed. 2005: 178–98).
7 For his own account of his appearance on *Arrêt sur images*, see Bourdieu (1996a). For a very different account of Bourdieu's appearance and its role as a spur to his subsequent critique of television, see Schneidermann (1996, 1999).
8 That said, it should be remembered that when, in 1905, Einstein published the four articles that would revolutionize the field of theoretical physics, he did so from a position outside the scientific field proper, while employed as a patents clerk who had notably failed to pay the 'entry fees' Bourdieu took as a precondition for anyone even to lay claim to universal truth in the scientific domain.

Conclusion

1 Bourdieu's early commentaries on Weber's sociology of religion offer more detailed insights into the influence of Weber on the genesis of the concept of 'field'. See Bourdieu (1971b,d).
2 For an exemplary deconstruction of the metaphysical and essentialist assumptions behind notions of culture, cultural identity, historical and social determination, see Derrida (1998).

Bibliography

Books and articles by Pierre Bourdieu

The following includes only those books and articles referred to in the foregoing study. For a complete bibliography of Bourdieu's work, see Delsaut and Rivière (2002).

In keeping with convention, Bourdieu's journal, *Actes de la recherche en sciences sociales*, will be abbreviated in the form *ARSS* throughout.

Bourdieu, P. (1958) *Sociologie de l'Algérie*, Paris: Presses universitaires françaises, 'Que Sais-je?' no. 802.

—— (1962) 'Célibat et condition paysanne', *Études rurales*, 5–6: 32–136.

—— (1962a) 'La Hantise du chômage chez l'ouvrier algérien: prolétariat et système colonial', *Sociologie du travail*, 4: 313–31.

—— (1962b) 'Les Sous-prolétaires algériens', *Temps modernes*, 199: 1030–51.

—— (1963) 'La Société traditionnelle: attitude à l'égard du temps et conduite économique', *Sociologie du travail*, 1: 24–44.

—— (1963a) *Travail et travailleurs en Algérie*, Paris, The Hague: Mouton (with A. Darbel, J.P. Rivet and C. Seibel).

—— (1964) *Le Déracinement: la crise de l'agriculture traditionnelle en Algérie*, Paris: Éditions de minuit (with A. Sayad).

—— (1964a) *Les Etudiants et leurs études*, Paris, The Hague: Mouton, Cahiers du centre de sociologie européenne (with J.C. Passeron).

—— (1964b) *Les Héritiers: les étudiants et la culture*, Paris: Éditions de minuit (with J.C. Passeron). [translation: *The Inheritors: French students and their relation to culture*, trans. R. Nice, Chicago, IL: The University of Chicago Press, 1979.]

—— (1965) *Rapport pédagogique et communication*, Paris, The Hague: Mouton, Cahiers du centre de sociologie européenne (with J.C. Passeron and M. de Saint Martin). [translation: *Academic Discourse*, trans. R. Teese, Stanford, CA: Stanford University Press.]

—— (1965a) *Un Art moyen: essai sur les usages sociaux de la photographie*, Paris: Éditions de minuit, 2e édition (with L. Boltanski, R. Castel and J.C. Chamboredon). [partial translation: *Photography: a middlebrow art*, trans. S. Whiteside, Cambridge: Polity Press, 1990.]

—— (1967) Postface to E. Panofsky, *Architecture gothique et pensée scholastique*, trans. P. Bourdieu, Paris: Editions de minuit, pp. 136–67.

—— (1967a) 'Sociology and philosophy in France: death and resurrection of a philosophy without subject', *Social Research*, XXXIV, 1: 162–212 (with J.C. Passeron).
—— (1968) *Le Métier de sociologue: préalables épistémologiques*, Paris: Mouton-Bordas, (with J.C. Chamboredon and J.C. Passeron). [translation: *The Craft of Sociology: epistemological preliminaries*, trans. R. Nice, New York and Berlin: Walter de Gruyter, 1991.]
—— (1969) *L'Amour de l'art: les musées d'art européens et leur public*, 2e édition revue et augmentée, Paris: Éditions de minuit (with A. Darbel and D. Schnapper). [translation: *The Love of Art: European art museums and their public*, trans. C. Beattie and N. Merriman, Cambridge: Polity Press, 1991.]
—— (1970) 'La Maison kabyle ou le monde renversé', in *Echanges et communications: mélanges offerts à Claude Lévi-Strauss à l'occasion de son 60e anniversaire*, ed. J. Pouillon et P. Maranda, Paris, The Hague: Mouton, pp. 739–58.
—— (1970a) *La Reproduction: éléments pour une théorie du système d'enseignement*, Paris: Editions de minuit (with J.C. Passeron). [translation: *Reproduction in Education, Culture and Society*, trans. R. Nice, London and Beverley Hills: Sage Publications, 1977.]
—— (1971) 'Champ du pouvoir, champ intellectuel et habitus de classe', *Scolies*, 1: 7–26.
—— (1971a) 'Disposition esthétique et compétence artistique', *Temps modernes*, 295: 1345–78.
—— (1971b) 'Genèse et structure du champ religieux', *Revue française de sociologie*, XII, 3: 295–334.
—— (1971c) 'Le Marché des biens symboliques', *L'Année sociologique*, 22: 49–126.
—— (1971d) 'Une Interprétation de la théorie de la religion selon Max Weber', *Archives européennes de sociologie*, XII, 1: 3–21.
—— (1972) *Esquisse d'une théorie de la pratique: précédée de trois études d'ethnologie kabyle*, 2e édition, Paris: Seuil 'Points', 2000.
—— (1973) 'Les Stratégies de renconversion: les classes sociales et le système d'enseignement', *Informations sur les sciences sociales*, XII, 5: 61–113 (with L. Boltanski and M. de Saint Martin).
—— (1974) 'Avenir de classe et causalité du probable', *Revue française de sociologie*, XV,1: 3–42.
—— (1976) 'La Production de l'idéologie dominante', *ARSS*, 2–3: 3–73 (with L. Boltanski).
—— (1976a) 'Le Champ scientifique', *ARSS*, 2–3: 88–104.
—— (1976b) 'Les Modes de domination', *ARSS*, 2–3: 122–32.
—— (1977) *Algérie 60: structures économiques et structures temporelles*, Paris: Editions de minuit. [modified translation: *Algeria 1960*, trans. R. Nice, Cambridge: Cambridge University Press, 1979.]
—— (1977a) *Outline of a Theory of Practice*, trans. R. Nice, Cambridge: Cambridge University Press.
—— (1977b) 'Questions de politique', *ARSS*, 16: 55–89.
—— (1977c) 'Sur le pouvoir symbolique', *Annales*, 32–3: 405–11.
—— (1978) 'Le Patronat', *ARSS*, 20–1: 3–82 (with M. de Saint Martin).
—— (1979) *La Distinction: critique sociale du jugement*, Paris: Editions de minuit. [translation: *Distinction: a social critique of the judgement of taste*, trans. R. Nice, London: Routledge and Kegan Paul, 1984.]
—— (1980) 'Le Capital social: notes provisoires', *ARSS*, 31: 2–3.

Bourdieu, P. (1980a) *Le Sens pratique*, Paris: Editions de minuit. [translation: *The Logic of Practice*, trans. R. Nice, Cambridge: Polity Press, 1990.]

—— (1980b) *Questions de sociologie*, Paris: Editions de minuit, nouvelle édition augmentée d'un index, 1984. [translation: *Sociology in Question*, trans. R. Nice, London: Sage, 1993.]

—— (1981) 'La Représentation politique; éléments pour une théorie du champ politique'; *ARSS*, 36–7: 3–24.

—— (1982) *Ce que parler veur dire: l'économie des échanges linguistiques*, Paris: Fayard. [modified translation: *Language and Symbolic Power*, Cambridge: Polity Press, 1991.]

—— (1982a) *Leçon sur la leçon*, Paris: Editions de minuit.

—— (1983) 'Vous avez dit "populaire"?' *ARSS*, 46: 98–105.

—— (1984) 'Espace social et genèse des "classes"', *ARSS*, 52–3: 3–15.

—— (1984a) *Homo academicus*, nouvelle édition augmentée d'un postface, Paris: Editions de minuit, 1988. [translation: *Homo Academicus*, trans. P. Collier, Cambridge: Polity Press, 1988.]

—— (1984b) 'La Délégation et le fétichisme politique', *ARSS*, 52–3: 49–55.

—— (1986) 'La Force du droit: éléments pour une sociologie du champ juridique', *ARSS*, 64: 5–19.

—— (1986a) 'La Science et l'actualité', *ARSS*, 61: 2–3.

—— (1987) *Choses dites*, Paris: Editions de minuit. [translation: *In Other Words*, trans. M. Adamson, Cambridge: Polity Press, 1990.]

—— (1987a) 'The historical genesis of a pure aesthetic', *Journal of Aesthetics and Art Criticism*, XLVI: 201–10.

—— (1987b) 'L'assassinat de Maurice Halbwachs', *La Liberté de l'esprit*, 16, special no. *Visages de la Résistance*, pp. 161–8.

—— (1987c) 'L'Institutionalisation de l'anomie', *Cahiers du Musée national d'art moderne*, 19–20: 6–19.

—— (1988) 'Flaubert's point of view', trans. P. Parkhurst Ferguson, *Critical Inquiry*, 14, 3: 539–62.

—— (1988a) *L'Ontologie politique de Martin Heidegger*, Paris: Editions de minuit. [translation: *The Political Ontology of Martin Heidegger*, trans. P. Collier, Cambridge: Polity Press, 1991.]

—— (1988b) 'Penser la politique', *ARSS*, 71–2: 2–3.

—— (1988c) 'Pour que vive une télévision publique', *Le Monde*, 19 October, p. 2.

—— (1989) *La Noblesse d'état: grandes écoles et esprit de corps*, Paris: Editions de minuit. [translation: *The State Nobility*, trans. L.C. Clough, Cambridge: Polity Press, 1996]

—— (1989a) 'Mouloud Mammeri ou *La Colline oubliée*', *Awal*, 5: 1–3.

—— (1989b) 'Tombeau pour une ambition', *Le Monde*, 11 May, p. 2.

—— (1990) 'Droit et passé-droit: le champ des pouvoirs territoriaux et la mise en oeuvre des règlements', *ARSS*, 81–2: 86–96.

—— (1990a) 'La construction du marché: le champ administratif et la production du "politique du logement"', *ARSS*, 81–2: 65–85 (with R. Christin).

—— (1990b) 'La Domination masculine', *ARSS*, 84: 2–31.

—— (1990c) 'Le Sens de la propriété: la genèse sociale des systèmes de préférences', *ARSS*, 81–2: 52–63 (with M. de Saint Martin).

—— (1990d) 'Pour une télévision publique sans publicité', *Le Monde*, 29–30 April, p. 2.

—— (1990e) 'Un Placement de père de famille: la maison individuelle, spécificité du produit et logique du champ de production', *ARSS*, 81–2: 6–33.
—— (1990f) 'Un Signe des temps', *ARSS*, 81–2: 2–5.
—— (1991) *Language and Symbolic Power*, trans. G. Raymond and M. Adamson, Cambridge: Polity Press.
—— (1991a) 'Un Analyseur de l'inconscient', preface to A. Sayad, *L'Immigration ou les paradoxes de l'altérité*, Brussels: Editions DeBoeck-Wesmael, pp. 7–9.
Bourdieu, P. (1992) 'In Conversation – Doxa and Common Life', *New Left Review*, 191: 111–21 (with T. Eagleton).
—— (1992a) *Les Règles de l'art: genèse et structure du champ littéraire*, Paris: Editions du seuil. [translation: *The Rules of Art: the genesis and structure of the literary field*, trans. S. Emmanuel, Cambridge: Polity Press, 1996.]
—— (1992b) *Réponses: pour une anthropologie réflexive*, Paris: Editions du seuil (with L.J.D. Wacquant). [translation: *An invitation to reflexive sociology*, Cambridge: Polity Press, 1992.]
—— (1993) *La Misère du monde*, Paris: Editions du seuil. [translation: *The Weight of the World: social suffering in contemporary society*, trans. P.P. Ferguson, Cambridge: Polity Press, 1999.]
—— (1994) *Libre-échange*, Paris: Editions du seuil and Les Presses du réel (with H.Haacke). [translation: *Free Exchange*, trans. R. Johnson, Cambridge: Polity Press, 1994.]
—— (1994a) *Raisons pratiques: sur la théorie de l'action*, Paris: Editions du seuil. [translation: *Practical Reason: on the theory of action*, trans. R. Nice, Cambridge: Polity Press, 1998.]
—— (1994b) 'Stratégies de reproduction et modes de domination', *ARSS*, 105: 3–12.
—— (1995) 'La Cause de la science: comment l'histoire sociale des sciences sociales peut servir le progrès de ces sciences', *ARSS*, 106–7: 3–10.
—— (1995a) 'La Violence symbolique', in *De l'égalité des sexes*, ed. M. de Manassein, Paris: Centre national de documentation pédagogique, pp. 83–7.
—— (1996) 'Des familles sans nom', *ARSS*, 113: 3–5.
—— (1996a) 'La Télévision peut-elle critiquer la télévision? Analyse d'un passage à l'antenne', *Le Monde diplomatique*, April, p. 20.
—— (1996b) 'Le Nouvel opium des intellectuels: contre la "pensée Tietmeyer", un Welfare State européen', *Liber*, 29: 16.
—— (1996c) *Sur la télévision*, Paris: Liber Raisons d'agir. [translation: *On television and journalism*, trans. P.P. Ferguson, London: Pluto Press, 1998.]
—— (1997) 'De la maison du roi à la raison d'Etat: un modèle de la genèse du champ bureaucratique', *ARSS*, 118: 55–68.
—— (1997a) 'Le Champ économique', *ARSS*, 119: 48–66.
—— (1997b) *Les Usages sociaux de la science: pour une sociologie clinique du champ scientifique*, Paris: Institut national de la recherche agronomique.
—— (1997c) *Méditations pascaliennes*, Paris: Collection Liber and Editions du seuil. [translation: *Pascalian Meditations*, trans. R. Nice, Cambridge: Polity Press, 2000.]
—— (1997d) 'Quelques questions sur la question gay et lesbienne', *Liber*, 33: 78.
—— (1998) *Contre-feux: propos pour servir à la résistance contre l'invasion néo-libérale*, Paris: Liber-Raisons d'agir. [translation: *Acts of Resistance: against the new myths of our time*, trans. R. Nice, Cambridge: Polity Press, 1998.]
—— (1998a) *La Domination masculine*, Paris: Editions du seuil. [translation: *Masculine Domination*, trans. R. Nice, Cambridge: Polity Press, 2001.]

Bourdieu, P. (1998b) 'The state, economics and sport', in *Culture, Sport, Society*, 1, 2, special no.
—— *France and the 1998 World Cup: the national impact of a world sporting event*, ed. H. Dauncey and G. Hare, pp. 15–21.
—— (1999) 'On the cunning of imperialist reason', *Theory, culture and society*, 16, 1: 41–58 (with L. Wacquant).
—— (2000) *Les Structures sociales de l'économie*, Paris: Collection Liber and Editions du seuil. [translation: *The Social Structures of the Economy*, trans. C. Turner, Cambridge: Polity Press, 2005.]
—— (2000a) *Propos sur le champ politique*, avec une introduction de Philippe Fritsch, Lyon: Presses Universitaires de Lyon.
—— (2000b) 'Sortir du néo-libéralisme', *Le Monde diplomatique*, July–August, pp. 10–13.
Bourdieu, P. (2001) *Contre-feux 2: pour un movement social européen*, Paris: Liber-Raisons d'agir. [partial translation: *Firing back: against the tyranny of the market 2*, trans. L.Wacquant, London, New York: Verso, 2003.]
—— (2001a) 'Le Mystère du ministère: des volontés particulières à la volonté générale', *ARSS*, 140: 7–11.
—— (2001b) *Science de la science et réflexivité: cours du Collège de France 2000–2001*, Paris: Editions Raisons d'agir. [translation: *Science of Science and Reflexivity*, trans. R. Nice, Cambridge: Polity Press, 2004.]
—— (2002) *Interventions, 1961–2001: science sociale et action politique*, textes choisis et présentés par Franck Poupeau et Thierry Discepolo, Marseille: Agone.
—— (2002a) 'The "Progressive Restoration"', an interview with Günter Grass, *New Left Review*, 14: 63–77.
—— (2002b) 'Projet d'intervention de Pierre Bourdieu dans l'exposition de Daniel Buren au Centre Georges Pompidou', in *Mot à mot*, ed. Daniel Buren, Paris: Editions du Centre Pompidou and Editions Xavier Barral and Editions de la Martinière, pp. C82–C91.
—— (2002c) *Si le monde social m'est supportable, c'est parce que je peux m'indigner*, entretien avec Antoine Spire, La Tour d'Aigues: Editions de l'aube.
—— (2003) 'Letter to the American reader', in Pierre Bourdieu, *Firing back: against the tyranny of the market 2*, trans. L. Wacquant, London and New York: Verso, pp. 9–10.
—— (2004) *Esquisse pour une auto-analyse*, Paris: Editions Raisons d'agir.
—— (2005) 'The political field, the social science field, and the journalistic field', in *Bourdieu and the Journalistic Field*, ed. R. Benson and E. Neveu, Cambridge: Polity Press, pp. 29–47.

Other works consulted

Adkins, L. and B. Skeggs, eds (2004) *Feminism after Bourdieu*, Oxford: Blackwell and The Sociological Review.
Ahearne, J. (2004) *Between Cultural Theory and policy: the cultural policy thinking of Pierre Bourdieu, Michel de Certeau and Régis Debray*, Research Papers, no. 7, Warwick: University of Warwick, Centre for Cultural Policy Studies.
Althusser, L. (1965) *Lire le Capital*, Paris: Presses Universitaires de France, nouvelle édition revue, 1996 (with E. Balibar, R. Establet, P. Macherey and J. Rancière).
—— (1965a) *Pour Marx*, Paris: Maspero.
—— (1984) 'Ideology and ideological state apparatuses: notes towards an investigation', in *Essays on ideology*, trans. and ed. G. Elliot, London: Verso.

Ambler, J.S., ed. (1991) *The French Welfare State: surviving social and ideological change*, New York and London: New York University Press.
Aparicio, J.C., M. Pernet and D. Torquéo (1999) *La CFDT au péril du libéral-syndicalisme*, Paris: Editions Syllepse.
ARESER (1997) *Quelques diagnostics et remèdes urgents pour une université en péril*, Paris: Liber-Raisons d'agir.
Armengaud, F., G. Jasser and C. Delphy (1995) 'Liberty, equality...but most of all fraternity', *Trouble and Strife*, 31: 43–9.
Austin, J.L. (1962) *How to do things with words*, ed. J.O. Urmson and M. Sbisa, Oxford: Oxford University Press, 1971.
Bachelard, G. (1934) *Le Nouvel esprit scientifique*, Paris: Quadrige and Presses Universitaires de France, 17e édition, 1987.
Bachelard, G. (1938) *La Formation de l'esprit scientifique: contribution à une psychanalyse de la connaissance*, Paris: J.Vrin, 16e tirage, 1996.
—— (1957) *The Poetics of Space*, trans. M. Jolas, Boston, MA: Beacon Press, 1964.
Bachmann, C. and N. Le Guennec (2002) *Violences urbaines: ascension et chute des classes moyennes à travers cinquante ans de politique de la ville*, 2e édition, Paris: Hachette Littératures.
Bakhtin, M.M. (1965) *Rabelais and his World*, trans. H. Iswolsky, Bloomington, IN: Indiana University Press, 1984.
—— (1981) *The Dialogic Imagination*, ed. M. Holquist, trans. C. Emerson and M. Holquist, Austin, TX: University of Texas Press.
Balibar, E. (2002) *Droit de cité*, Paris: Presses Universitaires de France.
Becker, J.J. (1998) *Nouvelle Histoire de la France contemporaine, vol. 19, Crises et alternances, 1974–1995*, avec la collaboration de P. Ory, Paris: Editions du seuil.
Benson, R. and E. Neveu, ed. (2005) *Bourdieu and the Journalistic Field*, Cambridge: Polity Press.
Berstein, S. (2001) *Histoire du Gaullisme*, Paris: Editions Perrin and Collection 'Tempus'.
Boltanski, L. and E. Chiapello (1999) *Le Nouvel Esprit du capitalisme*, Paris: Gallimard.
Bompaire-Evesque, C.F. (1988) *Un Débat sur l'université au temps de la Troisième République: la lutte sur la nouvelle Sorbonne*, Paris: Aux Amateurs de livres.
Brown, N. and I. Szeman, eds (2000) *Pierre Bourdieu: fieldwork in culture*, Oxford: Rowman & Littlefield.
Budgen, S. (2002) 'French Fiasco', *New Left Review*, 17: 31–50.
Bürger, P. (1984) *Theory of the Avant-garde*, trans. M. Shaw, Manchester: Manchester University Press.
—— (1990) 'The problem of aesthetic value', trans. S. Whiteside, in *Literary Theory Today*, ed. P. Collier and H. Geyer-Ryan, Cambridge: Polity Press, pp. 23–34.
Butler, J. (1990) *Gender Trouble: feminism and the subversion of identity*, London and New York: Routledge.
—— (1993) *Bodies that Matter: on the discursive limits of sex*, London and New York: Routledge.
—— (1997) *Excitable Speech: a politics of the performative*, London and New York: Routledge.
—— (1997a) *The Psychic Life of Power: theories in subjection*, Stanford, CA: Stanford University Press.
—— (2004) *Undoing Gender*, London and New York: Routledge.

Bibliography

Butler, J., E. Laclau and S. Zizek (2000) *Contingency, Hegemony, Universality: contemporary dialogues on the Left*, London and New York: Verso.

Caillé, A. (1986) *Don, intérêt et désintéressement: Bourdieu, Mauss, Platon et quelques autres*, Paris: Editions La Découverte and M.A.U.S.S.

Caillé, A. and J. P. Le Goff (1996) *Le Tournant de décembre*, Paris: La Découverte.

Calhoun, C., E. Lipuma and M. Postone, eds (1993) *Bourdieu: critical perspectives*, Cambridge: Polity Press.

Callinicos, A. (1999) 'Social theory put to the test of politics: Pierre Bourdieu and Anthony Giddens', *New Left Review*, 236: 77–102.

Champagne, P. (1990) *Faire l'opinion: le nouveau jeu politique*, Paris: Editions de minuit.

Champagne, P. and D. Marchetti (1994) 'L'Information médicale sous contrainte. A propos du "scandale du sang contaminé"', *ARSS*, 101–12: 40–62.

Delphy, C. (1984) *Close to Home: a materialist analysis of women's oppression*, trans. and ed. D. Leonard, London: Hutchinson.

Delsaut, Y. and M.C. Rivière (2002) *Bibliographie des travaux de Pierre Bourdieu, suivi d'un entretien sur l'esprit de la recherche*, Pantin: Le Temps des cerises.

Derrida, J. (1998) *Monolingualism of the Other: the prothesis of origin*, trans. P. Mensah, Stanford, CA: Stanford University Press.

Desai, M. (2002) *Marx's Revenge: the resurgence of capitalism and the death of socialist statism*, London and New York: Verso.

Diamond, H. (1999) *Women and the Second World War in France, 1939–1948: choices and constraints*, Edinburgh: Pearson.

Dixon, K. (1998) *Les Evangélistes du marché: les intellectuels britanniques et le néo-libéralisme*, Paris: Raisons d'agir.

Durkheim, E. (1894) *Les Règles de la méthode sociologique*, Paris: Flammarion, 1988.

—— (1897) *Suicide: a study in sociology*, trans. J.A. Spaulding and G. Simpson, London: Routledge and Kegan Paul, 1952.

—— (1903) 'Secular Morality', in *Moral Education: a study in the theory and application of the sociology of education*, trans. E.K. Wilson and H. Schnurer, New York: Free Press of Glencoe, 1961, pp. 87–102.

—— (1957) *Professional Ethics and Civic Morals*, trans. C. Brookfield, London: Routledge and Kegan Paul.

Duval, J., C. Gaubert, F. Lebaron, D. Marchetti and F. Pavis (1998) *Le 'Décembre' des intellectuels français*, Paris: Liber Raisons d'agir.

Eagleton, T. (1990) *The Ideology of the Aesthetic*, Oxford: Basil Blackwood.

—— (1991) 'From Adorno to Bourdieu', in *Ideology: an introduction*, London: Verso, pp. 125–58.

Ellwood, W. (2001) *The No-Nonsense Guide to Globalisation*, London: Verso and New Internationalist.

Fanon, F. (1961) *Les Damnés de la terre*, préface de Jean-Paul Sartre, présentation de Gérard Chaliand, Paris: Gallimard, 1991.

Ferry, L. and A. Renaut (1985) *La Pensée 68: essai sur l'antihumanisme contemporain*, Paris: Gallimard.

Forbes, J. and M. Kelly, eds (1995) *French Cultural Studies*, Oxford: Oxford University Press.

Forrester, V. (1996) *L'Horreur économique*, Paris: Fayard.

Foucault, M. (1977) 'Intellectuals and power', in *Language, counter-memory, practice, selected essays and interviews*, ed. D.F. Bouchard, Ithaca, NY: Cornell University Press, pp. 205–12.

Fourcade-Gourinchas, M. and S.L. Babb (2002) 'The rebirth of the liberal creed: paths to neo-liberalism in four countries', *American Journal of Sociology*, 108, 3: 533–79.

Freeland, C. (2001) *But is it Art? An introduction to art theory*, Oxford: Oxford University Press.

French, J.D. (2000) 'The missteps of imperialist reason: Bourdieu, Wacquant and Hanchard's *Orpheus and Power*', *Theory, Culture and Society*, 17, 1: 107–28.

Garnham, N., ed. (1980) *Media, Culture and Society*, special number on Pierre Bourdieu, vol. 2, no. 3.

Gerth, L. and C.W. Mills, eds (1948) *From Max Weber: essays in sociology*, Oxford: Oxford University Press.

Gramsci, A. (1971) *Selections from the Prison Notebooks*, trans. and ed. Q. Hoare and G. Nowell-Smith, London: Lawrence and Wishart.

Giddens, A., ed. (1972) *Emile Durkheim: selected writings*, trans. A. Giddens, Cambridge: Cambridge University Press.

Grasskamp, W., M. Nesbit and J. Bird (2004) *Hans Haacke*, London: Phaidon.

Grossberg, L. (1992) *We Gotta Get Out of this Place: popular conservatism and postmodern culture*, New York and London: Routledge.

Grunberg, G. and E. Schweisguth (1996) 'Bourdieu at la misère: une approche réductionniste', *Revue française de science politique*, 46, 1: 134–55.

Habermas, J. (1962) *The Structural Transformation of the Public Sphere: an inquiry into a category of bourgeois society*, trans. T. Burger, Cambridge: Polity Press, 1989.

Halimi, S. (1997) *Les Nouveaux Chiens de garde*, Paris: Liber-Raisons d'agir.

Hall, S. (1977) 'The hinterland of science: ideology and the "sociology of knowledge"', in *On Ideology*, Centre for Contemporary Cultural Studies, London: Hutchinson, pp. 9–32.

—— (1988) *The Hard Road to Renewal: Thatcherism and the crisis of the Left*, London and New York: Verso.

Hamon, H. and P. Rotman (1984) *La Deuxième gauche: histoire intellectuelle et politique de la CFDT*, Paris: Editions du Seuil and Points.

Harvey, D. (2003) *The New Imperialism*, Oxford: Oxford University Press.

Hatton, R. and J.A. Walker (2000) *Supercollector: a critique of Charles Saatchi*, London: Ellipsis.

Hegel, G.W.F. (1821) *Philosophy of Right*, trans. T.M. Knox, Oxford: Oxford University Press, 1969.

Hennessy, R. (2000) *Profit and Pleasure: sexual identities in late capitalism*, London and New York: Routledge.

Hochschild, A.R. (1983) *The Managed Heart: commercialisation of human feeling*, London, Berkeley, CA and Los Angeles, CA: University of California Press.

Husserl, E. (1913) *Idées directrices pour une phénoménologie et une philosophie phénoménologique pure, tôme premier, introduction générale à la phénoménologie pure*, trans. P. Ricoeur, Paris: Gallimard, 1950.

—— (1948) *Experience and Judgement: investigations in a genealogy of logic*, rev. and ed. L. Landgrebe, trans. J.S. Churchill and K. Ameriks, London: Routledge and Kegan Paul, 1973.

Jameson, F. (1984) 'Postmodernism, or, the cultural logic of late capitalism', *New Left Review*, 146: 53–92.

Jardine, L. (1996) *Worldly Goods: a new history of the renaissance*, London: Macmillan.

Jardine, L. (1997) 'Modern medicis: art patronage in twentieth-century Britain', in *Sensation: young British artists from the Saatchi Collection*, ed. B. Adams, L. Jardine, M. Maloney and J. Shand-Kydd, Royal Academy of Arts, London: Thames and Hudson, pp. 40–8.

Kahn, J.F. (1995) *La Pensée unique, édition revue et augmentée*, Paris: Fayard.

Kant, I. (1790) *Critique of Judgement*, translated with analytical indexes by J.C. Meredith, Oxford: Oxford University Press, thirteenth impression, 1991.

Laclau, E. (1990) *New Reflections on the Revolution of our Time*, London and New York: Verso.

—— (1996) *Emancipation(s)*, London and New York: Verso.

—— (2005) *On populist reason*, London and New York: Verso.

Laclau, E. and C. Mouffe (1985) *Hegemony and Socialist Strategy: towards a radical democratic politics*, London and New York: Verso.

Lahire, B., ed. (1999) *Le Travail sociologique de Pierre Bourdieu: dettes et critiques*, Paris: Editions La Découverte.

Le Doeuff, M. (1987) 'Ants and women, or, philosophy without borders', in *Contemporary French Philosophy*, ed. A. Phillips Griffiths, Cambridge: Cambridge University Press, pp. 41–54.

Le Goff, J-P. (1999) *La Barbarie douce: la modernisation aveugle des enterprises et de l'école*, Paris: Editions La Découverte.

—— (2002) *La Démocratie post-totalitaire*, Paris: Editions La Découverte.

Le Goff, J-P. (2002a) *Mai 68, l'héritage impossible*, préface de F.Gèze, postface inédite de l'auteur, Paris: La Découverte and Poche.

Lenin, V.I. (1899) *The Development of Capitalism in Russia: the process of the formation of a market for large-scale industry*, in *Collected Works*, vol. 3, London: Lawrence and Wishart, 1960.

Lenin, V.I. (1902) *What is to be done? Painful questions of our movement*, trans. J. Fineberg and G. Hanna, introduction by R. Service, London: Penguin Books, 1988.

Lévi-Strauss, C. (1958) *Anthropologie structurale*, Paris: Plon.

—— (1962) *La Pensée sauvage*, Paris: Plon.

—— (1973) *Anthropologie structurale deux*, Paris: Plon.

Loesberg, J. (1993) 'Bourdieu and the sociology of aesthetics', *English Literary History*, 60, 4: 1033–56.

Lukes, S. (1973) *Emile Durkheim, his life and work: a historical and critical study*, Harmondsworth: Penguin.

Lyotard, J-F. and J. Rogozinski (1986) 'La Police de la pensée', *L'Autre journal*, 1: 27–34.

McNay, L. (1999) 'Gender, habitus and the field: Pierre Bourdieu and the limits of reflexivity', *Theory, Culture and Society*, 16, 1: 95–117.

McRobbie, A. (2002) 'A mixed bag of misfortunes? Bourdieu's *the weight of the world*', *Theory, Culture and Society*, 19, 3: 129–38.

Marchetti, D. (2000) 'Les Révélations du "journalisme d'investigation"', *ARSS*, 131–2: 30–40.

Marx, K. (1857) *A Contribution to the Critique of Political Economy*, trans. S.W. Ryazanskaya, Moscow: Progress Publishers, 1970.

—— (1867) *Capital: a critique of political economy, vol. 1, book 1, the process of production of capital*, in *Collected Works*, ed. Karl Marx and Frederic Engels, vol. 35, London: Lawrence and Wishart, 1996.

—— (1975) *Early Writings*, London: Penguin.
Marx, K. and F. Engels (1845–6) *The German ideology*, London: Lawrence and Wishart, 1965.
Mauger, G. (1995) 'L'Engagement sociologique', *Critique*, 579–90: 674–96.
Mauss, M. (1950) *Sociologie et anthropologie, précédé d'une Introduction à l'oeuvre de Marcel Mauss par Claude Lévi-Strauss*, 6e édition, Paris: Presses Universitaires de France, 1978.
Merleau-Ponty, M. (1942) *The Structure of Behaviour*, trans. A.L. Fisher, London: Methuen, 1965.
—— (1945) *Phenomenology of Perception*, trans. C. Smith, London and New York: Routledge, 2002.
Michard-Marchal, C. and C. Ribery (1982) 'Pierre Bourdieu: "Questions de politique" ', in *Sexisme et sciences humaines: pratique linguistique du rapport de sexage*, Lille: Presses universitaires de Lille, pp. 161–72.
Moi, T. (1991) 'Appropriating Bourdieu: feminist theory and Pierre Bourdieu's sociology of culture', *New Literary History*, 22, 4: 1017–49.
—— (1994) *Simone de Beauvoir: the making of an intellectual woman*, Oxford and Cambridge, MA: Blackwell.
Moriarty, M. (1994) 'Structures of cultural production in nineteenth-century France', in *Artistic Relations: literature and the visual arts in nineteenth-century France*, ed. P. Collier and R. Lethbridge, New Haven, CT: Yale University Press, pp. 15–29.
—— (2003) *Early Modern French Thought: the age of suspicion*, Oxford: Oxford University Press.
Mouffe, C. (1993) *The Return of the Political*, London and New York: Verso.
Mouriaux, R. and F. Subileau (1996) 'Les Grèves françaises de l'automne 1995: défense des acquis ou mouvement social?' *Modern and Contemporary France*, N.S.4, 3: 299–306.
Nietzcshe, F. (1969) *On the Genealogy of Morals and Ecce homo*, trans. W. Kaufmann and R.J. Hollingdale, New York: Vintage Books.
Onfray, M. (2002) *Célébration du génie colérique*, Paris: Editions Galilée.
Pascal, B. (1966) *Pensées*, translated with an introduction by A.J. Krailsheimer, London: Penguin.
Pinto, L. (1998) *Pierre Bourdieu et la théorie du monde social*, Paris: Albin Michel.
Plato (1924) *Meno*, in *Laches, Protagoras, Meno, Euthydemus*, trans. and ed. W.R.M. Lamb, London: Heinemann and Loeb Classical Library.
Ramonet, I. (2000) *Géopolitique du chaos*, Paris: Gallimard and Folio-Actuel.
Rancière, J. (1974) *La Leçon d'Althusser*, Paris: Gallimard and Collection Idées.
—— (1983) *Le Philosophe et ses pauvres*, Paris: Librairie Arthème Fayard.
—— (1995) *Disagreement: politics and philosphy*, trans. J. Rose, Minneapolis, MN: University of Minnesota Press, 1999.
—— (1998) *Aux Bords du politique*, Paris: La Fabrique-Editions and Gallimard Folio-Essais.
—— (2000) *Le Partage du sensible: esthétique et politique*, Paris: La Fabrique-éditions.
—— (2003) *Les Scènes du peuple (Les Révoltes logiques, 1975–85)*, Lyon: Horlieu Editons.
Reynolds, S. (1996) *France Between the Wars: gender and politics*, London and New York: Routledge.
Robbins, B. (1993) *Secular Vocations: intellectuals, professionalism, culture*, London and New York: Verso.

Roos, J.M. (1996) *Early Impressionism and the French state (1866–1874)*, Cambridge: Cambridge University Press.
Rosenberg, J. (2000) *The Follies of Globalisation Theory: polemical essays*, London and New York: Verso.
Ross, G., ed. (1996) 'Debate: the movements of autumn – something new or déjà vu?', *French Politics and Society*, 14, 1: 1–27.
Sartre, J.P. (1960) *Critique de la raison dialectique, tôme 1, théorie des ensembles pratiques*, Paris: Gallimard.
Schneidermann, D. (1996) 'Réponse à Pierre Bourdieu: La Télévision peut-elle critiquer la télévision?', *Le Monde diplomatique*, May, p. 25.
—— (1999) *Du journalisme après Bourdieu*, Paris: Fayard.
Shusterman, R. (2000) *Pragmatist Aesthetics: living beauty, re-thinking art*, 2nd edition, New York and Oxford: Rowman & Littlefield.
Skeggs, B. (1997) *Formations of Class and Gender*, London, Thousand Oaks, New Delhi: Sage.
Smith, T.B. (2004) *France in Crisis: welfare, inequality and globalization since 1980*, Cambridge: Cambridge University Press.
Smith, W.R. (1998) *The Left's Dirty Job: the politics of industrial restructuring in France and Spain*, Pittsburgh, PA: University of Pittsburgh Press.
Spivak, G. (1988) 'Can the subaltern speak?', in *Marxism and the Interpretation of Culture*, ed. Cary Nelson and Lawrence Grossberg, Basingstoke: Macmillan, pp. 271–313.
Stallabrass, J. (1999) *High Art Lite: British art in the 1990s*, London: Verso.
Stiglitz, J. (2002) *Globalization and its Discontents*, London: Penguin Books.
Swartz, D. (1997) *Culture and Power: the sociology of Pierre Bourdieu*, London and Chicago, IL: University of Chicago Press.
Touraine, A., F. Dubet, D. Lapeyronnie, F. Khosrokhavar and M. Wieviorka (1996) *Le Grand refus: réflexions sur la grève de décembre 1995*, Paris: Fayard.
Veblen, T. (1912) *The Theory of the Leisure Class: an economic study of institutions*, new edition, London: George Allen and Unwin, 1924.
Verdès-Leroux, J. (1998) *Le savant et la politique: essai sur le terrorisme sociologique de Pierre Bourdieu*, Paris: Grasset.
Wacquant, L., ed. (2005) *Pierre Bourdieu and Democratic Politics: the mystery of ministry*, Cambridge: Polity Press.
Wallis, B., ed. (1986) *Hans Haacke: unfinished business*, Cambridge, MA: MIT Press.
Waters, S. (2003) *Social Movements in France: towards a new citizenship*, Basingstoke: Palgrave Macmillan.
Weber, M. (1904–5) *The Protestant Ethic and the Spirit of Capitalism*, trans. T. Parsons, London and New York: Routledge, 1992.
—— (1968) *Economy and Society: an outline of interpretive sociology*, 3 vols, New York: Bedminster Press, 1968.
Werbner, P. (2000) 'Who sets the terms of the debate? Heterotopic intellectuals and the clash of discourses', *Theory, Culture and Society*, 17, 1: 147–56.
Wieviorka, M., ed. (1992) *La France raciste*, Paris: Editions du seuil.
Wolff, J. (1983) *Aesthetics and the Sociology of Art*, London: George Allen and Unwin, second edition 1993.
Woodmansee, M. (1994) *The Author, Art and the Market: re-reading the history of aesthetics*, New York: Columbia University Press.

Wu, C. (2002) *Privatising Culture: corporate art intervention since the 1980s*, London: Verso.
Žižek, S. (1999) *The Ticklish Subject*, London: Verso.
Zola, E. (1866) *Edouard Manet: étude biographique et critique*, in *Pour Manet*, ed. J.P. Leduc-Adine, Paris: Editions Complexe, 1989.
—— (1880) *Le Roman expérimental*, Paris: Garnier-Flammarion, 1971.

Index

Adkins, L. 99
Ahearne, J. 32, 127, 135, 137–8, 171 n.1
Althusser, L. 10, 36, 50–1, 53, 90–1, 93–4
Aristotle 73

Babb, S.L. 17
Bachelard, G. 40, 44, 62
Bachmann, C. 83–4
Bakhtin, M. 136
Balibar, E. 30, 159
Baudelaire, C. 121, 122, 124–6, 130, 134
Blair, T. 95
Boas, F. 123
Boltanski, L. 79, 85
Boltanski, L. and E. Chiapello: *Le Nouvel Esprit du capitalisme* 8–9, 15, 34, 36
Bourdieu, P.: the aesthetic 36–53, 118–19, 120–40, 167, 168; 'Bourdieu petition' 21, 27–30, 142; corporatism of the universal 80, 141–61, 168–9; discursive montage 134, 135–9; field 9, 29, 34, 76–97, 126–7, 146–9, 156, 160, 164–5, 167–9; gay and lesbian movement 108–9, 173 n.2; gender 98–119, 165, 167; globalization 3–4, 11–22, 25, 154, 162–4; habitus 9, 36–53, 93–4, 96, 101–3, 110–11, 113–14, 117–18, 120, 122, 134, 137–9, 153, 165–7, 168; hexis 47, 48; homology 61–2, 82, 90–7, 101–8, 117–18, 165, 168; Kabylia 37–41, 44–5, 55–6, 87, 98–9, 101–5, 111, 113, 120, 137, 139; legitimate culture 32–3, 120, 132–3, 137; the market 122–3, 126–34; Marxism, attitude to 23–4, 26, 31, 34, 36, 50, 51, 58–9, 65, 91, 94, 164; the performative 54–75, 108–11; political field 54–75; position-taking 90–7; practice 9, 34, 36–53, 54–75, 118, 120, 134, 137–9, 166–7; race and ethnicity 145, 148–9, 150–4, 158, 166, 173 n.5; Raisons d'agir Collective 2, 7, 29, 88, 156, 171 n.7; republicanism 4–5, 13, 14, 16, 21, 22, 26–33, 64, 121, 132, 142, 155, 165, 169; scholastic point of view 32, 38, 42, 143, 146–7; Socratic anamnesis 63–3, 65–72, 166, 169; Socratic dialogue 149–55, 157–8; 'specific intellectual' 6–7, 9, 88; the state 23–6, 79–80, 87–8; symbolic domination 9, 42–3, 46, 51, 101, 111–17; theory effect 56, 67; works, *Acts of Resistance* 2, 10–14, 142, 'Célibat et condition paysanne' 99, 114, *Contre-feux* and *Contre-feux 2* 2, 3, 11, 14, 76, 'Delegation and political fetishism' 64, *Le Déracinement* 60, 172 n.1, *Distinction* 37, 40, 55, 82, 85, 95, 99, 100–1, 102, 106, 111–18, 122, 134, 135–7, 138–9, 143, 166–7, *Esquisse d'une théorie de la pratique* 91, 94, *Firing back* 2, 10–14, 77–8, 162–3, *Free Exchange* 121, 123–4, 126, 133–7, 139, 145–6, 148, *Homo Academicus* 29, 61, *The Inheritors* 31–3, 99, 102, *In Other Words* 66–7, 69–70, 130, *Interventions, 1961–2001* 3, 16, *An Invitation to Reflexive Sociology* 90, 94, 'The Kabyle house or the world reversed' 40, 55, 87, 99, 139, *Language and Symbolic Power* 2, 41, 52, 54, 55–6, 63, *The Logic of Practice* 40, 42, 44–5, 111–12, *The Love of Art* 33, 37, *Masculine Domination* 5, 98–111, 117, 165, 'La Nouvelle Vulgate planétaire' 55, 'On symbolic power' 92, 93; *On Television and Journalism* 2, 13–14,

Bourdieu, P. (*Continued*)
144–5, 154–8, 'On the cunning of imperialist reason' 153–4, *Outline of a Theory of Practice* 38–9, *Pascalian Meditations* 41, 42, 47–50, 64, 142–4, 145, 146–9, 164, 167, *Practical Reason* 79–80, 145, 146–9, 'La Production de l'idéologie dominante' 79, 85, 120, *Propos sur le champ politique* 3, 54, 68, 89–90, 'Questions de politique' 47, 56, 63–4, 99, 102, 149, *Reproduction* 31–3, 99, 102, *The Rules of Art* 2, 123–31, 143, *Science of Science and Reflexivity* 92–3, 144, 155, 'Social space and the genesis of "classes"' 54, 57–9, 92, *The Social Structures of the Economy* 2, 40–1, 42, 74–5, 76–90, 93, 94, 96, 165, 168, *Sociology in Question* 32, 67, *The State Nobility* 2, 82, 94, *Travail et travailleurs en Algérie* 60, *The Weight of the World* 2, 77, 144–5, 149–55, 163, 166
Buren, D. 123, 138–9
Bürger, P. 120, 134
Butler, J. 10, 36, 98, 109–11, 167
Butler, J., E. Laclau and S. Žižek: *Contingency, Hegemony, Universality* 159–60

Caillé, A. 17, 21, 148–9
Calhoun, C. 122
Callinicos, A. 14, 26
Carles, P. 156
Champagne, P.: *Faire l'opinion* 3
Chirac, J. 4, 19–21, 22, 31
Collège de sociologie européenne 61
Common Agricultural Policy (CAP) 162–4
Confédération française démocratique du travail (CFDT) 18
copyright law 128

De Beauvoir, S. 99
Le Décembre des intellectuels français 29
De Gaulle, C. 12, 19–20, 69, 107
Deleuze, G. 88
Delphy, C. 98, 103–4
Diamond, H. 107
Dreyfus Trial 6, 121
Dubet, F. 5
Duchamp, M. 134
Duclos, J. 47
Durkheim, E. 37; *Professional Ethics and Civic Morals* 24–5, 87–8

Eagleton, T. 36, 42, 45–6, 130–1
Emin, T. 132
Esprit 18; '*Esprit* petition' 18, 28–30
European Economic Community (EEC) 12
European Union (EU) 17, 18, 21, 25, 26, 162–3

Fanon, F. 60
Fassin, E. 30
Ferry, L. 145
Finkielkraut, A. 145
Flaubert, G. 121, 122, 124–31, 134
Fondation Saint Simon 18
Forrester, V.: *L'Horreur économique* 16, 18
Foucault, M. 6–7, 51, 88–9, 142–3
Fourcade-Gourinchas, M. 17
Fourier, C. 65, 112
Freedland, C. 135
French, J.D. 154
French Socialist Party 3–4, 19, 20, 22, 152
Front national (FN) 21, 67–9, 144, 149, 151–2, 166

Garnham, N. 5, 36
Giddens, A. 95
Gilroy, P. 154
Giscard d'Estaing, V. 74, 77, 79, 80, 83, 85
Gramsci, A. 10, 34, 36, 53, 62–3
Grossberg, L.: *We Gotta Get Out of this Place* 16, 19, 53
Grunberg, G. 151
Guillory, J. 122

Haacke, H. 121, 124–5, 131, 133–7, 139, 141–2, 148
Habermas, J. 129–30, 132, 142–3, 155
Hall, S. 10, 154; *The Hard Road to Renewal* 15, 16, 19, 34, 36
Heartfield, J. 134
Hegel, G.W.F. 91, 159; *Philosophy of Right* 24, 80, 147–8
Heidegger, M. 41
Helms, J. 121, 133
Hennessey, R. 104, 116
Hochschild, A.R. 114–15
homeless, the (*les sans-abri*) 159
Husserl, E. 39, 42–4, 60–1

Impressionists 125, 129, 130
International Monetary Fund (IMF) 2, 7, 13, 16, 25

Jameson, F. 132, 133–4, 135
Jardine, L. 124
Johnson, L.B. 14
Jospin, L. 21
Juppé, A. 27; 'plan Juppé' 18, 27–30, 96

Kahn, J.F.: *La Pensée unique* 17–18
Kant, I.: *Critique of Judgement* 37–9, 42–5, 53
Kennedy, J.F. 14
Keynesianism 3, 19, 25–6

Laclau, E. 10, 70–1, 159, 160, 161
Laclau, E. and C. Mouffe: *Hegemony and Socialist Strategy* 15–16, 34, 36, 54, 57–9, 66, 68–9, 70–2, 110, 165
Lahire, B. 5
Le Doeuff, M. 99
Le Goff, J-P. 7–8, 15, 33–4
Le Guennec, N. 83–4
Lenin, V.I. 61, 63, 65, 72, 108, 172 n.2
Le Pen, J-M. 21, 67–9
Lévi-Strauss, C. 38
Loesberg, J. 37, 40, 45

McNay, L. 100
McRobbie, A. 153, 154
Mallarmé, S. 40, 44, 120
Manet, E. 121, 122, 124–31, 134
Mapplethorpe, R. 133
Marchetti, D. 3
Marx, K. 40, 65, 115, 147–8, 159
Mauss, M. 57
Medici, C. 124
Merleau-Ponty, M. 42–4
Michard-Marchal, C. 99
Mitterrand, F. 3, 18–19, 20, 137
Moi, T. 99–100
Moriarty, M. 129, 172 n.4
Mouffe, C. 10, 160–1
Le Mouvement des chômeurs 72–4

National Endowment for the Arts (NEA) 133
neo-liberalism 1–4, 7–9, 11–35, 36, 41, 53, 71, 74, 76–90, 94–6, 149, 165
New Criterion 133
'Nouvelle Sorbonne' 6
Nouvelles questions féministes 98

Onfray, M.: *Célébration du génie colérique* 7

Pascal, B.: *Pensées* 47–9
'pensée unique' 17–23; *see also* Kahn, J.F.
Plato: *Meno* 65, 150
Pollock, J. 138
postwar compromise 3, 8, 15–16, 26, 34
public sphere 129–32, 141–61, 169; *see also* Habermas, J.

Ramonet, I. 18
Rancière, J. 9, 10, 54, 73–4, 110, 159–60, 161, 169–70
Rand Smith, W. 3–4
Reagan, R. 4, 15–16, 17, 19, 53
Renaut, A. 145
Reynolds, S. 105–6
Ribery, C. 99
Robbins, B. 4–5
Rodchentko, A. 134
Roos, J.M. 125, 129–30
Roosevelt, F.D. 14

Saatchi, C. 121, 124, 131, 132
Sartre, J-P. 6, 172 n.1
Schweisguth, E. 151
Serrano, A. 133
Shusterman, R. 139–40
Skeggs, B. 100, 110–11
Smith, T.B. 22
La Sociologie est un sport de combat 1, 156
Spinoza, B. 91, 94
Spivak, G. 88
Stallabrass, J. 121

Taylor Wood, S. 132
Thatcher, M. 4, 15, 17, 19, 20, 22, 57–8, 74, 110
Third Way 95
'Tobin tax' 25, 171 n.7

undocumented immigrants (*les sans-papiers*) 159–60

Van Gogh, V. 138
Veblen, T. 123
Verdès-Leroux, J.: *Le Savant et la politique* 5–6
Vichy France 106–7

Wacquant, L. 55, 153–4
'Washington Consensus' 4
Waters, S. 159
Weber, M. 60, 164, 173 n.1

Werbner, P. 154
Whiteread, R. 132
Wieviorka, M.: *La France raciste* 154, 173 n.6
World Bank 2, 13, 16, 25
World Trade Organisation (WTO) 2, 7, 13, 25, 162, 163
Wu, C. 121

Young British Artists (YBAs) 121, 124, 131–2

Žižek, S. 116
Zola, E. 124–31, 134, 142; 'J'Accuse' 6, 121, 126–7; *Pour Manet* 128–9; *Le Roman expérimental* 128

eBooks – at www.eBookstore.tandf.co.uk

A library at your fingertips!

eBooks are electronic versions of printed books. You can store them on your PC/laptop or browse them online.

They have advantages for anyone needing rapid access to a wide variety of published, copyright information.

eBooks can help your research by enabling you to bookmark chapters, annotate text and use instant searches to find specific words or phrases. Several eBook files would fit on even a small laptop or PDA.

NEW: Save money by eSubscribing: cheap, online access to any eBook for as long as you need it.

Annual subscription packages

We now offer special low-cost bulk subscriptions to packages of eBooks in certain subject areas. These are available to libraries or to individuals.

For more information please contact webmaster.ebooks@tandf.co.uk

We're continually developing the eBook concept, so keep up to date by visiting the website.

www.eBookstore.tandf.co.uk